FREEDOM AND CIVILIZATION

FREEDOM

AND

CIVILIZATION

BY

BRONISLAW MALINOWSKI

GREENWOOD PRESS, PUBLISHERS
WESTPORT, CONNECTICUT

Library of Congress Cataloging in Publication Data

Malinowski, Bronislaw, 1884-1942.
   Freedom and civilization.

   Reprint of the ed. published by Roy Publishers, New
York.
   Bibliography: p.
   1. Civilization.   2. Liberty.   3. Democracy.
4. Totalitarianism.   I. Title.
HM101.M24 1976   301.2   76-40226
ISBN 0-8371-9277-3

Originally published in 1944 by Roy Publishers, New York

Reprinted in 1976 by Greenwood Press, Inc.

Library of Congress Catalogue Card Number 76-40226

ISBN 0-8371-9277-3

Printed in the United States of America

Preface

FROM the early days of the rise to power of Hitler, Bronislaw Malinowski was an outspoken opponent of National Socialism. He began at that time to devote much attention to the analysis of war, from its development and throughout history to its disastrous present-day manifestations, and gave many lectures on the subject, attacking at the same time the totalitarian regimes as states organized for "chronic preparedness for war in the interests of war." This resulted in the early banning of his books in Germany.

In America, one of his first analyses of war was given in the Oration* at the Phi Beta Kappa exercises at the Harvard Tercentenary in 1936, and after his return to this country on sabbatical vacation at the end of 1938, he lectured with increasing intensity on the dangers of totalitarianism for humanity and culture.

After the outbreak of war in 1939, Malinowski remained in the United States, having been appointed to Yale University. He became more and more absorbed in analyzing the present world issues and in calling attention to the disasters which would result from a totalitarian victory. He was profoundly disturbed by the lack of realization among students of the significance of the war and the consequences of a totalitarian victory; both in 1941 and 1942 he suggested the organization at Yale of a discussion group of students and faculty, for the clarification of the issues and aims of the war and the questions of the coming peace. He felt a grave moral responsibility towards young students who might be going into the army, and believed they should be given the opportunity

* Published under the title "The Deadly Issue," *Atlantic Monthly*, December, 1936.

v

to understand why and for what they must fight. Unfortunately, this plan was not realized.

As the war progressed, Malinowski became increasingly preoccupied with the problems of the peace settlement. He wholeheartedly endorsed the principles enunciated in the Atlantic Charter, and believed that the future safety and well-being of mankind could only be achieved by means of a world federation. The most serious consequence of the present war, he felt, was the destruction of "the fundamental values of loyalty, decency and all ethical principles." He felt very strongly that it was his duty to make a contribution, based on wide anthropological experience, to present-day planning and discussions, through a clear analysis of the fundamental issues which face humanity in this world crisis.

This book is thus the final expression of my husband's basic beliefs and conclusions regarding war, totalitarianism and the future of humanity. The direct incentive, however, for writing it came when he was invited by Dr. A. W. Bray to speak at the Rensselaer Chapter of the Society of Sigma Xi in January, 1941. He chose as his subject "Human Nature, Culture and Freedom", and when beginning to write up this lecture* for publication, he became so absorbed in the theme that he decided to write a book on "Freedom". He continued to work with great concentration on it until the beginning of April, 1942, and then carefully put his material in order and laid it aside, intending finally to complete the book in the following autumn. He died suddenly five weeks later.

Since I had followed with my husband the day-by-day growth of "Freedom", and had discussed and read it with him in its various stages of development, after his death I began to arrange the material for publication. This entailed first of all the insertion of numerous additions and corrections which my husband had made in the manuscript. My primary objective has been to avoid editorial rewriting, since this is liable to alter or obscure the original thought of the author. The entire material of the book was written by my husband; certain chapters required the amalgamation of two or three sections, or the incorporation of his supplementary drafts. I have deliberately refrained from removing certain minor repetitions—which my husband in his final revision would certainly not have left—since elimination of them would have necessitated a reformulation of his argument.

---

* See "Human Nature, Culture and Freedom" in *A Revaluation of Our Civilization,* to be published shortly by the Rensselaer Chapter of the Society of Sigma Xi (Argus Press, N. Y.).

I know my husband would have wished to make certain acknowledgments. His indebtedness to various writers is expressed in the statement which I quote below, dictated by him for inclusion in his own preface:

"In some of the recent books and articles, the historian, Shotwell; the economist and jurisprudent, Walton Hamilton; the lawyer, Corwin; the philosopher, John Dewey, have made contributions towards the problem of freedom which I could endorse from A to Z. Needless to say perhaps, all that Bertrand Russell has written on the subject is in my opinion unimpeachable. It is also interesting that writers and thinkers mainly concerned with the course of political affairs: Mr. Walter Lippmann, for instance, Miss Dorothy Thompson, Professor F. Schumann, Professor Gilbert Murray, and Harold J. Laski, and above all, Sir Norman Angell, are able in each case to use the concept of freedom in a manner which the anthropologist would fully endorse, in that the concept could thus be used for any type of society and any type of evolution. I would especially like to acknowledge my indebtedness to those writers whose books and articles I have read while drafting this essay. The agreement of their views with mine allowed me to proceed with greater confidence. The recent book by Professor Irwin Edman which came to my hands only after most of my arguments had been framed would have saved me a great deal of trouble and intellectual random behavior had I read it earlier. It is an excellent presentation and correct in practically all its conclusions and even *obiter dicta*. As far as I know, however, no anthropological contribution to freedom has yet been made. An article by Professor Franz Boas recently published cannot be considered as in any way satisfactory."

He would, I know, also have wished to express his thanks to Dr. Mark May, Director of the Institute of Human Relations, Yale University, with whom he discussed part of the manuscript and through whose kindness he was provided with a research assistant; to Dr. Clark Hull, Dr. Phyllis Kaberry and Dr. Stephen P. Reed, with whom he reviewed certain sections of the book; as well as to his research assistants: Mrs. Evelyn Middleton, Mrs. Frances Wenrich Underwood, Mrs. Laura Willie, Mr. Howard Reed and Mr. Fred Sheppard.

On my own behalf, I would like to express my great appreciation to the Polish Institute of Arts and Sciences in America, whose generous help after my husband's death made it possible for me to undertake the preparation of the book for publication. I would like to thank Dr. Mark May for giving me secretarial assistance. I am also indebted to Dr. Phyllis Kaberry and Mrs. Lois Howard for their careful reading of the manuscript, and to Dr. Robert MacIver, Dr. Feliks Gross, Dr. Hortense Pow-dermaker and Mrs. Eleanor Kittredge for their advice and help. The sympathetic and understanding assistance of Mrs. Evelyn Middleton in the months after my husband's death I shall always remember.

VALETTA MALINOWSKA.

New York. March, 1944.

Contents

Part I

POLITICAL PRELUDE

ACKNOWLEDGMENTS

I WISH to acknowledge with thanks the kind permission of Professor Horace M. Kallen and Professor Walton Hamilton, to quote from their articles in *Freedom in the Modern World*, edited by Horace M. Kallen, 1928; of Messrs. Harper and Brothers, to quote passages from *What Is Freedom?* by Dorothy Fosdick; and of Messrs. Harcourt, Brace and Company, Inc., to quote passages from the articles of Professor F. Boas, Professor Robert M. MacIver and Professor J. B. S. Haldane in *Freedom, Its Meaning*, edited by Ruth Nanda Anshen, 1940.

Political Prelude

AN INQUIRY into the nature of freedom and its relation to human nature and to culture is not out of place in a fighting democracy. We are now engaged in a war against the greatest threat to freedom which humanity has ever known. We fight for freedom. Do we really understand what it is, appreciate its value, and realize that it is in fact the very foundation of our civilized life? We are surrounded by many magnificent slogans, some of them true and significant. We know that this is "a battle of free peoples against slavery"; we hear that this is "the fight for freedom"; we have been officially told that this war will establish "the four freedoms" firmly and permanently.

Yet the enthusiasm behind the slogans is not always as real as one might hope. We still often find the negative attitude that the war has to be fought and won only because this country had been attacked. Some people are looking for a "new order" to match Hitler's own. Many are not aware that the New Waves of the Future are fundamentally futile except to the pro-Nazis. In our democratic unpreparedness, we have failed to mobilize spiritually. This unpreparedness is natural since democracy is the denial of both war and preparedness. Total war is the most funda-

mental contradiction of everything which a democracy believes
to be true, real and valuable.

We must examine whether the charter of our Old Order cannot supply us with convictions as firm and beliefs as dynamic
as those of the false and meretricious totalitarian doctrine. In our
democracies we are living by truths and beliefs as old as mankind.
We hold to the values with which humanity started on its cultural
career, developed, and established its present cultural level.
Among these values, freedom, equitable dealing, submission to
agreements and to laws have always occupied the place of honor.
In all his endeavors to discover new principles of knowledge, new
devices, and new forms of social organization, man, primitive and
on his road to progress, has always been controlled by the freedom
of order, of initiative, and of achievement. This is the Old Order
of human evolution, an order which we still continue in our
democratic way of life. In this order, peace and its permanent
foundations have always been associated with the really productive phases of evolution and history. In this order the distinction
between the individual and the community did not appear as a
conflict, as an opposition in which one of the two must be suppressed, but as a complementary relation of give and take. In this
order the submission to rule, law, and moral principle did not
mean bondage, but enlightened interest, as well as ability of self-
expression.

In these times of sophistication and relativism it is the duty
of an anthropologist to restate and reaffirm the existence of certain values and principles which are indispensable to the very
process of maintaining and advancing culture. Such principles
must be incorporated into the collective conviction which is the
basis of our will to win this war—a conviction which, in view of
the Fifth Column tactics of our enemies, we must maintain with
never-flagging vigilance. The conviction that freedom, justice,

and democracy supply the best conditions for sound cultural development, must become part of that peace, the winning of which is as important as victory in war. This peace must contain permanent guarantees of all our social and moral values, of which freedom is the most valuable.

On December 7, 1941, there occurred the event which plunged the United States into war. The unforeseen, treacherous, long-planned and well-prepared attack on Pearl Harbor; the simultaneous drives in Malaya, the Philippines, and Hong Kong will make the date, as President Roosevelt put it, infamous for Japan and the Axis. The date indeed throws into clear relief the difference between the aggressors and those attacked, between countries who honestly lived and worked for peace and those who are responsible for war because they prepared for war.

The date is also significant as well as tragic for the United States, the British Empire, and the Netherlands, provided that the right conclusions be drawn and the right lessons learned. The first and most important lesson contained in the slogan "Remember Pearl Harbor" is that preparedness always wins. This lesson really means that unless we are prepared for peace after victory, and prepare so effectively as to make future wars impossible, we shall have to prepare for war everywhere; that is, we shall be forced to kill democracy throughout the world. This is the reason why the events here registered affect deeply the subject matter of the present analysis.

In our present world of mechanical superefficiency, preparedness is invincible. Let us face the facts. At Pearl Harbor, Manila, Hong Kong, and around Singapore, we found four of the strongest powers of the world facing a relatively small, exhausted, and economically poor country. Yet this country was able in the first round to beat its strongest enemies on every point and in every battle. China, the British Empire, the United States, and the Dutch

East Indies represent more than a billion people, about three-fourths of the world's economic resources, and more than one-half of its industrial output. The Japanese are outnumbered ten to one in manpower; and as regards potential wealth, and technical and economic efficiency, they simply do not count in the long run. Yet just because war at present is a short-run affair, preparedness, aggression, initiative, and indeed treachery can win the day and are winning the day.

What we rightly describe as treachery is, from the aggressor's point of view, choosing his time, preparing where to strike, and striking hard and ruthlessly, while at the same time weakening his opponents in purpose and lulling them into a sense of security. All this is infamous measured by the standards of any decent, normal policy of the democratic order, where agreements, pledged undertakings, and principles of law are valid. Yet the principles of modern warfare once admitted—freedom of armaments; freedom of insidious propaganda and the creation of fifth columns; the so-called balance of power, that is, international anarchy—it becomes evident that in such a world and to those who approve of it, the Japanese way of winning the war is nothing but wise strategy and effective tactics. All this also applies to every move of Germany and of Italy, ever since the beginning of the present war.

Thus, if at the next peace table the victorious democracies leave the world to international chaos, and once more allow the principle of preparedness to flourish, the democracies themselves will be faced with the alternative, prepare or perish. We may try again new experiments in superisolationism. Great Britain may try to believe once more in the existence of the Channel, and buttress this belief by trying to erect a Maginot Line in the air. The United States, establishing more or less imaginary barriers across the Atlantic and the Pacific, may once more retire into a defensive policy of isolation. In the next war any democracy, however well isolated, will be beaten, destroyed, and enslaved in the first round of a new, a bigger, and a better Blitzkrieg.

To recognize this it is enough to compare the events of 1941 with those of 1914. Is it best then for every country, above all for the great, peaceful, and freedom-loving democracies, to prepare? Obviously preparedness nowadays can only be carried through by adopting fully and completely the totalitarian system at home. Any country which does not mobilize all manpower, all wealth and all spiritual resources will not be prepared. Preparedness means nowadays the full, determined, wholehearted training of a people, body and soul, mind, conscience and convictions, for war. It means also the development throughout the nation of the spirit of aggression, of brutality, of ruthlessness, and of contempt for law, agreement, and obligation.

Thus unless we establish some fundamental guarantees for freedom, law and honesty in international affairs; and if we retain the principle that war is the only instrument of international policy, we shall stand at the crossroads of a truly destructive alternative. The democracies will have the choice, either to perish by the sword of their enemies, or to perish in preparing their own weapons of defense. In building up their preparedness they will have to sign their own death warrant as democracies, as free people, as decent people.

There remains, however, the third road, the road which leads to a free democratic world, to a Commonwealth of United Nations determined to preserve a lasting peace. The ideology embodied in Wilson's plans for a really effective League of Nations is not a utopia. It is a feasible plan which means merely the establishment of international law and order within a humanity which today has already grown into an integrally interdependent whole.

In the analysis of freedom which follows, we shall see that this moral, legal, political, and cultural reality must always be considered with reference to an integral community, living under a system of law and order. We shall see that in human evolution freedom is found first on a tribal scale. Through war, historical vicissitudes, conquests, and the diffusion of cultures, the social unit about which freedom can be predicated, and in which it flourishes or is curtailed, gradually widens. We shall see that political organization, that is, a central system of legislative, juridical, administrative and military powers, must follow the extent of real common interests.

At the present stage of human evolution the world as a whole is united by a network of common interests, of interdependencies of one nation on the others and of all nations upon each other. This community of interests is political in that wars and international disputes cannot be localized. It is economic in that raw materials as well as the products of industry must have one large world market, or else we shall have perpetual economic warfare, with unemployment, depressions, and crises throughout the world. In matters of health and technology, of science and crime, the world is equally interdependent. The infectiousness of disease, of crime, of spiritual corruption, of falsehood, has become worldwide. All this means that we must work for the prevention of "local incidents" and the outbreak of wars. If democracies are fighting, they must fight for the final abolition of war and the reconstruction of humanity, on some revised and sound Wilsonian principles.

The old Wilsonian League of Nations failed because it was not universal, had no real legislative competence, and no means to enforce its decisions. The New League must have full legislative competence in international relations, and its laws and administrative decisions must be sanctioned by force. The main task of such a league would be the prevention of preparedness for war as well as effective quelling of any international hostilities. It would also administer all those international concerns which demand a centralized control. The New League would above all supply the indispensable political, economic, and moral equivalent of war by providing elastic legislative mechanisms based on deliberation and free discussion which would allow peaceful change by voluntary agreement.

A political organization on a world scale entails far-reaching sacrifices on the part of each component community. The sacrifices, however, are not so great as the enemies of world order often allege. The fundamental problems hinge around the analysis of what we may have to surrender if we accept the road of peace, and what we know we shall lose if we establish at the peace table a treaty which is bound to breed new wars. In this analysis some of the principles implied in this plan will be discussed. It will be shown that all major crises in culture are the danger foci of freedom, of democracy, and of the pursuit of happiness. The absence of that freedom which only order in international affairs can guarantee, must inevitably bring about the absence of freedom in national life, under our present conditions of technical efficiency and of development in means of control, violence, and destruction. Only by preventing war through international reorganization can we place freedom on a sound basis and abolish all temptations, all justifications, all possibilities for the introduction of totalitarian methods in the constitution of this country and of all other countries.

There are still one or two points to be made in connection with our watchword, "Remember Pearl Harbor". We are all united in action for the pursuit of war until victory. Yet such a surface solidarity in practical or pragmatic pursuits probably hides a considerable amount of divergencies in opinion, in sentiment, and in purpose with reference to the ultimate issues involved, above all, to the end of the present struggle. This country has been attacked, and all agree that it must be defended. But ask the questions, "What are we fighting for?", "What is the new world order we desire?"—and the answers are by no means clear and unanimous. I submit that a surface conformity with underground currents of divergent opinions, ideals, and aims, has its great dangers.

In the first place, there is the fundamental danger inherent in the tragic role of a democracy forced into the pursuit of the most antidemocratic action on a gigantic scale, that is, total war. All wars, civil and international; all revolutions, especially those carried out by violence, are likely, as history shows, to tempt nations and peoples into the road of imperialism, of dictatorship, of new military ventures. Violence breeds hatreds of one class by the other, of one nation by many others. The mechanics of violence give a precedent and engender an antidemocratic morality through the lessons of their efficiency. For, once we have recourse to violence, we always find that ruthlessness, quick decisions, complete subordination and discipline, and the obedience to supreme command, are in the short run more effective than appeals to public opinion, deliberation, voting, and any consideration given to the conscience and opinion of individuals or groups.

Thus a war which is being fought on such an enormous scale, which penetrates into every aspect of human life, as total war inevitably does, may breed those very forces in our own community against which we are fighting. This danger is the more threatening because it is unavoidable. It is the very danger against which the isolationists of yesterday were warning. It is an important half-truth and as such it may produce very dangerous results, especially at the moment, when a sound and enlightened opinion in this country may make or mar the establishment of the only end worth fighting for, that is, the establishment of a permanent peace based on a world organization for peace. This point will be fully treated in the following arguments. We shall see that all action is in itself a temporary surrender of freedom. A collective action like the present war, carried on on a total scale, must in many ways as effectively eliminate freedom as it must eliminate laziness, treachery, dishonesty, and desertion.

This does not mean that we should submit to a foreign dictator's demands and commands because war causes a partial and temporary abrogation of freedom at home. We shall not become Hitler's slaves by consent and by surrender simply because we may be afraid temporarily to surrender to our own self-chosen discipline. The moral is that we must prepare for the full exercise of freedom when freedom again can and must be exercised. Because war means temporary slavery in its pursuit and may mean, if totalitarianism wins on the field of battle or of principles, world slavery as its permanent result, we must draw the correct conclusion: abolish war now and forever; insist on "America first" as the country which will lead the Commonwealth of Nations on its determined road to permanent peace.

The practical suggestion contained in these arguments is that for the duration of hostilities compensatory mechanisms of free discussion and planning should be established. In this the academic profession, which by assumption may be free and untrammeled, can be especially useful. There are many points in the planning for peace which it is difficult for those immediately concerned with public responsibilities to discuss now. One of the most difficult questions arises from the fact that fighting on our side, fighting gallantly and most helpfully, there is Russia, a people for whom we feel both gratitude and admiration, yet a people who are now governed by a system which even the best attempt at being euphemistic, bland, and conciliatory will not allow us to describe as democratic. The mere academic scribe can express the hope either that the present rulers of Russia will change the form in which they are now ruling their people, or else that the nations of Russia will replace the present system by one which is not fraught with the dangers of totalitarianism. Such a hope cannot be voiced too loudly in public by an official spokesman.

Thus a committee or many committees of protective vigilance are necessary under present conditions. In these committees, democratic types of thought and conscience ought to be cultivated. Such committees ought to watch over the clear dangers of the present moment. Even within the fighting democracies there is a danger of the means getting the better of the end, that is, of the establishment of imperialisms and totalitarian methods out of the present war impetus. There is danger of losing sight of our ultimate end: fighting a war to end war. There is a danger of moral and intellectual exhaustion.

After the war we shall have once more to recognize that discipline has to be balanced by the essence of freedom, that is, untrammeled initiative, criticism, and even dissent. The recognition of the value of hierarchy will have to make way for a belief in equality. The instrumentalities of secrecy, censorship, and planned General Staff decisions will have to give way to open discussion. It is enough to remember what happened in England and America, in France and indeed in the rest of Europe after the first World War came to an end in 1918, in order to realize how dangerous the process of spiritual demobilization can become. The surge of passions, the relaxation of purpose, especially of moral purpose, the aversion to further planning, since war planning had become so irksome—all this may lead to the breakdown of a consistent, purposeful drive towards the achievement of the real fruits of victory. By this I mean naturally the drive towards the achievement of permanent peace. The new isolationism and the new imperialistic greeds in every victorious community are the natural fruits of postwar lassitude. Thus we must concentrate on postwar planning, especially those of us who can contribute but little towards the winning of the war through direct physical contributions.

The very definition and analysis of freedom as here developed will convince us that the formation of purpose, the vision of ends, and the subordination of means to ends are the very essence of all liberties. We shall also see that under present conditions it is possible to establish cultural mechanisms which are related to future planning, to long-run policies, to untrammeled discussion, which will not interfere with the conduct of practical affairs, and yet will provide the compensatory forum of conscience and thought necessary to counterbalance the effects of war.

On the purely intellectual side, the most important point for academic workers is to clarify the issues involved. We have thus to analyze such concepts as "democracy", "freedom", the meaning and ends of civilization, "the American way", and "the pursuit of happiness". We have to show the realities which correspond to these words. For there is another great danger in the present situation, the danger of inflation in ideals, and of contempt for ideas, that contempt which is bred by over-familiarity. Such words as democracy and freedom have already become slogans of quick currency constantly repeated by those who believe in them, as well as by those who accept them only under the pressure of circumstances. The spiritual foundations of public opinion have to be watched with the same eternal vigilance with which we look after the physical foundations of our national defenses. Thus the Ivory Tower in which detached discussion is possible, in which we are still allowed to think clearly, to deliberate honestly, and to face facts squarely, has its definite value in the present world at war.

In such discussions it would also be important that not only such of us as are already convinced of the truth and righteousness of our cause should participate. Those who doubt, those who are uncertain, those even who courageously and honestly believe that there are valuable elements in fascism, nazism, communistic totalitarianism, and other waves of the future, should be allowed to participate on full rights of citizenship. I personally believe unreservedly that the testimony of facts and principles is on the side of those who are convinced that the national decision, that is, the national action of this country is right, not only in sentiment but also in the light of dispassionate scientific truth. I am deeply convinced that the United States of America, Great Britain, and their allies are fighting for their freedom, for that of other nations, and that of humanity at large. Yet the war will be fought once more in vain unless the final purpose of the free nations becomes embodied in a fully implemented organization of humanity for peace and freedom. I therefore should like to challenge and to invite the utterance of contrary opinions. Open and direct discussion is preferable to suppressed, hole-and-corner scheming.

Personally I believe that war and totalitarianism are incompatible with freedom and with the constructive exercise of culture. I also believe that without freedom and democracy, civilization cannot survive, still less advance. Hence I believe that victory for the democracies and the full world-wide maintenance of democratic principles in national and international affairs are the minimum conditions of freedom, that is, a human civilization alive and advancing.

The arguments of the following pages will turn round the question of what freedom as an attribute of the cultural process is. We shall see that it is possible to give a clear, scientific definition of freedom and that this definition allows of the solution of many of the wider, even philosophical problems connected with this concept; it also can be applied concretely and definitely to the most urgent need of the present world situation. Although political freedom is not the only type of freedom in culture, yet its absence destroys all other liberties; and at present the battle of freedom is fought between the two principles, that of democracy and of totalitarianism. Unless this latter is not merely beaten but also destroyed and its reappearance precluded once and forever, we will have to face a period of dark ages, indeed the darkest ages of human history.

Part II

FREEDOM IN SCIENTIFIC ANALYSIS

1

What Are We Fighting For?

IN THE previous pages it was shown clearly and conclusively that this question must be answered and answered scientifically. A call was made there for intellectual vigilance and for a mobilization of scientific thought and academic activities on the urgent issues of the day. Among other deficiencies of our unpreparedness, we have also failed to mobilize spiritually. There is no doubt that all around us we hear the slogans of "Fight for freedom", "The struggle of democracies against slavery", "The need of establishing justice and decency in the world". Yet when one of us raises his voice to affirm such values as "freedom", "justice", and "democracy", he does it at the risk of being accused of the academically unpardonable sin of "value judgments" or "suffering from a moral purpose".

There are many who condemn value judgments in the vested interests of academic futility, laziness, and irrelevancy. The best remedy here is to recognize that the soundest test of an adequate theory is always to be found in practical applications. The student of society and of human culture has, under present circumstances, the duty to draw practical conclusions, to commit himself to views and decisions referring to problems of planning,

19

and to translate his conclusions into definite propositions of statesmanship.

There is no doubt, however, that the ultimate decision in any matter of action, collective or individual, implies an element which cannot be proved by scientific argument. Medical science can demonstrate that certain forms of diet are indispensable, while other dishes are harmful. The decision whether you prefer to gorge yourself with fried capons soused in Burgundy and steer towards stomach ulcers and arthritis, or on medical advice keep to a reasonable diet, remains with the individual. It is possible to demonstrate that morphia, cocaine, and chronic alcoholism may become dangerous habits; but you cannot demonstrate that their use is not worth the price paid in health and moral integrity.

The student of human behavior can show that democracy, freedom, and justice are essential factors in all creative and constructive processes of culture. He can prove that no progress in matters economic or scientific, moral or artistic, is possible without true freedom. He can clarify the concepts, adduce factual evidence, and demonstrate the relationship of such realities as freedom, democracy and progress, economic, intellectual, and spiritual. After all this has been done, there enters the value judgment. Some may prefer destruction and mass murder to activities which are creative and constructive.

The history of today proves that tastes for cruelty, brutality, contempt, and hatred exist in human nature, and can be fostered so as to stifle and destroy Christian ethics, demands of a humane and just treatment of human beings, and even aspirations to security and prosperity. The final decision as to whether you prefer a world of Hitlerism, or the "American way", or the British type of life rests with the individual and many individuals. Yet such a judgment is only too often made through agencies of collective confusion rather than of scientific clarity. To establish this clarity in the complex problems of democracy, freedom, human culture, and human nature is the task of contemporary humanism. This task is the more urgent because we have to face now a world in which large-scale confusion has been achieved by means of a thoroughly planned and well-executed campaign of totalitarian propaganda.

The real issue, however, on which the value judgments of Americans, Britishers and other fighters on the Democratic side are going to be put on trial, is the price of freedom. One thing can be demonstrated scientifically: this is the essential dependence of all freedoms and every freedom and freedom in general upon the elimination of collective violence. Chronic insecurity, incessant economic disturbances, and the gospel of brutality and might is right, are inevitable in a war-ridden world, but are the direct antithesis of freedom. The price to be paid for this consists, as we know, in an institutional change. This implies a considerable degree of renunciation of national conceit, of self-satisfied reliance on one's isolated and glorious sovereignty—in short, the translation of ordinary principles of law, ethics and co-operation into the sphere of international affairs. Here the choices will be between the romantic values, that is, the sentimental appeal of national pride and self-satisfaction on the one hand, and the real interests of one's own self, one's family and all the people within our national boundaries and outside of them.

Peace, security and international law, sanctioned by a collective police force responsible only to the executive powers of the Superstate, are the only cultural devices which can prevent the recurrence of total war. The price to be paid for this is the collective agreement by all the citizens of each state, large or small, weak or powerful, to surrender part of the sovereignty of its state. This is in reality a small price to pay for the enormous advantages gained. The advantages are freedom from want and freedom from fear. These are the conditions under which initiative, public and private utterance, play, art, and independence of association flourish in culture. The price to be paid is the sacrifice of collective conceit.

The choice of freedom for the key concept of our analysis and around which it must turn, is imperative. Freedom is the most dynamic, essential, and general factor in the problems of to-day. Democracy is freedom in action. Freedom of conscience is the essence of religion, and religion is the core of civilization. Cast off Christianity, and religion enters as the Nordic myth of Aryan superiority, the ritual of Hitler worship, and the Nazi ethics of domination. Proscribe God through the anti-God campaign in Russia, and you will worship the spirit of Marx and his gospel at the shrine of Lenin's embalmed body. "Fascism is the new religion of the Italian people" was proclaimed by Mussolini, who graciously tolerated Christianity among his people, but who preached the true religion of the Black Shirt.

The principle of the self-determination of nations, groups, and persons can be defined only by making clear how far the freedom of collective decisions has to be related to rights of minorities and to legitimate claims of individuals. Justice, again, which is the spirit of laws, is the balancing and the portioning out of freedoms. Security is freedom from fear; and prosperity, freedom from want. We shall even be able to come near to the definition of that most elusive concept, the pursuit of happiness, and relate it to our description of freedom in terms of human needs and their satisfactions.

Freedom as the driving force of the cultural process challenges us also theoretically because it is the most difficult to define. Philosophers and political thinkers, theologians and psychologists, students of history and moralists have used this word with an excessively wide range of meanings. This was due very largely to the fact that the word freedom for very definite reasons has an emotional appeal and a rhetorical weight which make its use very handy in harangue, moral sermon, poetic appeal, and metaphysical argument. In propaganda and in the appeal to what is best and what is worst in human nature, the word freedom is used under the false pretense that this appeal is founded on profound wisdom and even on scientific cogency. Since it is also used in scientific or near-scientific reasoning, the word "freedom" leads a hybrid existence. The duty, therefore, of making clear scientifically to what realities the word freedom can be legitimately applied, and where it appears out of bounds insofar as any semantic legitimacy is concerned, is not to be shirked. We cannot allow the basic concept which controls the main issue of to-day— over which nations are at war, and over which they will have to determine a peace which will seal the future destinies of mankind—to remain vague, elastic and unviable to an extent which allows it to be prostituted in any argument or counterargument.

Freedom is a quality of the cultural process as a whole and it is a quality which cannot be predicated with reference to any specific aspect of the process, nor yet to any partial phase thereof. The distinctions of political, legal, or economic freedom introduce some confusion and are impossible simply because political power, economic pressure, and legal restraint are fundamentally interrelated. Within the framework of a concrete situation we may isolate things legal, as when a policeman arrests an individual *in flagrante delictu* of speeding, trespassing, or "committing a nuisance". Even then, in the real world in which we live, it is important to know whether the policeman will accept a substantial bribe, in which case economic and legal factors intertwine; or whether the arrestee is a Senator, a Lord, or a higher police officer, perhaps even a member of the Gestapo, in which politics override law and make economics unnecessary. If, however, we consider freedom with reference to the working of human culture as a whole, or with reference to the cultural constitution of a particular society, we shall be able to define the concept in a manner which precludes any ambiguities and solves more of the quibbles, contentions and uncertainties.

I submit that the real difficulty is due to the fact that no definition in terms of individual psychology or individual behavior can be given, because all individual freedoms, as all aspects of individual action, are related to the actions of others. They are also related in this to the instrumentalities necessary for action, that is, to systems of organization, to techniques, to mechanism, and also to words, that is, to speech, thought, deliberation and agreement.

In other words, freedom is an attribute of organized and instrumentally implemented phases of human action. Its great emotional potency is due to the fact that human life and indeed the pursuit of happiness depend upon the nature and the efficiency of those means which culture gives man in his struggle with the environment, with other human beings, and with Destiny herself. Hence unless we refer freedom to the techniques and technicalities of culture, and unless we understand it in terms of anthropological analysis, we shall never be able to establish the real semantic criteria in the distinction between legitimate and illegitimate uses of this word. Freedom is a symbol which stands for a sublime and powerful ideal. The same symbol, however, may become a dangerous weapon in the hands of the enemies of freedom.

We can predicate freedom with reference to three integrally related phases or aspects of human action. First of all we can speak about the freedom of conscience, of thought or purpose; about the freedom of speech, of the press, of the written word. All these are what might be called the freedom of framing the purpose, individual or social. The second phase about which freedom can be predicated is human action. Lastly, since human action is always purposeful and anticipatory of results, we also predicate freedom with reference to the results or the fruits of human endeavor. In this sense freedom is closely related to prosperity; to the effective exercise of political influence, that is, democracy; and to such fundamental rights as *habeas corpus*, freedom of worship, and the freedom of reaping the benefits of arts, recreation and all public amenities. All this already implies the definition of the term.

Freedom can be defined as the conditions necessary and sufficient for the formation of a purpose, its translation into effective action through organized cultural instrumentalities, and the full enjoyment of the results of such activity. The concept of freedom therefore can only be defined with reference to human beings organized and endowed with cultural motives, implements and values, which *ipso facto* implies the existence of law, an economic system and political organization—in short, a cultural system.

Our definition of freedom is composed of three links: purpose, which is embodied in the charter of an institution; instrumentalities, which include the men who work, the tools they use and the rules by which their work is carried to its conclusion; and result or effect, which is the function of the institution. The essential nature of freedom thus conceived is pragmatic. Freedom comes into being when the activities of organized behavior follow human choice and planning. Freedom is determined by the results of action as well as by its prerequisites. The individual's freedom consists in his ability to choose the goal, to find the road, and to reap the rewards of his efforts and endeavors. Those men are free who are able to decide what to do, where to go, or what to build. All claims for freedom remain idle and irrelevant unless planning and aiming can be translated into an effective execution through well-implemented and well-organized behavior. The determining conditions of freedom are therefore to be found in the manner in which a society is organized; in the way in which the instrumentalities are made accessible; and in the guarantees which safeguard all the rewards of planned and purposeful action and insure their equitable distribution.

Any definition in terms only of choices, of maturing and deciding on motives, or even of thought begs the question whether a decision however mature, wise, just or ethical can be effectively carried through. Definitions in terms of mere instruments, mechanical, social or spiritual, beg the question of purpose and result; for the freedom of instrumentalities is in the hands of those by whom the instrumentalities are used and controlled, individually or collectively, and is dependent on whose purpose is carried out, on who enjoys the results and how the results affect others. Sorcery in a primitive culture and a machine gun in our higher civilization give man the freedom to kill. They imply also the freedom of other people to be killed. This example shows not only that our definition is a minimum one as regards its scope and comprehensiveness, but that it must always be supplemented with regard to co-ordination or relating of purposes and ends. Definitions of freedom only in terms of results achieved, of the enjoyment of a higher standard of living, prosperity, ambition, exercise of powers, and pursuit of happiness in general beg the serious question referring to both purposes and instruments. The freedom of the abuse of power and parasitic enjoyment of wealth in complete idleness implies instruments of exploitation, enslavement and subjection of others. Such freedom is probably enjoyed most fully by Mr. Schickelgruber, the few remaining Oriental despots and perhaps a couple of war profiteers.

Our insistence therefore is on choice, or the formation of a purpose; on instrumentalities or the means to the end; and on enjoyment, or the end achieved and controlled. Only when freedom of thought or of inspiration becomes embodied in an active performance does it become relevant to the student of organized behavior, that is, of culture. The freedom which we need to understand is that powerful force which moves men to deeds, which inspires martyrdom and heroism, which precipitates revolutions and mobilizes nations into wars. Hence we insist on considering freedom only insofar as it refers to action, that is, to a decision which through full scope of being implemented becomes a reality of human behavior.

Clearly, since freedom of action means the conditions sufficient and necessary for the mastery of all circumstances inherent in the execution of purpose, freedom means power. Yet since freedom also means absence of restraint, it implies for every individual a condition of not being submitted to the power of others. It is evident therefore that the element of power, of efficiency, of ability to overcome obstacles, must be regarded as indispensable in any definition of freedom. Without some order—and order always implies a residue of authority if not coercion—freedom means anarchy. Thus submission to laws as well as the power to enforce laws and rules are indispensable in human behavior. It is equally evident that the real plus or minus of freedom is dependent on this legitimate use or on the abuse of power. When the work and effort of carrying out a task are imposed on the members of the group, and the advantages of this enterprise are enjoyed only by those who are in authority in the group, we have an abuse of power, through the differential distribution of advantage and effort respectively; and with it, a denial of freedom to those who have done the work.

It is clear from this that we shall need to throw some light on the nature of the rules, norms of conduct, and sanctioned laws which bind co-operating groups, in order to differentiate between tyranny and order, between dictatorship and democracy; in short, between a culture based on the arbitrary use of violence as its main principle, as opposed to a community in which the laws originate from spontaneous and bilateral agreements, while some of the rules have to be accepted simply because they are technical rules of concerted and implemented behavior, or laws which are guarantees of existence and of the exercise of culture. We shall also be able to show that cultures differ as regards the quota of freedom which they give, and we shall see that this largely depends upon the integral constitution of a culture, or as we shall call it, on its charter. Cultures organized for the pursuit of collective violence; cultures economically founded on slavery; cultures chronically or occasionally facing crises, especially war crises, imply a type of constitution where freedom does not flourish.

Our definition will also appear more viable insofar as we shall recognize that a culture, primitive or developed, can always be analyzed into its component institutions, that is, systems of organized activities, each with a charter or collective purpose; with an organized personnel; with a set of specific rules; and each operating a portion of the environment and using special instruments determined by the charter. Certain types of such institutions, slavery for instance, a military cast or a strict hierarchy, are as a rule related to the general type and constitution of a culture; in these cases the charter of the culture is based on definite abrogations of freedom to certain sections of the community. The same analysis that allows us to point out the presence or absence of freedom as determined by the charter of a culture, will also help us to show which are the constitutional elements that guarantee freedom within the institution and which are those that preclude it. Freedom once more, defined with reference to an institution. can be followed up within that group and related to the scope of action and the guarantees of satisfaction enjoyed by an individual.

True freedom—the freedom of order, of action and of achievement—enters into the very texture of human life and of ordered, organized human societies. It is a reality to be found in the conduct of domestic life, in the processes of learning, in the acquisition of values, in the administration of justice, the protection of life and property, and in the cultivation of science, art, recreation and religion. In all this we find that freedom is a gift of culture. It might as well be said that culture is a gift of freedom, for from the very beginnings of humanity freedom is a prerequisite of the exercise, the maintenance and the advancement of cultural achievements.

2

Freedom in the Birth and Growth
of Culture

CULTURE from its very beginnings consists in the organized exploitation by human intelligence of environmental opportunities, and in the disciplining of drives, skills, and nervous reactions in the service of collective and implemented action. The earliest human groups, and the individuals which form them, achieve a much greater integral freedom of mobility and environmental adaptation, freedom of security and prosperity, by the use of tools, by following the principles of knowledge, and by loyalty to a system of activities started with a purpose and carried out concertedly.

In its earliest beginnings, as well as in its fundamental function throughout evolution, culture satisfies first and foremost man's basic needs. Culture thus means primarily the freedom of survival to the species under a variety of environmental conditions for which man is not equipped by nature. This freedom of survival can be analyzed into freedom of security and freedom of prosperity. By freedom of security we mean the protective mechanisms which culture gives through artifacts and co-operation and which endow the species with a much wider margin of safety. Freedom of prosperity refers to the increased, widened, and diversified power of exploiting environmental resources, allowing man to prepare for periods of scarcity, accumulate wealth, and thus obtain leisure for many types of activities which man as an animal would never have undertaken.

The advent of culture changes man the animal into man the artificer, man the organizer, and man the thinker, talker, and planner. Man the animal lives within an environment to which, like any other animal, he became adapted in the course of organic development. Like any animal he is subject to the determinisms of his environment and to the requirements of his organism. Precultural man enjoys as much freedom as any animal and he is subject to the same bondage of his own flesh and its needs, and of the environment with its gifts and potentialities which have to be exploited, as well as its dangers against which any animal has to protect itself.

Culture implies directly and immediately an initial installment in freedom. For culture can be defined as the artificial, secondary, self-made environment which gives man an additional control of certain natural forces. It also allows him to adjust his own responses in a manner which makes the new readaptation by habit and organization more elastic and efficient than the adaptation by reflex and instinct. This initial installment of freedom becomes then gradually developed, and increases into that extensive control of environment, the manipulation of natural forces, and the development of physical and mental faculties which have now made man into the master of this globe, as well as the slave of his own mechanisms and stupidities. The integral increment in freedom, as well as its denials, we can realize by comparing man's place within his physical universe with that from which he started at the birth of culture. The anthropoid species from which man started on his cultural career lived within a limited habitat, probably a tropical jungle. The original man-ape satisfied his needs,

feeding on a narrow and definite range of foodstuffs, protected
from environmental dangers by a small margin of adjustment.
The species was anatomically rather defenseless. Like all anthropoid apes, pre-cultural man has no natural weapons, no fangs,
claws, or horns. Nor is he protected by a thick skin or great speed
of movement. The ape man was thus vulnerable in his own body
and exposed to many dangers because of the long maturation of
the young.

Starting from such a somewhat unfavorable position, man,
through his cultural development, has now overrun the globe and
conquered all climes and all habitats. He is able to adapt to
arctic climates as well as to tropical jungles. He lives on moun-
tain slopes and inhabits small islands surrounded by an enormous
expanse of ocean. He has developed means to irrigate the desert
and to find his subsistence on wide steppes and prairies. Thus
taking freedom as the range of adaptive possibilities, we see that
it has extended man's control as far as the surface of the earth
allows and into the various elements where man was originally
unable to penetrate.

This was made possible through the development of instrumentalities and co-operative actions, which gave man control of elements and means of locomotion to which he was originally not
adapted. By the use of dug-outs, rafts, canoes, and later on of
sailing and power vessels, man has conquered the surface of the
water. He has developed means of diving and remaining under
the water through the diver's outfit and through the extremely
complex instrumentality of the submarine. Even more recently
man has also conquered the air, and through this has reduced
space in a manner almost incredible to those born in the last
century.

The integral freedom given to man as an animal species
through the development of his cultural instrumentality is thus

objective, tangible and specific. It consists in a more efficient and better-founded way of satisfying the innate biological desires of man, and in the indefinite extension in the range of human mobility. It is a new type of environmental adaptation. It is brought about by the use of tools, artifacts, machines, and weapons; by the organization of human beings in relation to the apparatus, and co-ordinating their actions through rules of concerted behavior; and by the development of symbolic means of communication, more especially of language, which allows man to cumulate his tradition and to transmit it from generation to generation.

Culture in its initial state grants the freedom to live in security and with a margin of surplus, while at the same time it implies obedience and submission to certain restraints. These restraints consist in the rules of technique and of knowledge how to exploit the environment and avoid its dangers. Bound up with these are the laws of custom and of social give and take. Ethical principles, partly implicit in submission to the supernatural, partly arising out of organized emotional reactions, impose also certain restraints from the very beginning of culture.

All such laws are as indispensable even to the most primitive forms of cultural behavior as they are inevitable. It is important to keep in mind that earliest man was as bound by his rules as is the member of our highly differentiated cultures of to-day. Neither ontogenetically nor phylogenetically is "man born free". The newborn infant is supremely dependent for his very life on the social and cultural setting of his family. As he grows up, the very essence of training and education consists in disciplining certain freedoms, in substituting habit for reflex, skill for random behavior, and in imparting symbolically the full range of technical, social, and moral tradition. Phylogenetically, man begins with culture, and culture begins with trammels. Man is thus not born free, as Jean Jacques Rousseau wanted us to believe. He is born to a new freedom which he can only achieve by taking up the chains of tradition and using them, for, paradoxically, these very chains are the instruments of freedom.

Earliest man also was unable to produce a single artifact by his own devices, to carry out the simplest activity alone, or yet to enjoy the fruits of his labors—to have his share when others got theirs—except under the guarantees of primitive customary law, of property and privilege. This statement may seem exaggerated only to those who forget that all the benefits of tradition as well as all the guarantees of well-being are social. The use of fire as well as its production had to be learned. Stone implements may be produced by one man as well as used by him, but the quarrying of stone, the knowledge where to find and how to use the materials and the techniques, and the principles of private property in tools and goods produced, imply the existence of early customary law, co-operation and tradition.

In all this man establishes a new self-made environment, to which in turn he readapts his own organism. This new artificial environment obeys a determinism of its own. There exist laws of cultural process, of the constitution of culture, and of the efficiency of concerted activities. Hence culture inevitably becomes a source of new constraints imposed upon man. The laws of cultural process are less rigid than those of nature or of the living organism, and are to be found in the relation between artifact, skill, idea, and rule of conduct. They also control as laws of economics the production, distribution, and consumption of goods. As laws of educational process they determine the mechanism of developing and training the young and transforming an infant into a tribal or national citizen. We find also a number of general laws of structure and function in the study of organized systems of behavior, or institutions as we call them.

Within the really existing human societies, no man ever acts alone. He is always a member of a group, or rather of several groups: the family, the neighborhood group, his professional associates, his municipality, his nation and his sovereign state. This applies to the most primitive savages, to university professors, bricklayers and party members of a Communist, Nazi or Fascist totalitarium. A culture functions therefore by means of a system of related institutions. The values of a culture are embodied in its ideals, mythologies, political constitution and economic ideology; its instrumentalities function through the balanced co-ordination and working of institutions. The standard of existence and quality of living depend on the scope, range, distribution and enjoyment of wealth, rights, power, art, science, and religion. Each member of an institution enjoys his own differential freedom in the measure to which he has a part in the planning, a full access to the means of execution, and a share in the rewards. Even in its smallest and most insignificant manifestations, freedom gives any and every member of a society the sense of achievement, and through this the sense of personal value. In a free culture people can form their purpose, undertake activities and enterprises, and enjoy the gains from work thus undertaken.

The leitmotif of all our arguments will be that all those constraints which are dictated by cultural determinism are as indispensable to successful behavior as are the laws of nature and of the organism. Freedom, indeed, consists in the lead and guidance which the rules and laws of culture give man. At the same time we shall see that most of those rules of cultural determinism imply the element of power, placed in the hands of one or of a few. This power can be abused in the form of wealth, of physical violence, and of spiritual intimidation, with regard to initiative and planning, or to the control of cultural instrumentalities, or else to the distribution of the benefits. In every case the distinction between the differential freedom of social organization and minor or major cases of bondage, slavery or oppression turns round the question whether the constraint is necessary for the successful execution of the activity, or whether it is exercised to the advantage of a few and at the expense of others.

As humanity advances, there open up new vistas for human desire, interest, knowledge, and belief. In this, the symbolic aspect of culture—the power to embody tradition into communicable texts; the power to tell tales about past events, past miracles and past achievements; the power to plan, to foresee, and to foretell—becomes the means of invention of new devices, planning of new activities, and the maturing of purpose and motive. From this is derived freedom of conscience, thought and speech.

Freedom also gives man the power to anticipate, and to establish values by the guidance of which man can engage in co-operative activities and does reach new goals and enjoy them under his guarantees of tribal or national citizenship. This type of freedom embraces legal and political planning as well as the shackles and leeways of tradition. Here enter the domains of knowledge, technology, religion, art, and organized recreation, which from their humble beginnings gradually develop and engage more and more of human interests, human ambitions, and human abilities.

Thus it seems clear, first and foremost, that the concept of freedom must always be referred to the increase in range, diversity and power in human planning. The ability to foresee and to plan ahead, that is, the ability to use past experience in order to establish future conditions corresponding to the needs, the desires and the aspirations of man, is the first essential prerequisite of freedom. All planning, however, all visions, aspirations, discoveries or inventions remain idle, insignificant, and, to the science of human behavior, irrelevant, if the instrumentalities for their realization are not present. The freedom of the spirit is either an empty phrase, or it means some definite change in the world of matter, of flesh, and of human circumstances. Finally, and as the anthropologist and the historian know only too well, all human endeavor, all hard work and effort can either be worthwhile or, once more, vain, irrelevant and unreal. This yes-or-no condition of human enterprise depends clearly on its integral success, and on the value of its success to the community, to the institution, and to its component members. The final results of human activities, the satisfaction which they bring to the group and its component individuals, can either be realized or set at naught. To discuss freedom without considering the gratifications and enjoyments of the results obtained is to confuse the work of a slave with that of a free man. Freedom in terms of the standard of living, of the enjoyments and gratifications brought by culture to its carriers, is as important as the freedom of purpose and the freedom of equipment in efficient action.

Thus the maintenance, the management, and the development of the psychological mainsprings in inspiration, invention, and contribution are the first and foremost conditions of freedom. The formation of social loyalties, on which every institution is built, is the second condition. The way in which the cultural values, that is, the enjoyment of economic, social, political, moral, and spiritual benefits, are distributed—in other words, freedom in the pursuit of happiness—is the last and perhaps the main condition of liberty.

This brief outline of the cultural background of our problem in evolutionary perspective was given to show first and foremost that not a single human act, relevant to the science of man, occurs outside the context of culture. In this sense freedom can only be discussed as an attribute of the cultural process. In its very beginnings and throughout evolution, culture grants certain leeways and opportunities, and imposes certain restrictions.

Freedom, therefore, is always a relative concept which implies balance and relation. It is the surplus value in integral achievement, over and above the unavoidable submissions to rule, norm, and restriction. It lies in the relation between the prerogatives of self and of others, for man is dependent on others both through tradition and through co-operation. To start the analysis of freedom by considering how an individual behaves within a short-range phase of activities, a phase arbitrarily cut out, must always lead to error. The error becomes even more serious when we rely on the subjective feeling of the individual under such conditions and try to imagine how he feels. It is essential to start from the objective and real context of freedom rather than to train a psychic telescope or microscope on that unobservable entity, the human soul in its emotional iridescences, as it observes itself in its own private microcosm.

Thus our concept of freedom is an induction from the concrete and specific manifestations thereof. It is an asset given to humanity through the organization of human beings into co-operative groups, who have to obey certain norms, who have to use implements and machines, who have to co-operate for a determined end. In all this they achieve the integral freedom of their purpose at the price of partial submissions and renunciations. The sacrifice is small for their share in such great results. To the extent that these submissions and renunciations deprive some members of an institution—whether this be slavery or serfdom, a military regiment, or the crew of a galley—from either the participation in planning and the building up of the purposes and decisions, or else in the enjoyment of the results, such a denial of initiative and of a fair share in the standard of living means a total or partial, a temporary or chronic abrogation of freedom.

Right through our analysis there runs the thesis that freedom is the successful unimpeded course of the cultural process, bringing full satisfaction of all needs. Freedom is neither more nor less but full success in action. It is activity spontaneously planned, efficiently executed, and enjoyed in its results by all those who have contributed. In all this we shall see that the integral constitution of a culture, whether for peace or war, for collective robbery or the internal development of arts, crafts, and industries, for a religion of cruelty and aggression or for a faith essentially humane and ethical, is the primary determinant of freedom or bondage.

Thus the distribution of freedom within society, the distribution which has to be referred to purpose, activity, and standard of living alike, is one of the concrete and specific problems which cannot be neglected. The use of power in physical constraint, in economic pressure, and in spiritual intimidation has to be studied at any level of human development. Our approach shows that freedom is essentially a positive quality of human behavior, the quality of the smooth, efficient satisfying of all, within the context of a given culture.

Although we have insisted throughout that freedom is specific, concrete, and a concept of balance and relation, this does not mean that we must speak in terms of "many liberties but no one freedom". Freedom indeed is one and indivisible. It is a general concept which, as defined above, indicates the conditions of human existence, giving man the maximum control to do through concerted and implemented action what he desires and needs, to do it efficiently, and to do it so as to satisfy and not to thwart his wants and his aspirations. All general freedom is a common measure of each specific freedom. The scientific approach, through the study of specific manifestations, must be combined with the equally scientific postulate of the search for a common measure and the most general formula covering all these specific cases. This brief anticipatory summing up of the essentials in the approach here adopted will allow us to deal more readily with a critical survey of certain current contributions to the problem of freedom.

Part III

THE MEANING OF FREEDOM

1

Freedom in Its Universe of Semantic Chaos

"THE world has never had a good definition of the word liberty, and the American people, just now, are much in want of one." Thus spoke Abraham Lincoln in his Baltimore address on April 18, 1864. His statement is as true and practically relevant today, as it was then. There reigns now as then a complete chaos in the domain semantically covered by the words freedom and liberty.

Freedom is not a word about which it is suitable to be flippant, supine, or confused in a fighting democracy. We are fighting for freedom. We believe in it. Our belief cannot remain vague or intuitive, if it is to be really efficient. Ours is an age where faith must be in harmony with reason. Totalitarianism is trying indeed to subordinate reason and thought to dictated truth. Its crude mysticism, its racial theories and political and nationalistic dogmas are being ruthlessly imposed on a nation of thinkers and workers. This is perhaps the most destructive aspect of totalitarianism in Germany and elsewhere. We cannot follow suit.

Freedom is an ideal which throughout human evolution has inspired the most sublime philosophies and creeds. It has also mobilized man into the greatest battles of history and led him

43

to the most significant and glorious victories. People have fought for this ideal and died for it gladly. Martyrs and heroes of humanity have perished at the stake and faced their ordeals of martyrdom for the sake of freedom of conscience, of religion, of national independence and of scientific conviction.

Yet even here freedom has always appeared as a double-faced goddess: for martyrdom means religious persecution, and a fight for liberty implies tyranny. Tyrants, inquisitors and dictators had also their own ideals, at times even an ideal of freedom which they were trying to impose on humanity. Thus at every stage of evolution and history, in every specific case under consideration, there is a need of dispassionate, well-briefed inquiry into where freedom resided and from where oppression came.

The word freedom is, therefore, not a mere counter or token of speech. It is a word as moving in poetry as it is powerful in the domain of live battle cries. Many have sacrificed, and at this very hour are sacrificing, the fundamental freedom of existence for the sake of freedom. Others give up their own personal freedom and languish or perish in prison or concentration camp, so as to testify to the value of freedom. The freedom from want, the freedom of security, the strongest emotional freedoms of friendship and family bonds have to be surrendered to this sublime yet ruthless ideal.

The fundamental problems of ethics, sociology and psychology revolve around this concept. At times it is almost felt that to define such a word is nothing short of sacrilege. Yet this is necessary, for the word is also capable of indefinite perversions. It is our duty to show where these perversions lie and how they can be detected and refuted. The alternative is simply to surrender to confusion and perversion.

Any attempt to discover a satisfactory concept of freedom makes clear the fact that we do not suffer from a dearth of definitions but rather from a surfeit. There reigns a chaos and confusion of meanings, and it will be necessary to put some order into this semantic chaos, and to eliminate a few unnecessary concepts. The intuitive emotional and subjective meaning of freedom, as felt rather than formulated by the man in the street, conceives of freedom as the ability to do what one likes or to do nothing. The claim that liberty is the absence of restraint, of trammels, and of hindrances is persistent. Were we to collect some of the finest poetic phrases, some of the classic epigrams, some of the famous sayings of moralists, theologians and orators, we would always find an emphasis on the subjective feeling of an unlimited scope for choice and expansion in thought, in action, in the affirmation of oneself.

Freedom as "absence of restraint" is also the common semantic measure of all dictionary or encyclopedic definitions. "Absence of restraint", "exemption or release from slavery or imprisonment", "exemption from arbitrary control", "the quality of being free from the control of fate or necessity"—these are some typical and recurrent lexicographic entries under the words "freedom" and "liberty".

A modified and moderate insistence on lack of trammels runs through a whole group of explicit and circumstantial arguments and definitions, characteristic of liberal and libertarian thinkers. They argue, define and interpret facts so as to make liberty synonymous with the absence of chains, removal of restraints, and the minimum control of the individual. John Stuart Mill might be taken as representative of this view. His main insistence is on the freedom of thought and speech, and in this his arguments are on the whole unimpeachable. Mill, however, and many other liberal thinkers, who insist that "more liberty and less law" are directly related, often forget that it is not the quantity of law which matters, but its nature. The extreme position verging on

anarchism adopted by some liberals fails to give sufficient recognition to the fact that the degree to which discipline is necessary
depends on many factors besides human goodwill. Thus the
intuitive approach and its elaboration into the concept of freedom as the minimum of law discloses at first sight that a certain
reconsideration is necessary, and certain additions have to be
made so as to eliminate the contradictory elements.

This brings us to the other and, in its semantic form, apparently antinomic definition of freedom. When we are told by
Cicero that "we are all the law's slaves, that we may be free",
the implication is clear: freedom can only be achieved through
restraint. Even Rousseau, who at one stage of his argument affirms
that "man is born free", tells us elsewhere that "he has to be
forced to be free". Again, Montesquieu tells us that "liberty is
the right of doing whatever the laws permit, and if a citizen could
do what they forbid, he would be no longer possessed of liberty".
It would be easy perhaps to quote parallel statements from many
liberal writers, in which they affirm on the one hand that freedom is based on the absence of restraint, and on the other that it
is due to the establishment of laws. Yet "slavery to law", "obedience to law", freedom through being "forced into it", freedom
born of restraint, are contradictions in terms of "freedom as
complete lack of restraint".

Not only that: the conception of freedom as a complete and
unrestricted submission to laws, political authority, the general
will or the national genius leads us into strange regions. We meet
the Hegelian concept, with its roots in earlier philosophies from
Plato onwards, until we arrive at that freedom which is now
being proclaimed as the gift of totalitarian political systems.
Mussolini declared in one of his moments of outspokenness "We
have buried the putrid corpse of liberty". Yet his blander and
more cunning spokesmen, especially when they addressed credu-

lous democracies or Fifth Column converts, insisted that Fascism can offer the fullest freedom of individual self-realization by merging the citizen with the corporate state.

A simple, common-sense reflection shows that there is and must be a co-efficient of power in the conception of freedom. We have seen that this is the case throughout our brief outline of how culture increases human freedom, from its beginning right through the course of evolution. Free action must imply some control of circumstances and of other people. Since freedom implies efficiency and success, it also must imply power. Complete weakness and inability to act, inefficiency in planning and in performance, are not compatible with the freedom of achievement. They lead only to the freedom of failure. Yet, if we were carelessly to identify freedom with power, we obviously would nurse tyranny, exactly as we land into anarchy when we equate liberty with lack of any restraint.

Taking "exemption from constraint" at its face value, it is clear that the greatest margin of freedom can be enjoyed by people who are to the greatest extent exempt from desire, passion and even impulse. Diogenes in his tub has been the ideal of a free man for generations and still remains so. A Neapolitan Lazzarone, replacing the portable tub with his portable basket, implies equally the philosophic freedom, looks for his *Lebensraum* in the rays of the sun and remains perfectly free to beg, to cadge, and to do nothing. None of these philosophers of free living would cultivate such additional hampering needs as thirst for knowledge, for art, for religious and social recreations. Even the ideal of poverty as preached and practiced by St. Francis and his followers does not satisfy us as the fullest expression of the concept of freedom.

Freedom as willing submission to restraint—any restraint and every restraint—is obviously a perverted concept. The solution here must be found, as was suggested several times, in the analysis of laws and authority. There are rules, norms and laws which are as inevitable for action as they are creative of freedom. There are other laws, such for instance as we find in any historical tyranny, in the Spanish Inquisition, in the modern corporate state of Hitler and Mussolini, which not only deny freedom but also destroy culture. Any purely formal juggling with such words as law, rule, trammel, and discipline is misleading in the theory of freedom. Rules or laws are clearly means to an end. They are instruments in the regulation of human conduct. We have to see how they are employed and for what purposes as well as with what results, before we can assess their contribution towards or their abrogation of freedom.

In our brief analysis of the birth and development of culture and of the freedom which it gives, we have seen that the specific extension of control achieved by early man refers to the disciplining of his organism and desires, as well as to the management of the environment. No wonder, therefore, that among the general conceptions of freedom, preached and practiced by humanity, we find one in which human beings achieve spiritual independence by rejecting the trammels of the flesh, of ambition, and of wealth. This is the freedom of the spirit which we find embodied in such philosophies as Stoicism, and in such religions as Christianity, Buddhism, and all those which deliver the soul from the trammels of the flesh. The freedom achieved by the union with the Absolute or with God is perhaps the main gift offered to man by those beliefs which promise compensation in the other world for the sufferings and injustices of this one.

Here we have also to list that freedom of mind which is to be found in submission to fate. "The willing is led by fate; the resistant is driven". Stoicism and allied philosophies have inspired many who are suffering from illness or from imprisonment to overcome the physical trammels of the body by the freedom of the spirit. Here freedom is achieved by affirming the independence of the spirit, by showing how through renunciation of desire, of hope, and of ambition, man can still remain free, although physically he is disabled or shackled.

Some religious systems attack the problem in an even more radical and positive manner. Christianity and Buddhism alike insist on the moral desirability of freedom from desire. The saintly Buddhist works his way towards Nirvana. The equally saintly Christian, like Origen, achieves his freedom by castration. The ascetic anchorite runs away from human passions, interests, and ambitions, and lives in his lonely hermitage, climbs a pillar in a desert, or enters a cave. All of them strive for the freedom of the road to the next world, the freedom from life, the freedom from the trammels of the body. In this the use of the word freedom has again a different semantic value. As such we accept it respectfully. We are not unsympathetic, unmoved, or unelated by the heroic struggle against the world, the flesh, and the devil.

It is necessary to realize, however, that this concept of freedom implies the rejection or denial of life itself. Were we to imagine a culture in which all the members were decided to wean themselves from existence, to suspend the reproductive process and to devote themselves to the mortification of the flesh—such a culture could not continue. It would die of inanition. Human cultures have from time to time produced religious sects inspired by such an ideal and practicing it. We know them from the Middle Ages, and they have occurred again in eighteenth and nineteenth century Russia. Such sects of castrates, anchorites and hermits are an interesting cultural epiphenomenon. They always, however, presuppose the existence of a community whose culture and whose freedom are based on different principles.

Hamlet's problem of freedom, "to be or not to be", is thus but a sideline of cultural inquiry. The freedom of suicide, individual or collective, is one which ends the drama of the stage and of life. Hamlet has to reject it in the interests of the continuance of the play. We have to reject it in the interests of the cultural continuity of mankind. Now, when humanity is on the verge of collective suicide, we must bend our thoughts on preventing it, rather than on pondering how it could best be executed by a spontaneous decision. In this we once more return to our fundamental assumption: freedom is to us an attribute of human existence, that is, of human action, and we have to consider it with reference to decisions to act, and not to end life or suspend action.

There is, however, an even more important reflection which occurs to a student of culture and of cultural processes, with reference to the freedom of philosophic detachment and of religious escape into Nirvana or the union with God. Such "purely spiritual freedoms" are not really detached from their material and organic setting. It is an illusion to think of them as free movements of the spirit, slipping out of its trammels of flesh and matter. In reality Stoicism, union with God, and all other forms of "spiritual escape" consist in a severe discipline of the body. They usually imply a long period of training and organismic drill. They are based on a religious tradition, which has to be learned and assimilated. They imply a series of rules and an apparatus in mysticism. In order to achieve any of these religious and spiritual freedoms, man has to submit to a system of ritual activities, at times lasting over years. He has to learn a system of verbal instructions, and has to submit fully to the doctrine and the ethics. He has to read or listen to philosophic arguments and religious sermons. Through all this he acquires the principles of self-control, of nervous and muscular discipline.

The serenity of thought and outlook, the sublime soarings of the mind are thus not disembodied motions of the soul. They correspond to concrete, tangible and definite cultural processes.

Once more we recognize that the real battle ground of freedom, as well as the workshop in which it is produced in all its qualities, forms and varieties, is culture. The spontaneous withdrawal from life cannot be achieved by a mere act of will. It has to be carried through by a detailed substantial process of training, which is a cultural process.

When we turn to the affirmation of freedom through heroic death, we are faced by a somewhat different yet essentially cultural context of action. "Give me liberty or give me death" is not the cry of a Buddhist or of an ascetic. It affirms freedom of conscience through opposition to unrighteous might, and not in withdrawal from life. The martyrs of religious conviction, the political heroes who died for their country or for the freedom of humanity, affirm rather than deny the claims of life. In such cases it is not even necessary to emphasize the fact that freedom is part of a historical, hence a cultural, process. People who sacrifice their lives on the altar of God or of the nation have to face physical force, political oppression and other forms of organized injustice and restraint. They also in their own mind and body have to develop conviction, faith, and heroism through a discipline closely resembling that of the ascetic. It is a discipline differently directed, having other aims and following other mechanisms, but it obviously implies a clear purpose, the ability to endure and to brave pain and torture, and through this achieve results which bring more freedom to others if not to the hero and martyr himself.

An important byway of the claim that mind can triumph over matter is to be found in the domain of magic and miracles. This represents the irrepressible desire of man to escape the laws of nature, to overcome the tricks and trammels of chance, and to defy destiny herself. This freedom of magic and miracles affects a vast domain of human culture. We shall have to discuss it more fully in another context; here we are only putting it on the semantic map of the various meanings of freedom.

In discussing these last types of freedom we find always that they do belong in the domain of liberties given by culture. Since our central thesis is to the effect that freedom cannot be discussed outside the context of culture, we need only to mention here that political organization, economic enterprise, the pursuits of science, religion and recreation may become fountainheads of freedom. They may also contain serious and grievous denials of freedom. To us culture in its political, legal, and economic organization is the main battle ground in the fight for freedom. Even when it comes to recreation and to the pursuit of art, poetry and music, freedom may be curtailed as well as expanded. We have only to remember the main pastimes of ancient Rome in which the slavery of the main actors supplied the entertainment of the spectators.

The difficulty which we meet at this point turns round the question whether we have to admit or to deny the existence of many liberties, a semantic evasion which often is used to prove that there is not one freedom. On this issue we have already declared ourselves. Freedom is one and indivisible. It is a general concept which embraces its several specific manifestations.

2

Analysis of the Multiple Meanings

WE HAVE made a survey of several regions of fact, real or fictitious, where human beings look for freedom and find freedom. Freedom, as we have seen, is often declared as residing primarily in the world of absolute existence; or else it is to be found in the escape from the trammels of this world; or in the defiance of fate or submission to it. We have taken such opinions and beliefs at their face value. We accepted philosophical or religious systems, semantic usage, and rules of grammar and lexicography very much as we found them. This somewhat uncritical acceptance leads obviously into that "chaos of semantics", into that confusion and impossibility to define, about which we have heard Abraham Lincoln complain.

We have now to introduce some order into the confusion. To do this it will be well to project our findings onto a synoptic chart. We see there all the several usages of the term freedom plotted out around a central entry which we label "core of freedom". Our chart therefore is an inventory of the various opinions and linguistic usages in which the term freedom figures. Were we to take the self-valuation of each system and each usage as it stands, our chart would also represent several groups of fact. We have

already an inkling that this cannot be the case. We would have
at least nine freedoms and probably these could still be subdivided, fragmented or minced up into other freedoms. For one
thing, we suspect from all our previous arguments that the very
central meaning, the "core of freedom", is a subjective figment.
It was necessary, however, to place it in this central position
because, as we shall see, it is a figment and a fallacy very deeply
rooted in human psychology, as well as in that trickery of words
which has caused so much trouble in man's thinking and even in
man's active behavior.

The fundamental principle which will help us to introduce
order into this semantic chaos, to eliminate fictitious uses of the
word, and to define it clearly and consistently, is that we have to
look for freedom in the realities of human action and to analyze
them in their cultural contexts. Looking at our diagram we see
therefore that the entry at its basis "freedom of culture" contains
that solid matrix of fact and event in which real freedom occurs,
through the additions which it receives from organized and
implemented behavior, and in the restraints inevitable or else
remediable. This entry B-2 is flanked by two others "freedom
of conscience" A-2, and "freedom of miracle" C-2 which are
also essentially processes of culture. They represent, however, not
the real pragmatic mechanisms in which an increase or decrease
of freedom in behavior is given. They are essentially compensatory mechanisms of culture in which man expresses his defiance
of fate or else the belief in his ability to control chance by way
of magic or of miracle. The middle tier in which we find entries
A, B, and C corresponds to those definitions of freedom which
have always occupied a central position in all philosophic, ethical
and psychological discussions. We find there that intangible core
of freedom felt intuitively, rather than capable of clear definition: the feeling of absolute absence of all restraint. This is

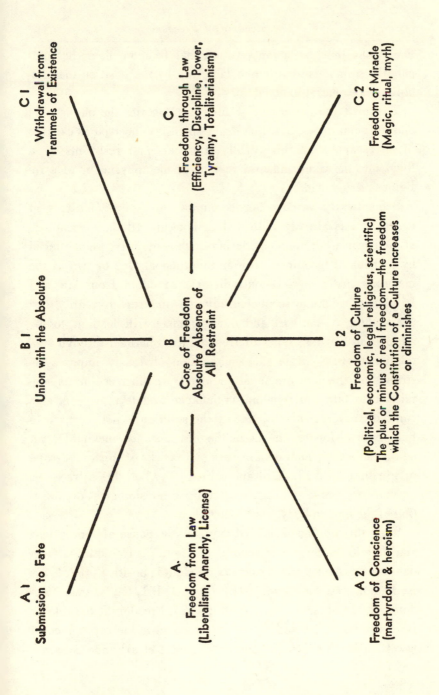

A1
Submission to Fate

C1
Withdrawal from Trammels of Existence

B1
Union with the Absolute

C
Freedom through Law
(Efficiency, Discipline, Power, Tyranny, Totalitarianism)

C2
Freedom of Miracle
(Magic, ritual, myth)

B
Core of Freedom
Absolute Absence of All Restraint

A.
Freedom from Law
(Liberalism, Anarchy, License)

B2
Freedom of Culture
(Political, economic, legal, religious, scientific)
The plus or minus of real freedom—the freedom which the Constitution of a Culture increases or diminishes

A2
Freedom of Conscience
(martyrdom & heroism)

flanked by the libertarian position that freedom flourishes outside the trammels of rule and law; and by the position that discipline is essential to freedom.

The third and upper tier of our chart contains the philosophic
and religious views, in which man's spirit is conceived as capable
of an escape from this-worldly trammels and restraints by a
flight into the transcendental regions of metaphysics or of a religious other-world.

Semantically we have here a number of groups of divergent
usage. It was already indicated that taking all these meanings
at their own word and considering them conjointly, we are faced
by a chaos of incompatibility and confusion. One or two of the
meanings are even self-contradictory. Freedom from law and
freedom through law seem contradictions in terms. In reality they
are nothing of the sort and our argument will lead us to the
affirmation that new types of freedom are obtained through submission to rule, while such submission obviously imposes restraints on freedom previously enjoyed. Again, freedom as submission to fate and freedom as defiance of fate may seem also
contradictory. Yet here obviously the solution is not too hard to
find. Submission to fate is in the last instance inevitable, yet
neither submission nor defiance are mere tricks of spiritual escape
or spiritual revolt. In hard and solid reality both these freedoms
mean a very active and highly disciplined physiological organization of the human body.

Right through the variety of views and expanse of conceptions
and definitions there run several clear-cut contradictions: freedom is negative (A and B) *versus* freedom is positive (B-2, C-2).
And again, freedom is subjective (B, A-1, B-1, C-1) *versus* freedom must be objective (C, A-2, B-2, C-2). Freedom is the release
from constraint (A and B) *versus* freedom is the acceptance of
law (C). These contradictions we can meet clearly and squarely

on our main principle; namely, that freedom can only be found in those additions to human efficiency and control which culture provides. To us therefore freedom is positive; it is objective; and it consists in the acceptance of law.

As regards the other confusion, we find that freedom is referred either to the spirit alone, or to the spirit controlling the body, or else to the spirit escaping the trammels of the body and of matter. Here we have already removed the confusion. We have definitely shown that all the "pure freedoms of spirit" are achieved not by any metaphysical shortcuts, but by mechanisms of training, ritual, ascetic drill and exercises. All such mechanisms in turn are based on traditional systems of philosophy, religion and mysticism. Thus, and with reference to our chart, we would have to pull down the positions A-1, B-1, and C-1 from their exalted heights and place them where they really belong—in the context of culture. Since as students of real human behavior we are interested in the freedom of the mind only when this freedom is expressed in action—the action which affirms conscience, conviction and patriotism, as well as philosophic aloofness, the union with God and independence from the flesh—we must study all forms of spiritual freedom in those processes where it is really effective. We see clearly, therefore, that the three upper entries in our chart belong to B-2, "freedom of culture". They are the additions to human control over the various obstacles, misfortunes and turns of chance and destiny, which are given to man through the creative additions of socially and culturally organized belief, thought and ritual.

In religion we find promise, planning, a prescription for life, and a code of rules. This is extremely real and of supreme importance to the individual and to society. We can show that in a Christian society inspired and permeated with faith, preaching it in ritual and observing it in its ethics, there are certain types of freedom, such as the freedom of the City of God. Faith also contains a promise, the real promise of compensation, reward, and payment in full of any deficiencies. In faith lies the prevention of injustice, exploitation and slavery.

The opinion that religion is the opiate of the masses is not true. In reality and historically, it is faith which brings about the brotherhood of man and gives celestial freedom. The effectiveness of faith lies in the extent to which it is a solace to the true believer, and how far it affects the mighty and the rich, the ambitious, greedy and lustful in their behavior.

In other words, since we refuse to take belief, semantic usage and philosophic system at their face value; since we submit them to scientific analysis in terms of what they really mean as phases in human behavior, we can bring the semantic figments of the upper tier down to the solid ground of observation, analysis and correct interpretation. We refuse to follow the fictitious detachment of our concept of freedom from its cultural context. In placing freedom where it belongs, we eliminate a considerable area of our semantic diversity and we reduce it to the one well-established basic position: freedom in the cultural process.

There remains still the middle section with its core of free-floating-freedom and its two wings, of potential anarchy, and discipline leading to despotism. Here two main problems emerge. First of all we shall have to analyze more fully this "core of freedom" which we have listed here. Since it corresponds apparently to a persistent emotional demand of the human mind, our analysis here will lead us to an interesting solution. We shall be able to show that the claim for this concept of freedom as a free-floating gift from fate to man is psychologically well-founded. It is almost as inevitable as the feeling which every one of us cherishes, that he is the center of the world. We have an analogous feeling about the supreme value of our own personality, about immortality, and about the categorical imperatives of our intellectual and moral judgment. We shall see that as a matter of subjective personal experience we inevitably claim freedom absolute, unlimited and ubiquitous. We shall also be able to relate this error of subjective mysticism to certain objective manifestations of culture. All phenomena of magic, all revolt against determinism, all desire for miracles—from primitive magic and totemism, through the Roman Catholic belief in saints, right up to Christian Science— are developed and practiced by mankind. This concept of free-floating-freedom is very deeply rooted and has been persistently practiced.

The second problem which emerges from our chart demands the solution of the antinomy of the liberal's freedom and the disciplinarian's liberty. Here we shall see that each taken apart contains an error of statement. Harmonized, both claims lead us directly to the study of what freedom in concrete human behavior really means. Since all human action inevitably embraces discipline, through submission to the rules of this action, we never find freedom from restraint in human behavior. And here comes the essential and crucial point of our argument. Those who attempt any definition of freedom in terms of negative categories and in terms of an absolute and unlimited absence of trammels, must be chasing an intellectual will-o'-the-wisp. Real freedom is neither absolute nor omnipresent and it certainly is not negative. It is always an increase in control, in efficiency, and in the power to dominate one's own organism and the environment, as well as artifacts and the supply of natural resources. Hence freedom as a quality of human action, freedom as increase of efficiency and control, means the breaking down of certain obstacles and a compensation for certain deficiencies; it also implies the acceptance of rules of nature, that is, scientific laws of knowledge, and of those norms and laws of human behavior which are indispensable to efficient co-operation.

The real denials of freedom come also from culture. Over and above the rules imposed by nature, by technique, and by concerted action, there exist in all human societies rules and laws which result from the abuses of social power. In some human societies such abuses, organized and codified, give rise to slavery, political oppression and to laws which are Draconic in their severity or perverted in purpose. The philosophic treatment of freedom must include such actual denials of liberty, although it may try to remedy them by indirect methods. The sociological conception of liberty must be primarily adjusted to those problems where freedom can be increased or diminished through the practical application of sound theory. The sound theory of freedom consists in the full realization that men must have scope for the choice of what they want to do and where they want to get.

Such freedom of choice becomes effective only when it is backed up by access to all the means, technical, economic and political, which allow purpose to be translated into action. Since all desire and all purpose aim not merely at action but also at what this action brings, the problem of how people are rewarded for their efforts is essential to freedom. Slavery always gives full scope for people to work, but it does not allow them to choose their enterprise nor yet to benefit by it. Rigid social distinctions embodied in such institutions as class, caste, serfdom, and feudal hierarchy limit both choice and the enjoyment of results, and at the same time impose highly differential distributions of effort. Imprisonment is a denial of freedom in that it eliminates even the formation of purpose, and trammels most types of activity. The scientific treatment of freedom must, therefore, focus on the core of the problem rather than hunt for the core of meaning.

3

The Concept of Free-Floating-Freedom

W E MUST proceed now to the consideration of the first problem
stated at the end of our previous section. The suggestion is often
made in literature that it is futile as well as impossible to define
freedom so as to cover all the uses of this word and to bring out
"the core of the meaning" on which all ordinary usages converge.
Hence we are told, since any attempt at defining must lead to
failure why not accept the intuitive meaning, familiar to everyone using the word? The reader will see clearly that in this
analysis we do not accept this point of view at all. Since, however,
it has not only been explicitly suggested, but also haunts many
arguments and approaches, it will be well to state the case for the
concept of free-floating-freedom fully and fairly, before applying
to it a critical and I trust a finally eliminating analysis.

It may perhaps be best first of all to show that we are not tilting
at windmills, nor yet even arguing against windbags. The suggestion that we must accept freedom as a concept intuitive and subjective, essentially negative and strictly individual, is to be found
in some of the best contributions to our subject. Remarkably
enough, freedom in such approaches appears as absolute and
substantial as it is also made intangible, emotional and personal.

To be fair to all such views and approaches, we shall try to show through a psychological analysis why it is that the claim for a free-floating-freedom is so persistent and pervasive.

"Freedom is a concept that has meaning only in a subjective sense. The person who is completely in harmony with his culture feels free. He accepts voluntarily the demands made upon him". (F. Boas, R. N. A.*, p. 376) In this opinion of a leading anthropologist we see a clear demand that the concept of freedom be accepted as a subjective state of mind. Freedom consists in the voluntary subjective acceptance by an individual of the demands made upon him by his culture. We shall see that such a suggestion has to be rejected for two reasons. First, it is difficult to see how we could observe such a subjective feeling of harmony in any scientific study of human beings or of human behavior. Secondly, such an approach is extremely dangerous, since we could make a very good case for Hitler's freedom on the assumption that Nazi indoctrination has taken roots in most German minds, and is making them accept Nazi culture and be completely in harmony with it.

One of the foremost living sociologists, Professor MacIver of Columbia, tells us that the word freedom "signifies an immediate datum, something that cannot be analyzed into component parts or reduced to simpler statements. It is a meaning we must simply recognize, simply accept". (R. N. A., p. 279) Here we find a clear invitation for the acceptance of the intuitive meaning given in that experience of freedom which we all know and recognize. Professor MacIver is even more explicit: "About this universal meaning [of liberty] there can be no doubt. The child knows it who is forced to work when he wants to play. The savage knows it who is prevented from following his tribal customs. The criminal

---

* R. N. A. refers throughout to *Freedom, Its Meaning*, edited by Ruth Nanda Anshen, 1940. (Harcourt, Brace and Company, Inc.)

knows it who is put behind prison bars. The property owner knows it who is not allowed to use his property as he pleases". (R. N. A., p. 285) Here again we are invited to rely on the intuitive knowledge of the child, the savage, the criminal, or the bloated plutocrat.

Once more I submit that this is not feasible. First of all I have not yet heard of an adequate instrument of observation, a psychoscope as we might call it, which would allow us to observe and to register the knowledge or the feelings of a child, a savage, or a criminal, or for that matter of any human being scientifically studied. In the second place it is perfectly clear that here we have a demand for accepting a reality for which the word "freedom" fits metaphorically, but which as a matter of fact cannot be allowed to exist in any well-ordered society. Education is nothing else but a gradual curtailment of the child's "freedom". The machinery of criminal law which is the foundation of order in human communities consists in the curtailing of "criminal freedoms".

Another writer, Professor Walton Hamilton of the Yale Law School, as eminent a thinker in jurisprudence as in economics, declares thus his skepticism: "For all our knowledge and understanding, we can no more define freedom than we can realize it. It is a general term, the core of which is an opportunity for man to make the most of himself in the fragment of the world about him".* Is not one Adolf Hitler "making the most of himself in the fragment of the world about him"? If this be freedom, it is a freedom of making the world about any one of us into fragments where freedom is not easy to find. Here once more we have the direct reference to the thoughts which are entertained by the individual. We have therefore an invitation to a subjective treat-

* Walton H. Hamilton in *Freedom in the Modern World*, edited by Horace M. Kallen, 1928.

ment of the concept. We have also an outspoken doubt as to
whether any definition is possible, and the semantic suggestion
that we must look for a core of meaning, which however is left
very vague in general. Dr. Hamilton's view here quoted is the
more telling, in that this writer, who starts so vaguely and con-
fusedly, is able in his excellent essay to develop an argument in
my opinion completely free from any mistakes, an argument in
which freedom is definitely related to real and concrete cultural
processes. Yet even this writer has to make his bow to the undefinable "core of meaning".

An eminent student of natural science, Professor J. B. S.
Haldane, opens his discussion of freedom with a high and
mighty claim to scientific exactness. "The first essential in any
scientific study is a possibility of comparison. The measuring
rod, the stop watch, and the balance are at the very roots of science. If our study of freedom is to have any practical results, we
must try to tackle the question, is A freer than B? A may be a bus
driver in New York, and B a bus driver in Belgrade, or B may be
a corporation vice-president, a poet, or A's wife in New York.
In almost every case we find the question unanswerable." Professor Haldane then proceeds to discuss the manifold dimensions
of freedom, such as reading the works of Marx, attendance at
movies, drinking alcohol after 10 p. m., and many other amenities
of life. He then inquires, "Who is to decide which is freer? Our
best plan will be to specify different possible fields of freedom,
so that we may be able to carry out comparisons within these
fields. The overall summary will inevitably be subjective, but
we can at least say that in some particular respect A is more free
or less free than B."* Here we find a queer mixture of assumptions and claims. The writer has decided beforehand that the

---

* J. B. S. Haldane in *Freedom, Its Meaning*, planned and edited by Ruth Nanda
Anshen, 1940, p. 447.

inquiry must remain essentially subjective. Yet he advises us to be equipped with stop watches, measuring rods, and balances. We once more register the psychoscope.

The point however with which we are here concerned is that freedom is considered with reference to an individual. Each individual has to be compared with an individual torn out of his social and occupational context, and checked up with another individual. This obviously would be an idle proceeding, besides being indefinitely cumbersome and redundant. We shall see that if we were to compare the organization of bus drivers and of corporation vice-presidents, we might reach certain conclusions even without a measuring rod or stop watch, which are not applicable to social studies. Science does not consist in the use of instruments of precision where these do not fit. It consists in the adjustment of methods of observation to the subject matter observed. It also demands that we study each phenomenon within its legitimate isolate, that is, the correct context.

Another really eminent and competent writer, this time a philosopher, insists on the negative character of freedom. Professor Horace M. Kallen informs us that "No political or social scientist has yet produced as far as I know, a description of freedom as a positive, intrinsic quality of the course of nature or the life of man".* (p. 2) And again: "I cannot too often repeat, history defines the liberties of man by no positive traits, only by the prohibition of certain types of obstruction or interference: religious, civil, personal, political and the like. Thus any action native or acquired, once impeded, then *un*impeded becomes a liberty. And it becomes a liberty only through the withdrawal, usually the forced withdrawal, of the impediment". (p. 272) This writer also suggests the subjective element in the definition of our concept: "Freedom seems to involve the way you feel when

* *Freedom in the Modern World,* edited by Horace M. Kallen. New York, 1928.

you are let go—whether in talking, eating, drinking, fighting, moving, or what you will. Without the restraint and its relaxation this feeling does not seem to occur; and as feeling is always an individual experience, the social definition of Freedom involves prohibiting interference, forbidding or removing obstruction or restraint, rather than characterizing a feeling". (p. 3) Here we have the clear recognition that it would be better to study freedom in its social implications. Indeed once more a great deal of what Professor Kallen writes about freedom in the excellent collection of essays edited by him and to which he makes two important contributions, is fully acceptable to us. The passages quoted however exemplify the subjective factor haunting most arguments on freedom, as well as a persistent negative quality which is attributed to freedom.

Let me quote one more contribution from an expert on the subject. Miss Dorothy Fosdick of Smith College has produced what Professor MacIver describes as "the best analysis of the subject within my knowledge". It is indeed a most useful survey of literature with very valuable critical contributions. It suffers however from the obsession that there exists "a core of literal meaning of the word"*—a phrase which reappears throughout the book. It also attempts to give a definition of this "core of meaning", a definition which should remain true to all possible usages as well as true to that feeling which we have when we utter the word liberty. "Behind every demand for liberty is this desire to escape from unwelcome external restraint". (p. 3) Here we note the distinction implied in the adjective "unwelcome", a distinction clearly referring to the subjective appreciation of the individual. We could rephrase it by saying that freedom is the escape from those restraints which we do not like.

"Liberty is held to be endangered or denied when some out-

* *What Is Freedom* by Dorothy Fosdick, Harper and Brothers, 1939.

side influence prevents the doing of what one desires to do, feels able to do, and has otherwise available means of doing". (p. 5) Here once more we find a multitude of contradictions. If a man has all the available means of doing something and wants to do it, what is this "outside influence" which can prevent his doing what he wants? We cannot really affirm that an individual has the means to perform an action and then postulate *Deus ex Machina*, jumping in and frustrating action. Clearly the term "means to do" has been insufficiently defined, or else a completely imaginary entity is brought into play.

"Liberty in any realm is the lack of restraint not merely on what men care to do at the moment but on what they may care to do. Liberty involves the continued existence of unclosed possibilities of choice even after one has been taken, allowing a person to continue to do what he wants even after he changes his mind. A man has liberty in any area when several liberties are open to him in that area". And again: "The condition of liberty in any area of experience implies that several alternatives of action remain open". (p. 11)

We must be grateful to Miss Fosdick for stating very clearly, very cogently and in detail the concept which fits perfectly well into the center of our diagram and which we have labelled "core of freedom: absolute absence of all restraint". Her statement also reveals how completely this concept is untenable. It is absolutely impossible to imagine any real case of human behavior to which Miss Fosdick's definition could be applied. If we imagine a case of individual behavior within a normal ordered system, we would find that no one is ever in possession of those "several alternatives of action" which have to remain open. No one disposes "the continued existence of unclosed possibilities of choice". Human beings in the course of their normal day have to eat and drink, to go to their office and work, to go to their recreation grounds and play and then to return home and after an evening's entertainment to go to bed. Follow up the life history of yourself or of anyone you know well and you will see that the human career consists in making one choice or the other and sticking to it. The more successful the career, the less "changes of mind" are necessary in it—or possible.

It is hardly necessary perhaps to continue our criticism. The statement here quoted expresses, as nearly as it can be done in the terms of conceptual analysis, that subjective and fictitious but very insistent demand for unlimited freedom which human beings cherish, and which no one ever experiences in real achievement.

The opinions here quoted are sufficient to show how obsessive the desire is to define the "core of meaning" of freedom. We have seen that all the writers quoted are inclined to accept the subjective or intuitive "knowledge", "feeling" or "desire" of the individual concerning what he means when he uses the word freedom. The core of meaning therefore would have to embrace all the usages and any linguistic usage of the word.

This corresponds closely to what we have done on our chart: we have a core of meaning on which all the possible predications of freedom converge. From this core of meaning also all the other meanings radiate. This core of meaning amounts, as we know, to something like an unlimited scope for a choice, never trammeled, never fixed, never in any way determined. The meaning therefore is also essentially negative. We have to postulate an absolute absence of restraint or else we might run counter to one or the other of the possible metaphorical combinations of word in which freedom figures. Such obsessive phrases as "do what you please", "do as you like", "do nothing", can only fit into such a vague, all-embracing definition as that formulated by Miss Fosdick in her excellent attempt to define the undefinable.

She makes quite clear the point that even one's own choice must never remain binding, or else there is no freedom in this popular demand for it.

We see therefore that we have here a concept of freedom built up out of elements essentially subjective and individual; a concept which is in its nature negative while at the same time it is absolute and substantial. I should like to add here that this concept is not merely constructed with avowedly subjective and personal elements of individual consciousness; it also refers invariably to short-run, small-phase moments of choice, decision, will or whim. It therefore neglects completely the pragmatic context of human behavior. It also disregards the fact that choice and decision alone are completely irrelevant to the individual, as well as to society and culture, unless they become executed through a successful and essentially rewarding action.

4

Freedom in Subjective Experience

BEFORE we proceed to sum up our reasons for a complete rejection of this "core of meaning", that is, the concept of free-floating-freedom, it will be well to indicate why human beings so insistently demand it in their feelings, intuitions and desires; and also why this semantic turn of language has left such a strong imprint on human thought.

The fact is that we, one and all, do feel such a craving for freedom, and that we demand it with all the emotional insistence of our being. Were we to hark back to the memories of our childhood, we would first and foremost remember how strongly we always resented the discipline of parental intervention, of any control by nurse, governess or servants. No one, savage or civilized, belonging to any class or group in society, could fail to remember from his own childhood and adolescence that the process of learning and training involved punishments as well as rewards. The punishments, whether by actual violence, parental or tutorial, or else by being deprived of certain privileges, at times of free movement or the exercise of personal preferences, were always resented as that "unwanted interference" which was felt and resented as actual constraint. Indeed, every parent and every educator knows quite well that in the training of the child it is best to proceed by the use of rewards rather than punishments. At the same time there is no doubt that punishments, restraints, and coercions are indispensable even in the education of the best and most amenable child, by the most enlightened and benevolent parent or teacher.

The best education makes work into play. Yet play contains always an element of make-believe, an element of "freedom" to do what the child wishes at the moment. The trick of successful education consists in the use of such freedom by turning it into the chains of spontaneously accepted desire to follow up a determined course of activity. The child may be given the "freedom" to imagine himself an adult. He then imposes upon himself certain rules and restrictions inherent in the game of playing grown-up. Much of the apprenticeship to life in primitive communities, as well as of the earliest techniques, of good manners and of adequate social conduct, can be taught to the child and ingrained in him through this use of certain imaginary freedoms, self-chosen but then firmly imposed. The child may wish to change the reality of the moment by playing travel, by impersonating such professions as that of a soldier, of a sailor, or even of a buccaneer. In such moods and within such activities he experiences the subjective freedom of choice, a freedom which insofar as it is put into action, gives him also the feeling of achievement and of power. Yet once more the freedom does consist in the acceptance of rules. Think as hard as you like, you will find that there is no game, no play, no imaginary pastime of child and adult alike which does not consist in the acceptance of rules, regulations and other self-imposed restraints. When the child indulges in listening to fairy tales or reads books of adventure and travel, he moves again in a world where actors in a magical, miraculous, or adventurous game are subject to new and specific determinisms.

In this analysis we discover two principles. The first is that a feeling for unlimited scope of choice, of self-expression and of embarking on a wide range of spontaneously chosen activities runs right through the earlier psychological stages of the individual. To this feeling there corresponds also a strong distaste, amounting at times to revulsion and revolt, against all interferences which cut into the playful activities. At the same time, and this is our second principle, since every game implies rules, once the child has made his choice he has to submit to the rules. Yet here also comes the important reservation: in infantile psychology choices are often picked and dropped easily, and there is no doubt that a demand for "unlimited choice", "for several choices remaining permanently open" enters very definitely into the infantile feeling of liberty.

This desire for absence of chains, of restrictions, and trammels never completely disappears from human psychology. Indeed, it becomes embodied into a persistent revolt against strict determinism as well as against arbitrary coercion from outside. Think of any concrete event in your own life, or in that of some near and well-known person. Most of what we do and want to do is determined by the needs of our organism, by the routine of our occupation, by the career which we have chosen and by the social and personal ties which we have formed in founding a family, in choosing our friends and in having to enjoy or endure our colleagues and professional associates. In this routine of living we are so definitely "slaves to habit" that we do what we have to do without raising the problem of freedom at all. Few of us feel that our freedom is seriously affected when the gong sounds for dinner and we have to change and go to the table or simply repair to where the place for us has been set. We eat our meal partly by habit, partly by appetite, but we do not categorize such an event under the head of freedom or constraint. It is only when some emotionally colored event looms ahead, pleasant or unpleasant, that the problem enters. We have made a decision to undertake a pleasant excursion to a spot of recreation. All is set for the trip and in the last moment someone in the family becomes ill or an unwelcome guest telegraphs his arrival which we cannot very well refuse. Under such conditions we always *feel* that we have made a decision, that we have all the means to carry it out, but that an "unwanted interference" from outside deprives us of the freedom to act. Once more the infantile revulsion and revolt against an attempt at our freedom resurges. Scientifically analyzed, we would have simply to say that the conditions necessary and sufficient for the execution of our plan had been altered. We cannot carry out the actions on which our desire was bent, simply because the means available are no more what they were a few moments ago. In our feeling however we arbitrarily and unscientifically put the full blame for our upset on the one new factor, because it was not foreseen, because it is unwanted, and because on the whole we resent that specific factor which deprives us of our means of travel. Means signify here of course all the conditions sufficient and necessary for the execution of our plan. Take again self-imposed decisions such as a visit to a dentist, an unpleasant interview, tax payment, or an examination—we feel not *free*, hence we have this desire to change again. Yet there is nothing more binding and trammeling than indecision.

The more we analyze any concrete case of disruption of our personal freedom, we shall find that in objective statement a new determinant of our behavior has arisen. This determinant is an integral part of what we might describe as the equipment or the means, or the conditions necessary and sufficient for the execution of our plans. It is unscientific to set it apart as a distinct and different reality, simply because emotionally we blame this factor and no other for the curtailment of our freedom.

As we know already, all action of human beings living within a culture can only be carried out in co-operation with others and in dependence upon them. Hence in any and every decision which I take, such as a decision to travel, to go to a theater, to start a new business or to change my career, I have to enlist the interests of others to make them accept my decision and to collaborate with me in its execution. Insofar as all this runs smoothly, insofar as we feel successful in what we do, we do not resent all the agreements, conventions, rules of manners and of morals which are implied in such action. Yet at every point where either the laws of nature or the needs of my organism, or the decisions of others thwart my desires, I have the tendency to hypostatize such an action or event, to single it out from all others, and to label it "constraint".

This psychological analysis brings also in relief why freedom is so frequently and persistently conceived of as a negative quality. Freedom is very much like health or virtue or innocence. We feel it most intensely after we have lost it. The man who enjoys health is certainly not aware of it and he would be the least capable of giving us a clear concept or definition. With health it is exactly as with freedom: we must lose it and then regain it in order to become aware of it. Yet would an intelligent doctor describe health scientifically as the "absence of disease"? This might be done by an old-fashioned practitioner of a hundred years ago who worked at "healing" and "disease" as economic factors in his existence and as "failings" of his clientele. Scientific medicine defines health in terms of normal metabolism on the basis of the normal anatomical and biochemical equipment of the organism. This parallel throws some light on the psychological approach to the concept of freedom. The violent affirmation of an absolute absence of restraint is due to the fact that the very enjoyment of freedom, like the enjoyment of health, of virtue, of innocence and of wealth, remains subjectively unnoticed. To take this subjective condition of the human mind as the basis of our scientific definition is obviously as absurd as to define air by the predications of a man who has been half stifled and is gasping for breath. In all the cases here mentioned it is the duty of science to give a positive definition and to give it in terms of those factors which determine a certain condition in nature or in human society and culture, rather than to resort to human feelings and to the subjective vicissitudes of human existence.

Our analysis could be made even more emphatic if we asked ourselves who are the people who write and sometimes even think about freedom. They are the artists and poets, the moralists and philosophers, the psychologists and students of personality. All such people live by imagination, and work very often from the armchair and in the armchair, using their own mental processes as the empirical subject matter of their analysis. Now an artist or a mystic who reaches out into the infinite and whose subject matter is pervaded either with religious inspiration, or with strong dramatic and emotional experiences of man, will tend to concentrate on the freedom of thought or fancy, of daydreams and of mystical expansion. He will very often forget that free-floating thoughts and ideas do not affect the course of human behavior unless and until they are translated into action.

Again, freedom often enters into the life events of people involved in strong emotional experiences. A man in love will claim the freedom of full realization of his feelings. He will reify every circumstance and absolutely any restraint, however adventitious, which drop an obstacle into the path of his sentiments. All men when they are hungry or exposed to cold wind and weather will react very strongly to the specific causes of their misfortune and resent them as obstacles to their freedom. In many cases their emotional distress, which is also a physiological deficiency, will drive them to crime or to revolt. They know what freedom means but freedom to them is again primarily an emotional reality. To the sober sociologist it is expressed in terms of economic conditions, political order and certain specific forms of organized commissariat and means of transportation.

We could speak of the oversensitive spots or moments of human existence in which the feeling for freedom and the idea of freedom obtrude themselves with imperative force. The young man in love; the unfortunate devil who through illness, drink, or misfortune is unable to support himself and his family; the individual who under strain of circumstances has to act and work against them, or must speed, breaking all rules of the road— such people know how terribly oppressive the obstructions, the restraints and the otherwise acceptable laws of human existence can appear. The same applies to the creative artist, the religious fanatic or mystic, as well as the man who has too much or too little power, and in his attempt to mobilize it resents any obstruction. In all such cases obviously the emotional reaction will be concentrated on one factor and one factor only. This will be torn out of its context, hypostatized and then labelled "*the* restraint". Freedom is in such circumstances very clearly felt as the absence of such a restraint and of any such restraints.

We thus see how it is that the personal feeling of being free receives a full citizenship in human subjective appreciations. We are driven towards accepting it and we demand it to be accepted at its face value. We see that the concept which arises out of this feeling must remain individual, subjective and essentially negative, referring to short but critical phases of human existence. We see also why this feeling does not allow us to translate the concept into an objective and scientific recognition: all that matters to the sociologist are the conditions under which human action can run smoothly and effectively, that is, freely.

The permanence and insistence of this sentimentally founded apprehension of freedom, which arises in childhood or even infancy, and remains imperative throughout human life, is also supported by linguistic mechanisms. All general concepts, such as "time", "space", "cause", "force" and "matter", are invariably reified and hypostatized both in metaphysics and in common linguistic usages. To the scientist however each such concept is essentially relational. It is an aspect of an objective process. In the ordinary home-parlance of the average individual however such concepts as "time", "space" and "force" are essentially subjective, and full of emotional values, since man reacts to them with strong feelings. Force, time and space, like freedom, justice and authority, influence and control vast domains of that reality in which human beings move and act. They are sources of influence; they determine our behavior; and very often they determine it in a manner propitious or else adverse to our desires. Hence they appear to act, to hold us in their grip, and to organize all aspects of reality in a manner to which we cannot help reacting emotionally. In the shorthand of ordinary speech it is inevitable that we use such concepts in a very personal manner. We endow them with an intention, with good and evil attitudes towards ourselves. Through speech, especially through the metaphors of speech, force and freedom, time and justice, matter, space and equality receive a substantial existence. They also are often conceived anthropomorphically.

All this is essentially true as regards freedom in its most general and widest meaning. Freedom has to be conceived as the conditions necessary and sufficient for the effective run of any process or any activity. Freedom is thus a category of process, of action and of rest. Used in this very general meaning it is almost synony-

mous with the concept of existence. It fits therefore any context
and every context. A word which lends itself for all uses becomes
to a large extent useless, except in metaphysics. The real scientific
task in the analysis, observation and definition of freedom is the
discovery of its legitimate context. As regards the term freedom
in its application to human behavior, we have already indicated
that this context has to be found in the organization of concerted
and implemented human action, and in its relation to all those
factors of effective action by which it is determined. Even thus it
remains a general concept and we shall have to make it very
much more specific in order to make it really useful. The most
important task in this specification of freedom will be the distinction between on the one hand the inevitable restraints implicit in all successful and viable action, and on the other those
forms of authority and discipline in which specific interests are
served to the detriment of the community as a whole and even
of the integrity of culture.

Returning to the semantic problem, we see that freedom as a
general concept, controlling all human action, must provoke
violent emotional reactions. Freedom allows and restraint for-
bids. Freedom inspires and restraint hampers and disrupts. Both
are felt as live forces, as anthropomorphic entities. Both are
subject to that most tricky semantic device: the creative metaphor of linguistic usage. In all such cases words used as metaphor
and personification impose a claim for the absolute existence of
their referents. Thus freedom, which is an aspect of the inevitable
determinism of human action and of the conditions under which
human beings act, becomes a live object, a statue with a torch,
an absolute goddess with a cornucopia of indefinite free choices,
of unlimited possibilities and gifts, real and magical.

Were we to follow this word in its actual usage and metaphorical development we would see, and indeed we have seen,
that it fits perfectly well into a variety of contexts, partly real,

partly imaginary. The testimony of language could be used to prove that freedom is an absolute and independent source of inspirations, affirmations and placets; even as restraint is a source of denials, interferences and caveats. In our emotional reactions, to which words are specially subservient, we like to blame restraint and praise freedom. It would be interesting to collect from more or less inspired and more or less confused literature a number of quotations to show how far the misuse of the term can go. We know that "man is born free, and everywhere we find him in chains". In reality he is not born free, since a human infant is superlatively shackled and dependent. Nor yet are men everywhere in chains, although we do find them shackled very often and very grievously right through human evolution and history, and at the present moment. But to predicate chains for everybody everywhere and at all times is to stultify the search as to where chains are really to be found.

To define freedom with respect to childish whims, to criminal tendencies, to the behavior of a lunatic or of a man running amok is essentially a linguistic liberty. People have discussed the freedom of angels to dance on a point of a needle. We might also speak of the freedom to travel to the moon and to eat it were it made of cheese. Grammar does not forbid us to use the word freedom in such a sentence. Nor is there any reason why we should not declare that some people enjoy the freedom willingly to submit to tyrannies. The "freedom to exercise excessive power and to tyrannize" is also a phrase. We might even say that Hitler has given the world the maximum of integral freedom. He is free to tyrannize all his subjects and to threaten the rest of the world. His subjects are free to murder all those who oppose them. And to the rest, to the Jews, Poles and German Liberals whom he has enslaved, he has given the sublime freedom of spiritual submission to a cruel destiny.

5

The Semantics of Freedom

HOW should we deal with the semantic problem here involved? The answer is simple. There is no inherent wisdom in language. The ontological argument that the nature of an entity is somehow contained in its name has long been rejected even in theology. It must be rejected in all scientific thinking. We have completely to throw overboard any meek acquiescence in dictionary meanings, in the dictates of epigram, metaphor and linguistic vagary. We have often stressed that in science we must run counter to linguistic usage. This is even more important in social science than in the study of matter or organism.

No word has to be so carefully defined from this point of view as the word freedom. In the examples just given we have indicated how dangerous a loose, intuitive or popular usage can be. A precise definition is necessary, since if we do not draw sharp lines round this fundamental concept, we may play into the hands of the enemies of freedom. Claim too little for freedom and you leave scope for slavery. Claim too much and you allow its foes to prove that it cannot exist anywhere, or that it can exist even in the worst tyrannies. This is not an imaginary or fictitious case.

The totalitarian propaganda has lived on play both with the word freedom and on the word freedom.

The physicist does not inquire through universal suffrage or a Gallup Poll what the meanings of his concepts are. He analyzes the processes of mechanics and he defines "mass", "force", "velocity", "acceleration", and "gravitation" by reference to observed realities and to their relations. The humanist must be even more determined and consistent in his rejection of popular usages, dictionary meanings and dictionary definitions. He uses words of an older citizenship and words linked with general discourse in sermon, in political harangue and in the task of molding public opinion. The sober light of reason is as indispensable, if not more so, when we deal with concepts liable to appear in heated dispute and perverted propaganda, as when we analyze the impersonal processes of mechanics and electricity.

A great many popular and literary uses of the word freedom therefore have to be rejected. At times the word is used in a meaningless context. At times it is referred to a real situation but then the word is used in a metaphorical sense, as when we say that people are free to be slaves. Once more we see that the most important scientific task is to be quite clear as to the context of our argument. We have to scrutinize whether such a context is real; whether it is relevant; and whether it represents a legitimate isolate of human behavior. In all cases we rejected freedom as an independent, substantial and spontaneous absolute. Such an absolute, holding the cornucopia of unlimited choices, does not exist in reality. It exists only in the metaphor of speech.

As regards the linguistic usage of this word our mandate is clear. We do not try to prevent the child, the metaphysician, the man in the street, or even the confused amateur or great poet from using the word freedom as he pleases. But we can state clearly and definitely that no argument can be regarded as scientific in which the word freedom is used in any other sense than as defining those cultural conditions under which human beings can mature their purposes, execute them efficiently and reap the benefits of their labors. Hence to speak about the criminal's freedom to murder, to rape, or to steal is simply an abuse of words. Instead of such an unscientific liberty with words, we have to affirm that the collective freedom of security demands that in every ordered society criminal tendencies to murder, to rape, and to steal should have no freedom. To speak about the child's freedom to do what he likes, or about the lunatic's freedom to behave as he is impelled to, is equally unscientific. We might as well speak of the centrifugal force of gravitation. The correct way to describe facts would be to say that education implies the disciplining of infantile moods, whims and drives; while social stability demands that insanity should be cured or kept under lock and key.

We have here briefly to refer once more to one aspect of human culture in which the idea of freedom, free-floating, pervasive and omnipotent, is actually embodied and standardized. All that we embrace under the heading of mythology, fairy tales, and folklore; the various beliefs in magic and miracles are built upon this conception of freedom. Not only in our daydreams and actual dreams, but also in the nursery tales we remember from childhood, and in primitive and civilized legends, we enjoy the magical freedom of levitation, the rapid transportation of the magic carpet, the freedom to move invisibly through space, the freedom to conjure up the ghosts and to command spirits. There is no doubt that the appeal of contemporary fiction in detective story, mystery tale, and in the exploits of wonderful and ever successful adventurers represents the same craving for unlimited freedom. It seems to be an essential ingredient of relaxation from the cramping force of determinism and logic, to enjoy the fictitious feeling of freedom. The whole universe must remain open and accessible to those who wish to enjoy that mental expansion which, moving on the line of least resistance and of wishful thinking, expresses our deeply ingrained craving for emotional freedom. Perhaps a good deal of the success of that most recent form of magical mysticism which we find in the doctrines of Nazism, Communism and Fascism, is due to the combination of real mechanical power on its executive side with the feeling of indefinite possibilities in sentiment, and lust for political and economic self-realization.

That this aspect of human culture is closely akin to insanity has been often suggested by psychologists especially of the Freudian brand. Indeed in my opinion they have gone too far. Yet within its legitimate limits the proposition remains true that the psychopath in his megalomania or paranoia claims the same type of freedom as Hitler or the modern quack or clairvoyant. Magicians, witches and miracle mongers of all times have lived and battened on the promises and pretenses to overthrow determinism. They always have found their innocent victims and many have been burned or executed as victims of this belief and suspicion. The desire for full freedom for one's self, and the suspicion that others can enjoy it at one's own expense, have always controlled a whole domain of organized human life.

We have tried to show the several sources which have contributed towards the concept of free-floating-freedom and we have indicated our critical reservations as to the feasibility of translating that vague emotional apprehension into a scientific concept. Thus free-floating-freedom remains a supererogatory epiphenomenon of human existence. In its semantic usages such a concept must remain indefinitely chaotic. It follows human feelings since it is born out of them. Like all emotional words it lends itself to indefinite metaphorical stretching. It remains forever unobservable since its real context lies in the inaccessible realms of subjective feeling.

It will be well quite briefly to sum up our main points of criticism. We start from the point just touched upon: the subjective fallacy. Here the reason for rejecting such a concept is the fundamental principle of all science: every concept used must be open to objective, that is, universally accessible, public, and factual observation. Hence an entity which by definition occurs only within the realm of personal introspection cannot be a subject of scientific discourse. All mental states which are postulated as occurrences within the private consciousness of man are thus outside the realm of science.

As a matter of fact it is easy to show that what a man wants, feels, and desires is not at all subjective in the sense here mentioned. Strong emotions as a rule break out into action. They invariably appear as physiognomic expressions and only the greatest control can allow "the man with a poker face" to hide what he feels. Even then such a concealment is invariably temporary. A strong emotion will affect a man's behavior towards the people he loves or hates, towards the circumstances he resents or enjoys—perhaps only in the long run but with very definite determinism. Thus emotional states of mind are by no means necessarily outside the scope of observable fact. The psychologist who remains satisfied with the assumption of an unobservable feeling makes therefore a false assumption. His real duty is to establish the relationship between the emotional state and its overt expression. He then ought to construct his definitions in terms of fact and not of the falsely assumed private and personal feeling. All this is not by any means the confession of an intransigent behaviorist. It is merely the statement of what actually occurs in human behavior; and of the scientific postulate, that facts which can be observed belong to the domain of scientific argument, and that hypothesis as to what happens in the unobservable domain of consciousness becomes scientific only after it has been linked up with human action. We reject therefore not so much introspection as psychoscopy or spiritual television.

We thus see in this why the concentration on the psychological aspect of freedom leads at times into the byways of the problem. There is however a world of daydreams, of intentions, good and bad, real or fantastic, where the human mind is subject to random meanderings of free association and of wishful thinking. We have not rejected this aspect of freedom from our analysis. All such states of mind are the raw material from which desires, purposes and motivations may crystallize. Insofar as this is the case; insofar as from vague, loose, disorganized visions, there emerges a purpose, that is, an initiative to act, we are again within the realm of the cultural process, which is social, implemented, and individual. Insofar as most human beings pass through states of mind which never become translated into activity, the student of culture is not interested in such aspects of human psychology. To make myself clear, I remind the reader that the meanderings of human imagination become translated into human action when they lead to the creation of written or oral literature, art, music, or dramatic performance. Such output is essentially a cultural activity.

Again, modern psychology, Freudian and otherwise, suggests that some mental processes are pushed back into the so-called unconscious. Even then they can become culturally significant or at least symptoms which affect culture. The occurrence of neurosis, of hysteria, of various "complexes" affects our psychiatric clinics and hospitals, and it also affects the course of ordinary work. Most of what happens in the human mind, conscious or unconscious, finds its expression in overt behavior, hence also in institutionalized, social reaction. Some of those daydreams and ambitions which cannot find normal expression on culturally acknowledged lines, lead to revolutions or to crime, to perversions or to underground activities. Everywhere we find that mental state, action, and integral cultural result have to be taken together. Far from being enthusiastic about the maximum freedom given to the daydreamer, modern psychology and sociology teach that we have to devise methods of treatment and education, from infancy onwards, in which the freedom of psychological and physiological drive or motive will be adjusted to the conditions of its legitimate realization.

We have thus states of mind which are purposeful and effective and as such subject to cultural analysis. We can discuss the problem of freedom only insofar as the state of mind makes an imprint on behavior, individual hence also collective. If we had only one case of neurosis, hysteria, or revolutionary and criminal obsession, it might remain individual. Since such cases occur always in large quantities, society must and does deal with them collectively.

The second fallacy with which we have recurrently dealt in our arguments is semantic. Social science is still burdened with the superstition that words contain their meanings. The use of words is by no means confined to scientific argument. When we borrow terms which are highly susceptible to emotional or mystical elasticities of meaning, and borrow them for scientific analysis, we have to submit them to a process of deflation and redefinition. Our semantic brief has now been made clear and precise. We have to use the concept of freedom only with reference to those contexts where man can and does manipulate the augmentations and diminutions of freedom. We have therefore to study freedom within its full cultural context. Remarkably enough we came to the conclusion that freedom, like many other positive concepts of human existence, remains least noticed and spoken about within those conditions where it really flourishes. Here as often, language becomes a false witness. We are never compelled to complain, to blame or to express our emotions about any free goods of nature and existence. This explains the negative coefficient so often implied in the use of such words as freedom, justice, health, prosperity and security. This last word, for instance, began to flourish and to be obsessive in human speech during the very period of human history when security almost vanished from the face of the world.

Closely related to the semantic fallacy is the one which we might describe as pragmatic. An analysis of real human behavior as we find it in day-by-day existence and in the human career shows that we neither crave for a constant change of purpose or for unlimited choices, nor yet, were we to crave for such a super-indeterministic condition, could we ever achieve it. The serious events of our life are determined for us by the conditions into which we were born, by our training and education from infancy on, by our choice of a career and mate, and a set of ideals and values. Even when it comes to trivialities we usually habituate to a certain brand of cigarettes, we prefer beer to wine or vice versa, we develop a taste in recreations, newspapers and party opinions. That situation in which man has constantly to choose and reject choices, to postpone decisions and reformulate them does not occur in the normal existence of a healthy member of a community and of those many institutions which constitute a community. The freedom of indecision, the free-floating-freedom, occurs as we know in pathological conditions of the human organism, and in those moments of relaxation or relapse into daydreams and free associations which run parallel to the serious course of human life. When occasionally we lapse into the inability to decide or to frame a problem, this is certainly neither emotionally nor conceptually freedom. It is always a process emotionally painful and pragmatically hostile to effective action.

To overcome another fallacy, that of freedom as an individual response *par excellence,* we could inquire as to the conditions under which we are made to feel restraints and trammels. We have quoted already certain minor events of personal life which we feel as attempts against our freedom: a cold, an indigestion, an aunt or a mother-in-law, a misunderstanding or a miscalculation might confuse our planning or upset our purpose. At times, semantically speaking such interventions would be described as "that nuisance" or that "run of bad luck". Sometimes we do declare that an "unwanted interference" has curtailed our freedom. We would certainly define as a real attempt against our freedom any serious accident, or a disabling disease or a criminal act such as a frame-up, a racket, or a trap. Persecutions by gangs, by political factions, by personal enemies, and above all by the political state, are felt and defined as major and serious attainders against our freedom. Here undoubtedly we would legitimately be led to inquire what freedom means in its dependence upon the occurrence of such outward restraints. In this we could follow each individual case piecemeal and then attempt a synthesis. Were we to try collecting thousands of millions of such cases, we would certainly embark on an unprofitable chase after innumerable minor and major cases of disturbance in human action. Instead of that, we can institute an inquiry as to the general conditions which foment accidents, abuses, avoidable cases of disablement and distress and other concrete and specific limitations of legitimate freedom. We know that such conditions vary from society to society, from community to community, and from institution to institution. We would find that certain forms of cultural constitution or political organization establish conditions of hygiene, preventive medicine and police service which largely prevent the occurrence of restraint due to bodily disability, ill health and accident. We have on the other hand cultures where there is no well-ordered organization of medicine, hygiene and hospital services. Again, we have cultures where legal and police organization is either ineffective or corrupt, and others where it is fundamentally honest and efficient. The general problem of a sound Constitution, of honesty and intelligence in the services of administration, social welfare and economics, is obviously one of the primary elements of constitutional and civic freedom. There are cultures which look after the interests of personal liberty. There are others which foster the abuse of political power, or corrupt police services, as well as the power of wealth, the encroachment of organized labor and other attempts against the average citizens' liberty.

Thus starting from the purely individual perspective and the emotional claims of personal liberty, we are led by a correct argument to the study of the cultural background.

If we consider the large-scale events which affect the community or the nation as a whole, we would find that there are two sources of national and collective restraint. First of all, the freedom of one and all is adversely affected by large-scale natural catastrophes. In the second place, the freedom of all or of large groups within a community becomes curtailed by certain historical events which affect the political, economic, or legal constitution of the group.

An epidemic, a pestilence, a volcanic eruption or an earthquake affects temporarily the freedom of the inhabitants, one and all. Disablement, destruction and death produced by such catastrophes constitute definitely "unwanted interferences" with human action and human existence. Here culture provides certain protective and anticipatory mechanisms, which are always an addition to collective freedom. The advances made by modern hygiene and preventive medicine; the scientific prevision of floods, fires, and even earthquakes and cyclones have at least improved our ability to foresee and to prepare for certain emergencies. Culture does not bestow on man environmental omnipotence. Culture however has from its very beginning given man an increase in his control of the environment, of his own organism, and of his destinies in general.

The catastrophes of human history are at times also engineered by man himself. The study of human evolution and history teaches us that at certain stages and under certain political and geographical configurations a peaceful community saw itself attacked and overwhelmed by stronger and more aggressive neighbors. War most certainly was not the chronic state of primitive humanity. Real warfare makes an appearance late in human evolution. Yet from a certain stage of development the phenomena of aggression and conquest, with such by-products as slavery, political subjugation, extortionate taxation, and various other symptoms of tyranny, are a chronic source of diminutions in freedom.

On the credit side we find a whole series of historical events as well as prehistoric antecedents thereof in which we see humanity fighting for freedom and achieving freedom. The interesting point to be registered here is that in long range historical perspective we see that the fight is always about small but tangible and real increments in freedom. All the battles for national or political independence, from the Greek stand at Thermopylae to the heroic resistance of the contemporary Greeks against totalitarian invasion, were fought for national self-determination. A nation, that is, a group with its own independent culture or way of life, thought and felt that it was worthwhile to sacrifice life, limb and property for the right to remain master of its own home. In the revolutions against domestic tyranny, freedom appears as the demand for a fuller share in the freedom to frame purposes and to enjoy the results or achievement. The battles for religious freedom appear to us nowadays very often as entirely futile; yet to the men of that time, the freedom to choose the form of their sacramental rite, as well as the freedom to determine the constitution of their own congregation and the text of their Holy Scriptures, appeared so valuable that no sacrifices were too great. The battles for the emancipation of slaves, serfs, and manual laborers have again all aimed at the threefold freedom of purpose, action, and benefits.

In all such historical events where we can register an increase in freedom we find on detailed and concrete analysis that freedom appears as a very definite attribute of human action. Free action is the one in which purposes are formed and organized; are translated into co-operative and implemented action; and the fruits of the action are distributed equitably among those who have participated in it.

We have seen throughout that the three phases or aspects of human action—purpose, execution, and results—are integrally related. They are only significant in this relationship. Yet under certain conditions of culture the instrumental sequence of purpose, action and enjoyment is not inherent in the course of events. It is possible to plan or to desire, yet to be prevented from enacting such plans or desires. A slave, a man at the point of the pistol or bayonet, or a man hypnotized can and must act without ever having willed such an act. And once more, a man can labor, risk his life, and sacrifice all his vital energies to obtain results which he will never be able to enjoy.

Whether we look at this problem within the context of individual action or in historical or evolutionary perspective, we have to realize that there is no full increment of freedom unless all the phases remain integrally related, and unless we can predicate freedom about each of them and all of them in their integral result.

Let us once more examine the three phases of freedom in human action. The purpose, as we saw, is nothing else but the planning of an activity for the achievement of definite results. Were we to consider here the freedom of conscience, of thought, or of belief, we would have to realize that historically this type of freedom means always the exercise in action and in life of any such prerogative. Freedom of conscience means the ability to follow the dictates of one's own moral purpose, in one's relation to others, to the universe or to God. The freedom of religious doctrine always implies the translation of such a doctrine into prayer, sacrament, ritual and ceremony. For the essence of belief is an active relationship between a man or a congregation and those sacred realities which they demand to worship in liberty. The freedom of scientific thought does not mean in any historical reality sitting in an armchair and thinking out one's own ideas. It means first and foremost the freedom to proclaim those ideas, the freedom of speech, of teaching and of persuasion. It means in real science also the freedom of research, that is, of access to laboratory, the field or the realities of human organization. In short, examine whichever type of freedom you like—of framing purposes, individual or social—and you will find that the claim to freedom of action is implicit.

When it comes to action we have already made the point that no relevant cultural behavior exists which is purely individual and which remains outside the social and material apparatus of culture. Thus freedom of action implies free access to material wealth as well as the scope for organization and co-operation. We shall have still to prove more minutely that all cultural initiative—whether this be an invention, a religious inspiration, a political principle or an ethical improvement—must become translated into an organized system of collective and implemented activities. Here freedom consists in the scope given to individuals and groups to organize and to implement all such purposes as they may choose. It resides in what is usually called "freedom of combination", a freedom enjoyed in democracies but denied in societies either where the state takes over all initiative or else where slavery, serfdom, or the caste system debar certain groups from any initiative and supply others with an excess of power.

Finally, the freedom of achievements and results refers to the standard of cultural enjoyment for the members of a community. Here problems of freedom hinge on such tangible and concrete facts as the distribution of wealth, the freedom of vertical mobility or the freedom of movement across certain territorial boundaries. Here also enter the problems of how far the finer gifts of culture, such as recreations, intellectual and artistic enjoyments, and all the religious and spiritual benefits, are distributed within the community.

In all this we see once more that no theory of freedom remains true to reality in which we concentrate on any one of the three phases and the processes to which freedom essentially refers. It is the essence of human action, in individual and collective perspective alike, that desire has to be satisfied in active behavior and that satisfaction consists in the consumption of goods, material and spiritual. It is however also a fact that culture, which gives all the integral freedom to mankind, can and does at times sever the connecting links between purpose, action, and results. This occurs when whole sections of a community are deprived of all the benefits of such cultural processes as education, the development of individual abilities and skills, and the possibilities of advancement in social status. Here the differential enjoyment of freedom can be very tangible and definite. We find communities where there is no free and universal education or else where education, instead of allowing each individual and each differential group to form and mature purposes, build up careers, and develop spontaneous loyalties, aims at producing human beings which are only means to an end. Such an education has always been given to slaves and to all of those who are by birth condemned to an inferior status. This type of education, in which people from the outset are condemned to be educated to become gun fodder or other pawns in the game of war preparedness, is now prevalent in all totalitarian regimes.

As regards action, liberty means personal choice and a full scope for group organization, with adequate access to all the necessary implements and legal privileges for organized activity. The negation of freedom we find once more wherever human beings are put into an extraneously determined place—in a galley, in a chain gang, in a factory, or in a platoon. Here again the totalitarian structure of modern civilization is a negation of freedom and a re-establishment of slavery.

As regards the liberty of enjoyment, that is, the liberty of one's fair share in the communal standard of living, we see that this is curtailed by the existence of parasitic privilege given to few at the expense of the many who are exploited. The extreme case of liberty in enjoyment without the price paid in a contribution either to planning or to the work done, is exemplified in the various parasitic groups of the idle rich or the hereditarily powerful. True democracy must always aim at the curtailment of all the unearned increments in power and wealth, and of the ability of consuming goods, material and spiritual, which have been produced by others. This obviously does not mean that we accept here a completely egalitarian concept of freedom or of political and economic constitution. The communistic dogma that the only class fit to enjoy privilege and prerogative is that of manual laborers, is as false in principle as it has proved fallacious in execution. Communism has established only a new aristocracy on the ruins of the old one and a new type of exploitation of the many by the few. The real reason for this is that Communism as a war regime has once more resulted in a totalitarian rather than a democratic constitution of culture. "War" here means the war of classes, but even in this form, any concept which organizes vast quantities of human beings on an emergency basis must introduce that excess of discipline, hierarchy, and centralization which is forever inimical to freedom in the sense of spontaneous initiative, free-chosen combination, and equitable distribution of results within the group organized for a definite purpose.

In all this we see that freedom appears as a definite configuration of cultural conditions which controls all types of human activity so as to make it both effective and rewarding. The denial of freedom is always embodied in political, legal, or economic restrictions or inadequacies which prevent human beings from maturing their purpose, realizing it, and achieving the results in the form of an adequate standard of living. Once more we see that our conception of freedom is positive and objective; it is essentially pragmatic, and implies a social and technical context. It implies always the benefit from action and responsibility for action by individuals and groups alike. The instrumentalities of freedom we find in the political constitution of a community, its laws, its moral norms, the distribution of its wealth, and the access to such benefits as health, recreation, justice, and religious or artistic gifts of culture. To scour the universe for possibilities of freedom other than those given by the organization of human groups for the carrying out of specific purposes, and the production of desirable results, is an idle philosophic pastime.

Part IV

FREEDOM AS A GIFT OF CULTURE

1

The Initial Installment of Freedom

IN THE COURSE of our argument and in our somewhat whimsical survey of the various fallacies inherent in the linguistic usage of our elusive concept, we have formulated a number of assumptions. Let us enumerate them once more. First, we assume that we are interested in existence, that is, in action. The freedom of the spirit must be left over and understood as a by-product of our definition of freedom in action. Secondly, we assume that any definition of freedom in terms of one individual and his exclusive interests is not viable, since one man's power is or may become the slavery of another, indeed of many others. We thus affirm that freedom must be predicated with reference to groups in co-operation. Thirdly, we also assume that the element of instrumentality, that is, of material goods, whether implements or consumers' wealth, has to be included in our definition. Man never acts under conditions of culture without the equipment of his material mechanisms, and in this he has to submit to certain rules inherent in the mechanism, while laws of ownership or of usufruct determine the rights of use and the limitations of abuse, as well as the distribution of benefits. We therefore defined freedom as the smooth and effective, as well as successful, run of an activity undertaken by a group of men who with a clear aim in view combine for the task, fit themselves out for action and achieve the desired end.

These assumptions are not arbitrary. We are discussing here freedom as a reality of human action; hence all freedoms to quit participation in life, in existence, and in co-operation remain outside the interests of a student of humanity as it actually continues its life, achieves its existence through culture, and works on the development of cultures. Yet this very affirmation of existence implies in itself those restrictions on freedom which arise from human nature, that is, man's animal nature.

In an earlier section we have already taken a bird's-eye view of the part played by freedom at the birth and during the growth of culture, and we have seen that the range and the scope of man's control of his conditions of living have enormously increased throughout the long period of evolution. The qualitative factor of freedom through culture appears from the very beginning. This can be best seen when we compare the basic freedom of survival as this is given to man and animal respectively. It will be well to define the concept of freedom with reference to animal behavior. In its essence, animal freedom hinges on the freedom of survival. Under conditions of nature the various species develop their anatomical and physiological equipments in adaptation to the environment, through natural selection and other mechanisms of evolutionary adjustment. We can say that an animal is free when through the full exercise of its specific adaptive activities it can satisfy its biological needs. This obviously means first and foremost that the animal can obtain from the environment and within its environment the satisfaction of hunger, thirst, sex, and rest. It also means that it can protect itself from dangers, as well as attack other organisms within its habitat. The problem of animal freedom thus involves the organism and its environment, including also the other organisms of the same species. The satisfaction of the basic biological needs is achieved by means of the special instrumental activities such as the flight of birds, the swimming of fish, the stalking, hunting, and attacks of birds and mammals of prey. Each animal species also reproduces through a periodic performance of courtship, of wooing and selecting, and of successful mating. With this a number of physiologically determined parental modes of behavior are related. All these instrumental activities are the essential part of the organic program imposed on a species in the course of its adaptive evolution.

Animal freedom, therefore, consists in the effective and successful pursuit of all the innately determined activities through which the animal satisfies its organic needs. Freedom in animal behavior therefore depends on the presence of a normal equipment in anatomy and physiology, as well as of those environmental conditions to which the organism is adapted. Freedom thus means that, given a specific drive, the animal has full scope for the execution of an instrumental activity and the full enjoyment of the results. The elements which curtail or destroy such freedom may consist in the destruction of some anatomical or physiological factors in the animal's equipment. An organism maimed, congenitally deformed, or too weak to hold its own in the struggle for existence is deprived of part of its freedom. When this goes beyond a certain measure, it destroys the animal's freedom of survival. Again, place the animal in captivity, that is, deprive it of that environment to which it is specifically adjusted, and once more you prevent it from carrying out its anatomically and physiologically founded instrumental behavior.

Thus freedom here means once more the smooth and effective run of a process which can again be analyzed into three phases. We have the initial drive which starts an activity; we have con-

ditions for an effective course of this activity; and we have the
reward of satisfactory results in the satisfaction of the drive. All
this implies healthy and normal conditions of the organism, the
presence of well-determined environmental conditions, and the
successful carrying out of the activity.

Animal freedom was here discussed somewhat at length, because it shows once more that any definition which would present
freedom as a revolt against determinism, or else supply it
with a negative co-efficient, does not fit animal behavior under
conditions of nature. We see here that freedom consists in obedience to the constraint of drives and to the natural laws of the
environment to which the animal is adapted. Freedom also
appears to us, wherever we look at the behavior of animals, as
the positive quality of action which achieves its end. Since the
freedom of survival is as necessary to man as to animals, human
freedom means neither indeterminism nor yet can it be regarded
as a negative quality.

Biological freedom implies the same tripartite division into
drive, action, and satisfaction, which we found in cultural freedom
as purpose, execution, and the enjoyment of results. Both biological and cultural freedom are also determined by the conditions of the organism and by the respective environmental contexts. This context consists of the secondary environment when
it comes to human behavior; and it is thus the study of man's
secondary environment, that is, culture, which gives us most
answers in all problems of freedom.

Returning to man as an animal, right through his evolution he
depends permanently and fundamentally upon the conditions
which we have defined as the basic freedom of survival. The
major part of man's activities is controlled by drives coming
from the body and forcing him to eat when hungry, to drink
when thirsty, to rest when tired, to sleep for about one-third of his

existence, to follow attractions covered by the words "sex" and "love", and also to exercise his muscular energies in some form of bodily action. It is well to remember that the moments of freedom to be free are very rare in human life. Human nature, that is, man's animal impulses, imposes on every individual a periodic rhythm of phases when he is impelled towards certain goals and repelled after he has satisfied the drive. The sated man or animal refuses to eat, and is only attracted by those conditions which allow digestion. The awakening from sleep moves the rested, healthy organism towards activities.

It is important to register the concept of biological freedom, which might be called the pre-cultural definition of freedom, because it contains the minimum definition of the concept and it applies to man as well as to animals. The evolution of culture, as we shall see, increases this type of freedom, which consists in an increased control by man of his own bodily determinism and of environmental circumstances. For this increase of freedom a price has to be paid in terms of submission to the laws of concerted and implemented behavior.

Man has overcome by culture the specific limitations of his adaptive equipment. Through the tools which he uses he supplements many deficiencies of his anatomy. The biddings of his physiology are regulated on the one hand by the formation of habits and skills, and on the other by the creation of artificial environments in which he can continue to breathe, move, eat and rest, screened off from the impact of dangerous or hostile influences of the environment. All this implies that freedom of adaptation in which certain determinisms of the environment and organism alike are readjusted or utilized.

Yet culture is not omnipotent. It cannot overcome the two fundamental determinisms to which man is submitted as a lump of matter and as an organism. On these two points man still re-

mains an animal and from this status he never can be completely
lifted. As a piece of matter, vital and animate, but still matter,
man is subject to gravitation, impact, and to all the physical laws
which govern matter, mechanically, chemically, thermically and
electro-magnetically.

As an organism moreover man is not free when it comes to
breathing, eating, drinking, sleeping, resting and the exercise of
brain and brawn, of eyes and ears, of mouth and nose. The core
of human drives and desires and of all culturally determined purposes remains biological. Thus man, like the animal, is not free
to defy the laws of nature. Nor is he free ever completely to de-
tach himself from his organic needs. The enormous extension of
freedom through culture in this respect consists primarily in the
reshaping of environmental conditions and resources, and in the
protective devices created by man against environmental dangers.

Culture thus provides man with the wider and larger instrumentality for the satisfaction of all his primary, that is, biological,
needs. It also makes him independent of certain environmental
trammels and dangers. In this there enters that increase in the
range of choice and purpose as well as in the efficiency of behavior which we define as the cultural increment in freedom. In
its emergent character, the evolution of mankind imposes also
new needs and gives rise to new desires and motives such as those
of intellectual curiosity, artistic impulse, and the religious need to
reach the supernatural. This increase in the standard of living
and in the conditions for its satisfaction is also part of the cultural
increment of freedom. The standard of enjoyment at various
levels of human development is closely related to that highly emotional, somewhat vague and comprehensive concept of happiness.
Happiness could be scientifically defined as the relation of the
full range of individual needs and desires within the context of a
given culture, to the opportunities for their satisfaction.

We shall see that our definition of elementary freedom in terms of the survival of an animal organism will retain its value in the discussion of human affairs. The permanent basis of all extensions of, and additions to, freedom remains the freedom of survival. For all the pursuits, whether of ambitious engineering, of profound scientific research or artistic creation, depend upon that constellation of circumstances which allows a group and all its component members to live with a full satisfaction of their bodily needs, and which protects them from the dangers of bodily mutilation and destruction. The freedom of survival thus consists of two fundamental installments: the freedom of security, that is, the freedom from fear; and the freedom of prosperity, that is, the freedom from want.

Starting from this latter, we see that culture from the very beginning provides those goods of consumption which allow man to satisfy his bodily necessities of hunger, thirst, rest and comfort. It also bestows upon human beings a margin of reliance upon the regular satisfaction of such bodily needs. This margin depends upon planning, storing, and the production of goods in advance of the incidence of a need. At the lowest level man remains physiologically satisfied if the conditions under which he produces his food and his clothing, his dwelling, and his calefaction remain unimpaired.

The real danger of destruction, either by natural forces, or by dangerous animals including micro-organisms, or by human enemies, creates the second great problem of culture. Under primitive conditions this determines the choice of habitat, the protective margin of distance or of barrier, and it leads men to live in groups which can unite when danger threatens. Any community which is permanently exposed to attack or to such catastrophes as earthquakes, tidal waves, volcanic eruptions, or cyclones enjoys but a small margin of security. More or less specific means of foresight and protective measures are developed.

I have insisted here upon the fact that security and prosperity are the basic conditions of all other freedoms given by culture. It shows first that the continuity in the concept of freedom as between animals and men is real. In the second place, the freedom of survival, that is, the twofold freedom of security and prosperity, remains the basic condition of evolution and progress. The archaeologist can show from magnificent remnants of extinct communities and cultures that in the course of evolution there has been disruption and annihilation of whole civilizations when the foundations of security and prosperity became destroyed. The student of history knows that wars and droughts, epidemics and natural disasters, as well as mismanagement of national resources, have led to the disappearance of specific cultures, the death of empires and the depopulation of whole regions.

At the present moment these facts should not be forgotten. We are now faced with the denial of the two fundamental freedoms in a manner so brutal and overwhelming that it is at times almost difficult to perceive its stark reality.

Security is shattered and for years the world has suffered from its absence, which was due to the wholehearted preparedness of the totalitarian countries for war, and to the unimaginative Maginotism of the imaginary defense lines of the democracies. Autarchy, disorganization and belated and purblind appeasement have wrought havoc with our political, economic, industrial and spiritual life. We are now even in this country living in actual fear of destruction, of brutality and death, as well as of poverty. The reduction in our foundations of prosperity will prove to the community as a whole and to every individual, how directly the freedom of all and the liberties of each are affected when security and prosperity are threatened by the catastrophe of total war. In the rest of the world there obtains nationwide starvation and a total abolition of personal freedom. Thousands of people are dying from hunger, exposure and lack of protection against epidemics; that is, from the denial of biological freedom in the satisfaction of primary organic needs. Fear and the constraint of brutality have made away with any dignity of man's personal sense of value, and have made the phrase "pursuit of happiness" mere mockery in countries subject to totalitarian rule.

Man once more is threatened in his animal, that is, basically human nature. This threat, however, not only affects man in his freedom of survival. It also disorganizes human groups, lowers their standards of life and happiness, their finer intellectual and artistic sensibilities, and their whole religious and ethical response to destiny. The point is not always clearly realized that the greatest horror of war does not consist in the destruction of human beings, in the waste of wealth, in the toll taken by mutilation, disease, poverty and disorganization. The greatest loss we are suffering is in the fundamental values of loyalty, decency and all ethical principles. Culture, in its finer spiritual aspects, cannot survive the shattering lesson of today that might is right; that brutality pays; that ruthlessness, perfidy, and the rule of force are the only moral arguments which matter.

All the values and all the increments in freedom which civilization gives to man imply also a great danger. We have now great concentrations of people, millions living in large towns, whole districts over-populated and living on a very high level of comfort. All such modern communities depend for their food, their calefaction, their clothing, their light and their water supply on complex and easily disrupted systems of reservoirs and aqueducts, of transport, and on industrial production in distant countries. Any serious disruption in this system threatens the survival of such groups. The high development of our modern techniques and engineering works gives present-day humanity an indefinitely greater control of its physical environment. For a modern community this environment extends indeed across the earth's surface.

In a country like the United States we have become so dependent on rubber and tin from the southwestern Pacific, on gasoline, its sources, its refineries and pipe lines or tankers, that any disruption in communications, in production, and transport not only lowers the standard of living, but disorganizes the very foundations of life. Let total war last long enough and the disorganization proceed unchecked, and people may be threatened with starvation, freezing, and darkness. Should the present war leave this country still outside the real miseries, the lesson must be learned that future wars, which will unquestionably cut much deeper into the substance of human life, must be prevented.

We could register point by point, and on a whole range of utilities, at this very moment and at the very spot where we are living, the increased vulnerability of man under conditions of total war. This vulnerability is the price for the extremely complex system of production and distribution, of technique, scientific control, and organization which has placed the resources as well as the amenities and values of the whole world at our disposal so as to raise our standard of living, material and spiritual. We have built an enormous superstructure of delightful and valuable refinements in our expectations from life, on the basis of the freedom of survival.

This basis consists in the elementary right of every organism to be well fed, protected from fear of destruction, from epidemics, and from savage brutalities exceeding anything which even a captive animal is ever made to suffer. This basis must be maintained. It can only be maintained if we recognize that the world is at present one, and the interests of all constituent communities of the human species united and interdependent. The Great Society is now established in its various branches all the world over.

International anarchy, which can mobilize such enormous forces of destruction and disorganization, has already annihilated large areas in our specific freedom. Unless we put this anarchy under the firm control of international organization we cannot hope for any future for culture and humanity.

The disruption of the biological basis of civilization through total war is inevitable. The freedom from want in the present world depends upon a world-wide, interrelated economic system. This system obeys laws of its own determinism. Such laws cannot be controlled, dictated, or overridden without annihilating the system as a whole. Yet at present all economic interests are subordinated, and have to be subordinated, to the use of violence in war.

Can we draw the moral? Have we learnt the lesson? Everything else must be sacrificed in the planning of a new world for humanity to come, in order to establish a minimum at least, a maximum if possible, of permanent security, and hence prosperity. For the two concepts, it is easy to see, are inseparable.

Preparedness and its companion, autarchy, have begun the disorganization ever since Fascism started on its career of organizing for war. The principle of world-wide economics is based on the laws that production of each commodity be fostered wherever the best conditions for it occur, while international exchange of goods be carried on in the interests of world economy as a whole. Preparedness demands that every political unit should be self-sufficient and independent of its potential enemies. Thus even in preparedness there is a clash between the prospective use of armed violence and the real interests of humanity.

As regards the other freedom, that of security, the only mechanism which could establish and guarantee this would be a system of international law, that is, an instrumentality which would prevent or solve conflicts and also be sufficiently strong to sanction its decisions by force. There is no need to prove that such security is not compatible with the principle of absolute state sovereignty and the balance of power.

The clash between might and right is to be found in the essential mechanisms of culture. Culture gives freedom. Culture also provides the means for its annihilation. This can be traced to the very beginnings of human organization and production of artifacts. The consumers' goods and the tools which constitute the wealth of mankind, primitive or developed, can be used in the satisfaction of man's needs. As soon as wealth becomes monopolized by individuals, small groups, or large institutions, it also becomes a means of exploitation. Most artifacts can be used as weapons to kill, to subdue, and to enslave, as well as tools for the production of goods. Science and communion with the supernatural open up new avenues of freedom to man. They can also be used, however, as means of constraint and the dependence of many upon few through the element of mystical fear, as well as through the use of organized techniques of intimidation.

Thus in the very nature of organization, implementation, and the creation of ideas and values, culture at the same time gives man the integral freedom of environmental control and opens avenues for the suppression of differential freedom to some members of the community. The distinction between freedom and oppression hinges upon the purpose of an organized activity, the means used and the distribution of results. At the one end we find the monopoly of force, of wealth, and of spiritual influence as the main sources of bondage. At the other end we find an equitable distribution of initiative, of instrumentalities, and of the standard of living. In the modern world these two opposed policies are represented by totalitarianism and democracy respectively. The distinction between monopoly and equitable distribution, however, can be traced to the very beginnings of culture.

We are thus led again to the leitmotif of our argument: the distinction between the rules and constraints which effectively establish freedom and those which abrogate it. Rules which arc intrinsically determined by the requirements of purposeful and concertedly executed action in which the results are equitably distributed, are rules of freedom. On the other hand, rules and principles of organization in which, through the monopoly of physical force, wealth, and supernatural influence, an individual or a group can compel others to act without giving the workers any share in planning or in the enjoyment of the results, are rules which deny freedom in its sociological sense.

We shall see that the rules of freedom are those which grow through a long evolution, through trial and error, and gradual adjustment, within groups organized for a definite purpose. Freedom in primitive communities is very definitely associated with a conservative attitude towards well-established rules and values. Even at a high level of development it is dangerous, theoretically and in practice, to associate freedom with subversive, disruptive, and revolutionary movements. This is perhaps one of the most pernicious twists in our modern approach to freedom. It will be well to substantiate our argument with a further survey of cultural processes, primitive and advanced. In this survey we shall try to make a clear distinction between rules accepted because they are intrinsically needed for the success of an activity, and rules sanctioned by coercion.

2

Differential Contributions to Early Freedom

W ITH these problems in mind we now pass to the consideration of some of the typical devices of primitive culture. Among the earliest artifacts and skills of primitive man, the discovery of fire, the production of stone implements, of artifacts made of wood, of clothes and of dwellings occupy a prominent place.

Fire, through the light which it sheds, through the warmth which it gives, through its uses in cooking, in bending and toughening wood, and cracking stone, is one of the basic cultural values of primitive man. Mythology and art have always associaated fire with freedom, from the myth of Prometheus and its primitive counterparts, to the torch wielded by the Statue of Liberty.

Early man produces fire by friction, in following the rules of knowledge and the norms of skill. In every primitive tribe people have to learn how to select the appropriate wood, how to shape it, and how to carry out the brief but difficult task of ignition. Were we to study the various uses of fire, we would see either that it always belongs to a household, that it is indispensable to people on a hunting or fishing expedition, or else that it plays some ritual part in a magical or religious ceremony. To understand its various uses therefore we would have always to place it within an organized system of activities, that is, an institution.

Fire as one of the basic devices of primitive culture is determined in its production, its uses, and its value by a system of rules which are always integrated with reference to a household, a team of hunters or fishermen, a totemic clan, or a magical fraternity carrying out a ceremony. In all such organized activities fire plays an essential part. The rules which people have to obey in its production, its appropriation, and the respect due to it, are primarily sanctioned by the fact that each member and the group as a whole desire the activity to be successful, and realize one and all that the result depends upon the careful carrying out of the rules.

The contribution of fire to freedom consists in that it extends the range of human action, and satisfies many bodily needs. At his home or campfire man can escape the rigors of extreme cold, he can rapidly recover from exposure to wind, rain, or snow. Fire is one of the principal devices which allows man to adjust to new environments and new climates. Through the light which it sheds, fire allows man to move at night and to ward off dangerous animals. Round the campfire people can talk, rest, or sleep in comfort and in safety. The domestic hearth gives warmth at night and allows man in his kitchen to transform inedible substances into palatable and nourishing food. Fire, indeed, gives an indefinite surplus of nourishing materials and of other utilities in consumption. It thus increases the range of what people can want, of what they can do, and of what they can enjoy.

The price which they have to pay for all this consists in the submission to the norms of knowledge and the rules of skill. Those who use it also have to submit to social rules of property and to the norms and taboos of value. Round the fire people have to dispose themselves according to age, rank, and authority. Its value in physiological advantages also leads invariably to a system of doctrine, mythology, and rules of respect towards the sacred element. Fire is as a rule protected from pollution, and specific types of fire have become centers of religious cults in primitive as well as highly derived cultures.

The same applies *mutatis mutandis* to another fundamental device of primitive culture, the stone implement. Stone is used as hammer, as cutting blade, as spear or arrowhead, and as axe or adze. This once more can be achieved only by obedience to the rules of where to find the material, how to shape it, and how to use the artifact. The technical rules are related to laws of property and of value. The individual who produces the axe or adze keeps it in his possession. Others respect his claim to ownership. The owner may give, exchange, or lend the article to his kinsman, friend, or neighbor. Such a transaction is always carried out according to definite social and economic rules. Each implement belongs to a system of organized activities—workshop or home, a hunting expedition, or a group of builders. Within each system people once more have to follow rules of knowledge, of technique, of co-operation, and of respect of property. Such rules are essential to the freedom of effective action.

Were we briefly to survey the domestic inventory of primitive man, that is, those artifacts which he uses in his daily life, we would always find some objects of wood, skins, or vegetable tissues used as clothing, and some kinds of personal ornamentation. They are all collected and produced according to the rules of primitive technique. They are owned personally: usually the man who produces them has also the claim to exclusive use. In satisfying human comfort, in protection against cold or wind, in the preparation of food by the use of domestic pots and pans, artifacts add to human freedom. Primitive clothing is sometimes very scanty, as is also the apparatus of cleanliness and hygiene.

Personal ornamentation enters early into human use and it serves to emphasize distinctions of sex, age, rank, and status. Here as elsewhere the material apparatus of culture partly satisfies some direct needs of the organism; it also becomes related to new, emergent needs such as those of social distinction, of the enhancement of beauty or dignity, and of functional transformation. A good deal of primitive ornamentation and clothes is used in tribal ceremonies, magical, totemic, or merely social. Masks, bodily paint, insignia, and ornamental symbols transform the actor into a mythical being or give him a special temporary status.

We have been approaching some of the earliest contributions to culture and to the freedom which it gives from its most tangible aspect, that of material artifacts. Yet at every point we have to register that the rules surrounding an artifact are always rules of social organization. Human beings produce objects, use them, own them, and value them, because such objects are an indispensable part of an organized concerted action. Such actions again do not mobilize human beings in a haphazard manner. We find that they are always performed by clearly defined, permanent human groups. The fundamental institution of primitive mankind and of mankind in general is the family or the domestic group. At early stages of culture the family is not merely the reproductive organization. It is also the principal educational institution and it fulfills a number of economic, legal, and religious functions. Of all forms of early organization, the family contributes the greatest quota of freedom in survival, since it is the organization which protects the long infancy of the young, equips them for life, and nourishes young and adult alike. For the domestic unit is the main organization for food production, distribution, and consumption. It is also the nucleus of kinship, that is, of the extended ties of blood on which a great deal of early organization is founded.

The material substratum of the family consists in the dwelling where the members live and of the domestic utensils which they use. This gives early man the freedom to rest and sleep, the freedom of protection against surprise attack, and a secluded spot for the round of daily life, as well as for many technical activities. The household equipped with domestic utensils is the place where human beings eat together, sleep at night, and from where they issue forth to their outdoor tasks.

The benefits of freedom which early man derives from his domestic institution depend upon the fact that all the manifold rules of common life are integrated into a system. This system again is related to certain biological endowments of the human organism, which supply the specific drives and physiological controls of the culturally defined rules of custom and law. The family starts with marriage. Under conditions of culture the attraction of sex is transformed into a social fact by the law of marriage. There is not a single culture, however primitive, where the permanent cohabitation of man and woman and legitimate procreation do not demand a contract which defines the relations of husband and wife as well as of parents and children. The law of marriage, the laws of descent, succession and inheritance, as well as the laws of kinship, constitute the charter of the domestic institution. This charter defines the duties of the members of the household.

Many of such duties are strongly backed by physiological impulse, sentiment, and inclination. Men and women are mutually attracted. This leads to the appearance of children, and the parental attitude towards offspring is also physiologically founded. Culture bases its decrees on innate tendencies and transforms these latter into rules sanctioned also by an organized vigilance of the community. In saying this we do not personify culture but merely state the universal facts of early social organization. We must also realize that human cultures, like any other evolutionary phenomena, are subject to the laws of competition and those of the survival of the strongest forms of organization. The immense advantages given to any type of primitive culture in virtue of a strong, well-integrated, and well-working organization of family and kinship would guarantee success and survival to a community thus organized. A primitive culture where the family was weak, rent by internal conflicts and dissensions, would have no chances of survival.

We thus register the fact that a well-integrated type of family, in which tribal law makes it a duty of the parents not merely to feed and rear the children, but also to educate them and equip them for life, is the source of basic and derived freedoms. This implies the strict observance of all the rules on which the organization of the family depends. Such rules include the taboos of incest, the economic division of labor between husband and wife, the duties of care and education of the young. They also imply that the children must submit to parental authority, and later on must help and assist their parents.

Tribal law defines also the relation of a newly founded family to those to whom it is related through husband and through wife. The new generation becomes invariably incorporated into a complex and extensive system of relationships to members of other families. This is the starting point of the system of kinship and clanship which provides an important aspect of early tribal structure.

We have mentioned here that the family implies the principle of authority. This is defined as between husband and wife, and parents and children. A new family is, as a rule, also submitted to the authority of both the husband's and the wife's parents, and directly or indirectly to the authority of the clan and the local group.

The problem of authority is intimately connected with the

differential freedom of primitive mankind. So far we have mostly spoken of the integral freedom given by culture, as an extended instrumental apparatus, to all those who manage this apparatus, do its work, and benefit by its existence. The principle of author- ity, however, means definitely a differential access to the benefits of freedom. Authority can be defined as the power of taking initia- tive and making decisions, of controlling the instrumentalities to carry out a decision, and it also means the privilege of distributing the results. We would find as a rule that in primitive domestic units authority is vested in the father. This is even the case when we study so-called matrilineal societies. There, some legal de- cisions are carried out by the wife's male kinsmen, usually her brothers. As a rule, however, these do not meddle in actual do- mestic affairs. Were we to inquire how far in primitive conditions there is scope for an arbitrary and oppressive exercise of domestic authority, we would see that at times minor acts of tyranny can be registered. Intimate acquaintance with any type of primitives shows us that they are as human as any other people and that oc- casionally we find men and women who are irascible, brutal, and arbitrary. In my own fieldwork I have known bullying husbands as well as regular shrews among the wives. Sometimes both par- ents are far from ideal towards their children, and there are also cases where the parents are oppressed by their children.

In spite of this however a regular, systematic or tyrannical abuse of authority is not to be found under primitive conditions. This is due largely to the fact that all the rules of conduct, when it comes to domestic relations and kinship duties as well, are founded upon some dictates of human nature; that is, they are founded physiologically. Husband and wife start their life with the initial premium on a mutually kind and beneficent treatment. For marriage, related as it is to the attraction of sex and the element of sexual gratification, permanently tends towards making the relationship valuable to either partner. The maternal affection for her offspring is also physiologically founded. During gestation and lactation the mother, animal or human, remains naturally attached and affectionate towards her offspring. The father of a family does not and cannot abuse his personal authority, because his subjects are his wife and children, towards whom his attitude is determined physiologically as essentially friendly and kindly. This sentiment is probably related to the husband's tender feelings towards his gestating and lactant wife. This is usually embodied into taboos and observances which a prospective father has to keep. The appreciation of paternity is also due to the fact that in most primitive cultures to be a father is both a duty and a privilege; it is enjoined by the community and it gives to the father a higher social and moral status.

In the second place an abuse of authority is never easy within small groups where people carry on their life face to face and in daily intimate contact. In the third place the conduct of husband and wife, and of parents and children within the family, is subject to the control of the patrilineal and matrilineal groups. In extreme cases of brutality husband or wife and the children as well are protected by their respective kinsmen and by their neighbors. There is also the possibility of divorce for either partner, while adoption and the removal of children from an unsatisfactory domestic atmosphere is not infrequently found. Although we cannot in any way and in any respect predicate paradisical conditions of freedom and beneficence in the primitive family, kinship group, or any other institution, we can say that there is a limited scope for tyranny and oppression or any other abuse of authority, and that early systems of customary law never countenance such abuses.

Reference was made to another type of early organization, the local group. For reasons of safety and of effective exploitation of the environment, early man lives as a rule in small but compact local communities. The members of such a group are usually organized on a charter which defines the relation of the group to its territory. It also lays down the boundaries of their lands and dictates to them the rules of common action in economic, religious, and legal needs. The authority in such local groups consists at early stages of development of a council of elders, at times also of a headman, hereditary or elected. Such groups as a rule look after the roads or paths in the territory they own conjointly, and the water supply. They sometimes increase the productiveness of the land by rudimentary works of primitive engineering, irrigation, terracing, fencing and suchlike. As a rule their territory is related to them through mythological or historical legends which also establish their legal right to ownership.

Here also we find that the local organization gives man the freedom of space and territory through the rules of how it must be exploited, and through the customary laws of private and communal ownership. All such rules are sanctioned primarily by the integral interests of the group as a whole and all its members. The headman, or the local council of elders, has to exercise his authority, partly in taking the initiative of a collective enterprise, expedition, or ceremony; partly in making decisions when conflict occurs between the component groups of the municipality. Such component groups consist first of all of individual households. The earliest local group is also differentiated into various economic teams: the group of hunters or of fishermen, the specialists in various arts and crafts, and the guilds of sorcerers, magicians, or other wielders of supernatural power. The local group is also divided into clans and kinship groups as well as age-grades, secret societies, and sex-linked organizations.

The fact that people even at the earliest stage are permanently organized for the carrying out of specific tasks is important for us in relation to the problem of freedom. Each group organized for the exercise of a special task has also its authority, its system of specific training, and its collectively owned property in land and artifact. The question of freedom at primitive stages is thus essentially linked with the use and abuse of authority in such groups. It became clear that at the primitive level there is very little scope for real oppression. For in every institution we have the same limiting factors: such groups consist of kinsmen, hence of people related by blood and the sentiment of blood, since kinship runs right through the structure of the tribe. In all the groups people depend very much on each other, hence the sanction of reciprocity or retaliation is always present. The high degree of mutual dependence between the leader and his followers is another factor which under primitive conditions prevents the abuse of personal authority. Primitive conditions also do not lend themselves easily to the accumulation of power either through physical force or wealth, or the use of spiritual intimidation.

To understand this better let us once more turn to the fact already mentioned in the previous chapter: the possibilities of misuse for coercion of the material equipment of primitive culture. In our analysis we have considered artifacts primarily as consumers' goods and as tools. In this they are related directly or indirectly to the basic needs of the human organism. Fire warms, it helps in cooking, and it protects the organism. Stones and sticks, shaped and adjusted, help to take up roots, to break objects, and to produce consumers' utilities. Dwellings, canoes, and roads serve to open up space, to adjust it to human living, and to submit it to man's control.

Yet it can easily be seen that artifacts are potential sources of control and constraint of others. For this they can be used in two forms: as accumulated wealth, and as means of physical constraint, that is, weapons. Ownership as the right to exclusive control of certain objects may be employed to make others dependent upon the owner. The individual who owns a dwelling is the master not only of the commodities, but also of the other inmates, either guests or familiars, whose residence and whose behavior become partially at least controlled by the master. A community which owns a territory, its places of vantage, and its means of communication can levy a toll, economic or social, by controlling the access and forbidding or allowing others to enter. Instruments of magic and of sacred power give the owners and wielders control over the rest of the community through the belief in the miraculous property of such objects or else in their dangerous potentialities. Thus the production, ownership, and accumulation of material wealth allows certain people to exercise influence, power, and control through the law of property.

Most artifacts can also be transformed into weapons of aggression, as well as means of defense. Even fire is used in many primitive communities as a means of constraint in the form of firebrands hurled at the adversary, especially in family quarrels. Fire can be used also to burn down dwellings and protective palisades, while higher culture has developed firearms, explosives, and the cruel fire throwers of contemporary warfare. Stone implements can be used as clubs, spears and arrowheads. Wood is used for pointed spears, arrows and clubs. Thus there is hardly any artifact which cannot be turned into a weapon, that is, into an instrument of bodily harm, coercion, and violence.

We shall see that it is the culturally determined concatenation of the three elements—material artifact or mechanism, the law or rule of organization, and the value or standardized purpose—which, related to each other in an institutional organization, can lead either to a constructive and peaceful use of man's culturally increased power, or else to its use for direct constraint through violence, fear, and economic coercion. This type of cultural mis-use constitutes the real threat to freedom, differential and specific, that is, affecting minorities and individuals, at times even the whole community, within a culture. At primitive levels the misuse of the cultural apparatus occurs only sporadically on a small scale, and it never becomes institutionalized. But it is important to show clearly that the potentialities of oppression and bondage enter with the very appearance of culture. We shall have to show the conditions in which a culture as a whole may develop tenden-cies to an increasing restriction of real freedom.

3

Value and Derived Needs

IT WILL be well at this point briefly to indicate what we mean by the emergent character of culture in evolution. We have been constantly faced by the fact that certain new needs arise as soon as man begins to exploit the environment through the roundabout method of using artifacts, organizing concerted activities, and living in socially constituted groups. Man acquires the need of possessing implements, dwellings and clothes, having skilled individuals and those who know where to find food, hunt animals and get raw materials. He acquires the need of order, of training the young and replenishing the larder.

Until now we have mainly concentrated on the relation of cultural services to man's biological needs. We have seen, however, that freedom consists in the enlargement of scope and efficiency of action. Every increment in cultural devices and proceedings, however small, gives man an additional scope to do something definite which he wants to do. In this, it is very important to be clear that the *want* is by no means arbitrary. Human wants refer primarily and permanently to the achievement of desirable results, by which we mean an act which directly or indirectly satisfies the biological needs of the human organism. In other words human beings, primitive and civilized, never strive except towards action, towards the pragmatic achievement of results directly or indirectly related to their needs.

It is at this point that cultural determinism enters, first and foremost in the form of substituting complex, linked, and roundabout sequences of action which are related to the primary needs of the human organism. It enters also in that the incorporation of such activities into human behavior creates new needs, instrumental, integrative, and emergent. Every one of such new needs or cultural imperatives constitutes, if you like, a new constraint or shackle. Every habit, whether in the form of a technical skill, a conventional manner, a law, or an ethical rule, contributes to that second nature of man which implies an additional determinism on his conduct.

In our conception of freedom we regard the expression "slave to habit" and the whole concept of bondage to the legitimate rules and regulations of culture as a preposterous misnomer. The reason for this is that all the new imperatives or derived drives are essential to effective action, that is, to the achievement of every installment of freedom. They are also indispensable to that close co-existence of human beings and to their collaboration which is the very essence of culture. The essence of culturally determined action is that it is part of a system related to needs, basic and derived.

We shall have to survey the nature of those derived needs and introduce one or two more realities of cultural constraint which increase freedom, and we must also determine the potentialities of abuse which reside in them. Let us first attempt to understand the mechanisms which establish instrumental drives in culture. Man wants to be warm. He wants to satisfy his hunger. He wants to be protected against dangers. Such needs are based in the physiology of the human organism. From the beginnings of culture these needs are satisfied through activities by which material objects and devices are produced so as to satisfy the primary needs. Primitive man has to hunt and kill animals, and to organize and determine to collect fruits or tubers in order to cook them and eat them. Fire, a stone implement, a spear, and a household, bound up as they are with the rules of organization and knowledge, are necessary instruments. Through experience and tradition man acquires the derived drives to produce these instruments, to own them, and to place a value on them. Each new derived drive is a new factor in freedom.

As soon as man begins to exploit the environment through the roundabout method of using artifacts, organizing concerted activities, and living in socially constituted groups, new needs arise. We can say that these new or instrumental needs come into being or emerge. They are new dynamic factors in the cultural process, parts of determinism. Regarded objectively, these needs are neither more nor less than laws of process which result from what we have called cultural determinism; from the individual standpoint, they are desires or motives. The physiological drive appears as the initial motive to action, and reappears in its final consummation; between these two stages enters a series of new impulses. Man has to follow all the rules, laws, and constraints implied in his tradition if he wants to gain the advantages. He also has to be guided by the rules of symbolic communication, that is, by the traditional lore and law of his tribe. In all this freedom is acquired not by evading the new determinism of derived cultural imperatives, but by accepting it, following it, and valuing it. Freedom also is in no way and in no sense negative. It is the positive quality of human behavior, and it is determined by the degree of conformity of this behavior to the rules of effective performance.

Right through any detailed anthropological analysis of early techniques, laws of property and inheritance, rules of co-operation and distribution, we would find the same phenomenon. There emerge processes which more or less indirectly satisfy the physiological needs of the organism.

Every phase of such a process, every rule of co-operation and ownership, every object necessary as a consumer commodity or as an implement, become appreciated or acquire value and are surrounded with rules of appreciation and respect. Education consists in the transmission of such rules and in the teaching of language, which is the main instrumentality for the framing of rules, precepts, and imperatives. Our thesis is that freedom is found in obedience to such laws. The various devices of social control validate the rules. Primitive knowledge, however piecemeal, defective and pragmatic, consists of rules how to exploit the environment and how to produce artifacts. The function of early belief, magical and religious, is to supply certain deficiencies of early knowledge and to satisfy certain needs which arise from man's intellectual and emotional systems of thought.

The concept of derived drive or imperative, that is, of culturally determined motive, refers clearly to rules of behavior as well as to products. Man has to produce his implements and he has to use them. The retention of all the rules of effective behavior is also ultimately derived from the physiological rewards reached at the end of a chain of linked responses. Here emergent cultural control consists in the real and objective organization of motives. At each step in a chain of activities man has to remain aware first of all of the integral unity of those activities, and also at every step he must have a strong and definite motive to carry out the partial activity of the linked chain.

It may be best here to start once more from the most concrete and tangible aspect of culture, that is, the artifact. Earliest man discovered that a long, thin piece of wood, a stick to put it prosaically, provided it be well selected of tough, hard and resistant material and pointed at one end, is very serviceable. It can be used as a lever. It can be used as a spear to hunt, or to kill fish. Indirectly it thus becomes associated with a wide range of acts which bring food, give safety, and lead to other bodily comforts.

The stick acquires value. Economically, value is the translation into terms of personal possession of an object collected, shaped, and constantly used, and the application to it of the laws of ownership. The rarity of an object is equivalent to the difficulty to procure it, either because the raw material is scarce or a great effort is needed to find it. Ownership means that man will not surrender such an object except in exchange for other goods or for services. Psychologically ownership implies a hold on an artifact and a clinging to it, and the fact that some of the desirability of these physiological gratifications, services and goods which are obtained through this artifact become attached to the artifact itself. Personal experience, as well as collective experience, embodied in tradition, hence also in rules of conduct and customary law, crystallizes into the psychological attitude of a human being towards a whole range of material objects. This attitude we can describe by the term value, which is equivalent to all derived motivation. Value constitutes therefore a new driving force which makes human beings produce, maintain, and hold in physical possession those objects which enter instrumentally into the exploitation of the environment.

Hence value becomes the drive to bodily effort and endurance and to the overcoming of fatigue. Such a drive is a necessary part of the carrying out of an activity. Thus knowledge and skill lead to ownership of goods and utilization of material. Following such a chain of responses we would find that in selection of suitable wood, in its preparation, in the rapid friction, in the production of the spark, and the nursing of the flame, man is moved by association of each differential response to the final result. This consists in the use of fire for warming cold limbs, for the cooking of food, or for protection against animals and the environment. The appreciation of fire when it is produced occurs because fire gives comfort, safety, and provides palatable and digestible food. Thus value supplies the differential motives at each step in the production of fire, or of stone implements, dwellings, and all other commodities.

We can define the concept of derived drive as an aim or end and the concept of value as the purpose. Value is thus the culturally determined driving force, the new cultural determinism from the point of view of individual action. Embodied in tradition and learned by every individual in every generation, we find the emergence of certain new motives which fulfill the same function as physiological drives. They move man to action. They determine the type of behavior, they guide the individual and control the group through a chain of linked efforts towards definite goals.

Value therefore is that attitude which organizes drives, emotions and the impulse to possess other people and objects. It is the culturally determined ability to see the end and the appreciation of the range of ends. The estimation of value enables man to choose wisely, that is, so as to utilize his personal ability in the elimination of certain choices or actions and in the achievement of self-realization. Value is the force which brings about the formation of differential motives for each phase of action, and their integration into a concatenated sequence leading to the end. Through value, man is thus able to choose among the existing systems for the carrying out of a well-determined purpose, to learn how to use the means and to reach results.

Value makes man produce artifacts, own them, that is, cling to them physically to the exclusion of others, distribute them and exchange them according to rules of equivalents, and consume them or use them as instruments of production. The value of an instrument is determined by all those services in goods produced and services rendered which become associated with it. The value of a sacred emblem, of a magical formula or of a prayer lies in its power to allay fear, to control chance and to summon supernatural help. Value is always kept alive by the principle of reinforcement, that is, of functional utility, in that the objects, activities and realities valued subserve in the long run the primary needs of the human organism. Value also is manifest in the existence of norms sanctioned, that is, used as valid because they are necessary to the successful carrying out of an action, because they are implicit in effective co-operation, or else because lack of obedience is met by punishment and full obedience by reward. The whole system of education is determined by value.

Value, the new driving force, has its prototype in animal behavior. This we can observe in an animal's attitude and behavior in relation to certain objects or acts, about which, when he is deprived of them, the animal gets angry. A dog sets value on a bone, and is angry when it is taken from him. Animals value their sexual pleasure, and fight or are angered when this is interfered with. Some animals again regard certain territory as their own, and will attack others which enter it. All these attitudes in relation to a certain object or act demonstrate the animal prototype of value.

Returning, however, to our analysis of value in general and the concept of the emergent in evolution, we can say that by value we mean the acquired realization of instrumental imperatives. In every type of behavior here outlined we find that the motive to a specific act may be far removed from a physiological drive, yet taking any such phase we could relate it, sometimes very indirectly and in a very roundabout manner, to a final physiologically rewarding consummation. The reward for the carrying out of this action is invariably twofold: it is partly determined by the physiological result of the whole integral chain, but also is safeguarded by a system of traditionally formulated rules.

It is the relation of value to the formation of purpose which is significant for us in our analysis of freedom. Since value is the driving force which is the source of human motivation, and hence of the formation of purposes, it is a vital factor in determining human action, and therefore also freedom. The whole course of human action throughout life is determined by values, economic, political, spiritual or legal.

We will here make a general classification of instrumental types of activity, closely related to the problem of freedom, and each of which is pervaded by the dynamic principle of value or acquired motive. In the first place we see that the material equipment of culture needs constant production or replacement; this leads to the economic aspect of human behavior. Secondly, the co-existence of human beings in close proximity implies the general imperative of the maintenance of order and regulation, that is, the legal aspect of human culture. Thirdly, the tradition of culture has to be transmitted; this occurs in the educational processes which take place usually during the earlier stages of human life but become also extended right through life. Finally as we have seen, each organization demands the existence of authority and direction: this is the political side of culture.

As regards the economic process, this can be subdivided into the phases of production, distribution and consumption of goods, that is, of objects adjusted to needs but which also imply an organic readjustment. The primary determinism in this is supplied by the biological needs which impose on every human group first and foremost the production of food and shelter and protection against cold, wind and weather.

Even in the most primitive cultures we find that economic activities are organized, either into systems related to institutions in which they occur incidentally, or else by mobilizing special institutions. With the organization, there develops a doctrine; as, for instance, how to produce fire and how to use it at home, in camp, or on an expedition. Man thus learns how to value fire.

In most cases the concerted effort of such a group is indispensable to the successful run of a primitive economic system. This means that the enjoyment of freedom from want, and, when it comes to protective constructions, of the freedom from fear, depends on the smooth working of a combined enterprise. The group and each individual have to obey the derived imperative of full effort, of adequate skill and of conscientious performance.

In such activities, we find that value in the economic sense makes its early appearance. The economist defines value as the product of scarcity and utility. A more dynamic definition in terms of general analysis of culture would be that economic value is the drive related to utility which compels man to search for utilities, and to put a considerable effort into the production of artifacts. Therefore we define value here as the incentive to effort. This is also related to value in ownership, that is, to the strength of the hold which an object has over a man, that is, of the hold which a man can exercise over an object. As mentioned already, private property appears very definitely on primitive levels. When it is surrendered it always implies a repayment, either in kind, or in terms of some other obligations of kinship, co-operation or social dependence. Economically, man depends upon his shaped sticks and stones, upon his knowledge how to produce them, and upon his right to use them exclusively and permanently. This dependence finds its economic expression in the rules of ownership. The individual does not surrender the object which he has acquired or produced except in exchange for goods and services. Nor does man easily relinquish his association with others provided that this rewards him through co-operation. Psychologically ownership, social loyalty, and faithfulness to rules of knowledge and skill are determined by the final result of cultural processes, that is, by physiological gratification.

The principle of property, in the last analysis, means that a man or woman has the exclusive right to a number of objects, and that these have a determined place in such a physical setting as a household, a canoe or a piece of local territory. Property means that one person is related in a definite manner to an artifact when its use is imperative in individual or concerted action. Imagine a community where the principles of personal property were not in force. This would mean in terms of physical performance that no one would be certain to find his digging stick, axe, spear, shield or piece of clothing when the need arises. This would also mean that in a complex, concerted action such as communal hunting, fishing or the manning of a canoe, there would occur an initial and perhaps a chronic disorder, incompatible with any efficiency in performance.

The roots of property as a legal principle which determines the physical relationship between man and his environmental setting, natural or artificial, are the very prerequisite of any ordered action in the cultural sense. Value again, as an economic principle, implies equivalence in utility, that is, ultimately in the use of certain objects. Its absence once more would destroy property, and through this, order. Economic value thus can be estimated in exchange, as controlling effort and as defining distribution and consumption. Such economic values show a political factor, since services, loyalties and goods can be acquired by exchange.

We have seen in the course of our survey of economic value that the concerted effort of a group carrying out an activity is essential for its success; we have also observed that the participants are dependent on the rules already established by tradition and practice, by which this activity is brought to a satisfactory conclusion. These rules of co-operation, regulation and order therefore become valued and appreciated, since without close adherence to them, the activity could not be successfully concluded. In the same way, value enters into all co-operation, for a man learns to depend on those who work with him, and values their concerted effort towards an end, which itself is of value.

Culturally all derived imperatives or values are taught through education and embodied in tradition. In education, values are recognized by the educator; and these values are in turn imposed in his teaching and accepted by the pupil. In many cases, economic values control the educational system, partly through the teaching of skills and knowledge which are worthwhile and through the imparting of techniques of production, of manipulation and the rules of exchange; partly also as cardinal systems of reward. Through education, therefore, in its varying stages and forms, the implanting of values, that is, of the secondary motivation of culture, takes place. For education is the transmission of all verbally incorporated doctrines, of knowledge, mythology and belief.

We shall later analyze more fully the processes of education and their relation to freedom. It is necessary however to stress here the importance and immense power of education as the principal mechanism for the implanting of values. Since values are the driving force and motivation of human action, we can see that the whole course of human life can be determined as a result of values instilled in the course of education.

Normative values are linked with political, religious and economic sanctions. In primitive communities, normative values show a tendency of centralization in divine kings and chiefs or supernatural magicians, who are also the leaders in the dominant tribal activities. When we come to activities, the value of coercion is evident. It is used as an instrument in all education.

Value, as we can see from all this, is not merely related to individual experience; it becomes also incorporated into tradition. In all cultures, however primitive, we find that the most useful types of commodity, the most important elements such as fire and water, and also the most important sociological principles of organization become surrounded by taboos, ritual, and ceremony. Not all tradition however is sacred. We find communities where economic value is supreme, as in certain tribes of Northwest America and Oceania, in China and in the United States of America. Again, there are other communities living on and by war, in the form of cattle raiding, occasional rapine and plunder attacks, conquest and levy of toll; in these the predominant values are those associated with military virtues and force. In still other communities, industry, arts and crafts and constructive activities are developed, and are the basis of their main values.

Primitive religion centers on the one hand on the vital crises of the human organism, and on the other hand it enhances the value of the crucial cultural achievements at any given stage of development. We find everywhere the sacrilization of such vital crises as birth, maturity, marriage, and death. We find also that round the fire as domestic hearth, as magical instrument, or as symbol of some divinity, there develop ritual, taboos, and myths. Many of the inventions are ascribed to mythological heroes or ancestors of the tribe. The production of food, and its magical or religious multiplication, as well as the control of wind, weather, and the fertility of the soil, produce such cults as totemism, nature worship, and the magical ritual of fertility. One of the most important functions of magic, religion and ethics, primitive or developed, is the establishment of fundamental and comprehensive values. The objects, the norms of conduct, the main canons of social organization achieve a transcendental importance by becoming linked with systems of belief and ritual practice, to which human beings are made to submit through the conviction that they have been revealed to man, that is, imposed upon man by beings or entities superior to him and controlling him with a power transcending human understanding and human control.

This point, that is, the emergence of mysticism or the submission of groups or individuals to a superior order, had to be registered here because it is on the one hand a source of new strength and new efficiency for mankind, while on the other hand it can also be misused by groups and individuals within a community, to impose upon others. The power of belief organized and implemented as it always is, becomes, as we shall see, one of the main instruments of oppression, even as it is one of the powerful forces of freedom. We need only to remember such extreme cases as the Spanish Inquisition, the fighting fanaticism of Islam, the religious wars of the Middle Ages and of modern history, as well as the indoctrination and mysticism of the contemporary totalitarian creeds, to realize how magic and religion can lead to the enslavement of the human mind. In primitive communities the main instrument of this is the belief in sorcery directed against human life and human success.

In each culture, the dominant values are associated with the dominant activities of that culture. Related to these there exists a number of dogmatic affirmations in doctrines, legends and myths, which are implemented and drilled for. The dominant cultural interest tends to be translated into values often embodied in religion, magic, art and in types of knowledge. We shall see that in a democratic culture, where the individual is submitted from earliest childhood to a multiplicity of differential influences, he forms his values by choice among the existing possibilities. In a totalitarian culture, the dominant values or ideals—the doctrines of might is right, of race superiority and the use of violence—are incorporated in the charter of the state and are instilled by means of indoctrination. We can show that a culture may aim at war, with destruction, disintegration and the gradual loss of its scientific, artistic and moral achievements, and may live on the power of the few and the perverted vanities of the many. Or else, with freedom at its very heart, a culture can further the development of science, multiply art and lead to the pursuit of happiness within a variety of independent institutions.

The relation therefore of value to freedom is clear. Value is the driving force which determines purpose, and freedom lies in choice of purpose, its translation into effective action and the full enjoyment of the results. We find thus that value is the prime mover in human existence. It pervades all forms of activity and is the driving force throughout culture. Man is moved to effort, not under an immediate physiological drive, but instructed by traditional rules, moved by learned motive and controlled by value. Man works to obtain the thing that he values, whether this be an object, a way of life or a belief. The way by which the values—freedom of conscience, of dogma, of devotion to ideals —are established is one of the main installments in freedom or bondage.

4

Freedom, Education and the Formation of Purpose

WE SHALL now survey the processes of training and education in evolutionary perspective primarily as the instrumentality which develops in every individual his second nature. Second nature is, in its widest sense, the body of acquired responses, that is, of habits which human beings have to form under the impact of cultural determinism. Education in the narrower sense, as the initial training received by the child within the family and his subsequent schooling in skills, in knowledge, and in tribal or national values, occurs at the early stages of individual development. It is carried out within definite social settings: the family, the play group, the various workshops where crafts and economic activities are learned by his apprenticeship. At higher stages of civilization we have the whole system of specialized educational institutions.

In the analysis of education we have to remember that it is always based on the use of punishment and reward. Here the teachings of modern experimental psychology of the behaviorist type are extremely useful. More especially the concept of reinforcement, that is, of the dynamic character acquired by the derived drives in virtue of the primary reward, has to be kept in mind. This means that the habits of feeding, walking, cleanliness, and safe behavior are rewarded or sanctioned by their functional utility. Over and above this intrinsic sanction of success there invariably enter also punishment and reward meted out by parents on children as an arbitrary factor in the process. Obedience to verbal commands and other instructions is rewarded by food, by praise, and by demonstrations of affection. Disobedience, slackness, or rebellion are punished by physical retaliation and by depriving the learning organism of food and of other bodily attentions.

Modern behaviorists and animal trainers of all ages have proved that even lower organisms can acquire habits by an adequate process of conditioning. Culture from this point of view has been and is a vast conditioning apparatus in which every act of apprenticeship, every acquisition of a new word or symbol, every entry into a co-operative group means the conditioning of the organism to the acquisition of new habits. A habit may be defined as an acquired co-ordination of sense organs, muscles, and nervous tissues, so that an organism, animal or human, responds in a predictable manner to a definite stimulus within a determined context of situation. Cultural norms differ substantially from the habits of animals. Unlike the rats, guinea pigs and dogs which we condition in a laboratory, human beings are conditioned or trained simultaneously from earliest infancy to the use or adoption of the use of material objects, to symbolic sounds, and the social norms of dependence and co-operation.

In most phases of human behavior the primary drives are present, and the gradual development of secondary drives is clearly sanctioned. In human cultures also there is a great variety and complexity in the coercive, regulating or conditioning forces. As regards rules of technology and technique, those rules of how to use one's muscles, hands, feet, eyes and also one's nutritive organs, the human being is trained from infancy, partly by punishment and praise, but mostly by the sanction of success and failure. Since success and failure here are usually linked up with primary needs for food, comfort or cleanliness, the automatic sanction of effectiveness is strong. The rules of social intercourse, on the other hand, are sanctioned from the outset, partly by the laws of give and take, of effective co-operation and co-existence, partly by organized authority. It is with these rules which imply the existence of organized authority that a student of freedom in evolution is mostly concerned.

Both methods of sanction produce new elements of cultural determinism. The infant and the child learn to respond to conditioned stimuli of command, request, or signal. Reward is inherent in the process of teaching; parental authority is accepted because it is the all-rewarding, only and ever-present source of all satisfactions. In certain aspects of education, primitive and civilized, a high degree of discipline is developed. The military drill of the barracks' square, some technical aspects of primitive discipline in difficult manual activities, the regimentation which occurs at initiation ceremonies into age-grade and secret societies, and the control learned in the observance of taboos, are examples of discipline at simple or higher stages of development.

The relation of education to freedom is clear. Exactly as culture gives mankind its integral increment of freedom through evolution, so in the life history of every individual through the stages from animal to infant, to the last word in contemporary culture, education bestows upon him the freedom of his tribal or national culture. Or else it deprives him of certain aspects of this freedom. We shall see that human beings can either be trained to be free, or trained to be rulers, tyrants, or dictators, or else they can be trained to be slaves. Thus the understanding of educational mechanisms and conditions is essential to our appreciation of the reality of freedom as it occurs differentially in human societies. Taking education in its widest sense, we see readily that it is a process which lasts through life. Every new status which an individual acquires, every new condition of life such as marriage, parenthood, maturity, and old age, have to be learned, in that the individual has to adjust gradually and by the acquisition of new attitudes, new ideas, and also new social duties and responsibilities.

In this widest sense the course of education transforms the immature, unequipped, and untutored young animal into a social being, a tribesman, or a citizen who emerges with abilities to think, to act, and to respond in co-operation with other human beings.

In order to think, a human being has to learn how to use verbal symbols and also how to obey the instructions of others within a concerted activity, or in listening to planning, commands, and narratives. Early in life the teaching of language enters as one of the most important integrative processes. He has to learn the full extent of tribal rules, of custom, of law, and of ethics. Through these processes of education the individual acquires what we call a moral sense or conscience, which implies the ability to organize emotional responses, to refer them to definite values, and to make them control the social give and take.

With reference to our concept of freedom we see that a man has to learn how to form his purposes. From the wide and chaotic range of ever-changing whim, impulse, or drive which leads to random behavior, the individual learns to select a limited range of fixed and determined values. Motive and purpose are always the acceptance of cultural value or its reinterpretation and at times revolt against it. Since these are related to the instrumentalities of his culture, the individual is able to make such learned motives and purposes effective. He can transform every one of his culturally determined motives into some action or system of behavior which will lead him to the results desired, unless he is deprived by constraint or by legal trammels from access to these results, such as occurs in the case of a slave, serf, caste member or unemployed pauper.

We see therefore that in any form choice is the result of a long process, essentially social, where from infancy the individual depends on others, learns from them and co-operates with them. Projecting this on a typical career of an individual, primitive or civilized, we see that earlier or later he has to make the choice of his career. Even in a primitive society there is a certain range within which choice can be taken. The man or woman may excel in physical strength. This will predispose him or her to devote more time to economic activities than to the cultivation of magical or religious interests. To specialize in these latter, intelligence, memory, and at times even certain abnormal characteristics are desirable. Some men become naturally tribal leaders in the organization of enterprise or in the direction of ceremonies. As civilization develops and institutions multiply and crystallize on definite purposes, the range of choice widens. There is a choice of becoming an artisan or craftsman, or a trader and merchant, or in higher cultures a member of a profession, a politician, clergyman, artist, or intellectual.

From the point of view of education it is important to note here that most of it takes the form of apprenticeship, except in very highly differentiated cultures where professional schooling precedes apprenticeship. Education as apprenticeship means that a man has to translate the choice of his career or interest into a social act: he has to join the institution in which his chosen type of activity is embodied. Freedom of choice thus is always related to the freedom of being accepted into the appropriate institution.

Even in primitive cultures a human being is not shaped in a wholesale, overall manner. Teaching and learning are not given as a lump installment. The first phases always occur round the domestic hearth. Later on the youngster, male or female, receives a good deal of apprenticeship to life through the play group of his local community. When he is strong enough to carry out certain easy economic tasks he may have to look after the cattle, carry out some domestic chores, assist his parents or kindred in simple agricultural tasks, join a hunting expedition, or practice at fishing. He passes then through tribal initiation ceremonies when they exist, or else becomes instructed in the tribal law through a more extended process of learning.

All this means that at primitive levels of development the human mind and organism are not submitted to a centralized, standardized molding of personality which might radiate from one center and submit the individual to the acceptance of a wholesale system of ideas, skills, and social values. Under primitive cultures the very fact of the multiplicity and variety of influences makes any one-sided spiritual enslavement or indoctrination impossible.

Another important insight which we gain from this analysis is that at any stage of culture the chances of spiritual freedom, that is, of a variety of points of view and ideological crystallizations, depend, first and foremost, upon the existence of a number of mutually independent institutions, which though related enjoy a considerable degree of autonomy. Indeed, in several educational devices of the primitives, we see that joining a new institution or passing through initiation ceremonies entails a definite attempt to break down the loyalties and interests acquired in earlier life and to introduce new values. The institutions thus each exercise an autonomous spiritual influence on the growing mind.

When a man or woman enters the contract of marriage, this also implies a new institutional allegiance. The law of marriage and kinship is invariably ingrained through specific teaching, through association with initiation ceremones, as well as through observation and gradual learning. The duties and obligations of marriage and parenthood have to be learned.

The contract by which the choice of marriage is realized gives the two partners a new installment of freedom. All the advantages of domesticity already discussed: the privacy and seclusion of the household, the physiological advantages of mating, the benefits derived from parenthood, constitute the freedom of the household. This is achieved by following the rules of behavior, by carrying out the respective duties of husband and wife, of parent and child, and by submitting to the integral system of the laws of marriage, family life, and kinship.

In the same way any choice in religious ceremony, in technical or economic specialization, in learning to wield magic or to manipulate the sacred, means that the individual has to join an organized group, a clan, a magical fraternity, a team of hunters, tillers, or fishermen, and submit to all the restrictions, rules of conduct, and rules of skill implied by the membership.

In every case we would see that the full freedom implies not merely submission to duties, development of skills and making prolonged efforts in hard work and discipline, but also gaining the rewards which result from the activity. Freedom, we see more and more clearly, means access to the formation of purpose, to the instrumentalities of an action, and to the results of this action. Freedom is a very concrete and specific set of guarantees granted to human beings by the customary law of the tribe or community, and by all those factors which help man in joining that type of organized activity for which he is fitted and in which he desires to participate. In anything which man does and chooses to do, he will not work, sweat, or shed blood except for an end which he values and which he is allowed to enjoy. Thus looking at freedom as it controls primitive cultures and following it through the various stages of evolution, we become more and more convinced that it is always a determined, positive, and specific quality of human existence.

In this concrete discussion of training and education we see quite clearly why the freedom of the child, in the sense of letting him do what he wishes and as he likes, is unreal. In the interest of his own organism he has constantly to be trammeled in education from acts which are biologically dangerous, or which are culturally useless. His whims, his fits of idleness or disobedience must be gradually curtailed, formed, and translated into culturally relevant choices. There is also no freedom in action except within the context of organized human groups, each of them agreed on an integral purpose, each working it out concertedly, and each distributing the results.

Our analysis also shows us clearly where the tangible and the real limitations to freedom occur. In human societies the child is born with what we might call a definite personal birthright. He is healthy and normal, or else sickly, deformed, or mentally deficient. He comes into existence with the potentiality for certain abilities, skills or integral pursuits. To this natural birthright which might predestine the primitive or advanced infant to a definite career, there is however added also the cultural birthright. The child is born into a family which enjoys a definite status, wealth, and position of power. This may be positive or negative. In a community organized on the basis of a caste system, or of slavery, or serfdom, or color-bar division, the social conditions of the infant may either trammel and hamper him from birth, or give him the unearned increment of initial privilege. This is the real plus and minus of freedom into which every individual is born.

In this we see once more that freedom is not a subjective or psychological "state of mind". In the case of an infant he does not know whether he is destined to grow up into a king, emperor or millionaire, or else to become a slave, a serf or a pauper. Yet objectively and with a determinism almost as inexorable as that of a physical or organic process, destiny is shaped for him by cultural conditions.

This determinism can be broken through only by a cultural cataclysm such as a revolution, or modified to a lesser extent if in a given system the determinism of birth can be compensated by the freedom of training. As a rule we find that in rigidly stratified systems there exist also rigidly differential types of training. The sons of slaves and of noblemen or landlords, respectively, do not go to the same schools, nor yet to the same workshops. They do not play with each other and they do not associate in later life. Yet to any extent in which training, schooling, and apprenticeship can compensate deficiencies in birthright, and level up the chances of parallel careers, we can register an addition to freedom. In primitive communities at the low level of development we find no caste or rank hierarchy to any tangible degree. Such distinctions as are implied in age-grades, secret societies, and sex-linked distinctions are the only equivalent of class or rank. Yet except for differentiation by sex which as a rule is functional rather than oppressive, we find that freedom of choice and of access to training is equally distributed.

It is only when through the development of monopoly in power, wealth and spiritual constraint the discriminative institutions of caste and rank, as well as of wealth and power, make their appearance, that freedom as regards birthright and the full development of personality becomes seriously curtailed.

The combination of birthright and advancement through training which grants and guarantees the access to results might be described as the charter of citizenship. By this we mean the individual's right to use his natural gifts as well as his trained skills and services; and to reap the reward. This concept is essential to our understanding of freedom. It is enough to think of the contemporary phenomenon of unemployment, where enormous percentages of populations, able to work, trained for work, and eager to work, are simply cast aside because there is no scope for their contributions.

Unemployment is in some ways one of the most acute and distressing forms in which the freedom of exercising one's abilities and skills is denied. Whether the unemployed receive the dole or a subvention, or whether they have to depend on charity, they are not free men in the most essential respect of the term. They have no freedom to do what they have prepared themselves for; nor yet to earn that reward which gives them the sense of dignity obtained by living from their legitimate efforts.

A somewhat different contemporary phenomenon of the denial of the charter of citizenship is to be found in that reduction of class status which led to the formation of the group of déclassés in Hitler Germany and in revolutionary Russia. Here we find people who are capable and trained for important public service, having high abilities and high qualifications. This very training and upbringing has been erected into an impediment and a discrimination against them. A definite reduction in the charter of citizenship is to be found in yet another form wherever culture imposes an inferior status on people who are differentiated by race. The racial doctrine now preached openly and shamelessly by the Nazis and some of their allies has introduced a new form of slavery and serfdom associated with the index of "race" and of nationality. Unfortunately it must be stated that even in democratic countries we would have to register oppression by color-bar and by differential institutions against those who are classified as colored. Democracy must imply certain elementary values of freedom as well as of equality. Democracy lives and thrives by the principle of universal education. It is clear, however, that as long as we have a discriminative birthright and a discrimination in citizenship, independently of the level of education, the freedom through education does not exist. This is a subject very actual now, since a fighting democracy cannot adopt the ideals of freedom and equality as one of its main war slogans while it denies and ill-treats these ideals in its domestic policy.

In our analysis of education in relation to freedom we have registered several points. The individual is never free or bond except through his relation to socially organized groups. His birthright is defined by his parentage. His educational opportunities depend on the status of his parents, on their wealth, and on their rank. His acceptance into co-operative groups is a social act in which he depends on others.

The act of choosing is once more determined by the range of purposes within a culture, and by social as well as personal conditions affecting the possibilities of this choice. We can say from this point of view that the birthright is the initial definition of the individual's meaning and purpose, attached to him by society. We can say also from this point of view that his opportunities of personal development depend not only on him, but very largely on the attitude of his fellow tribesmen or fellow citizens, especially on the attitudes of those groups whom he wants to join as a member but is only allowed to do so by their consent. In some cases his skills may be developed and his efforts utilized, while his social rewards as well as economic remunerations are curtailed. In all this we see that freedom consists in a full, harmonious, and comprehensive satisfaction of the primary needs as well as of all derived interests and expectations of the individual within an organized society. It is within the universe of discourse of freedom in its relation to culture as a whole, to its component institutions, to rank, status and the various rewards, economic, spiritual and recreational, that we can understand its real increments and diminutions.

We see also that over and above the integral freedom of culture we have always to keep in mind its distribution socially determined. Slavery gives more freedom to the master at the expense of the slaves. At times it allows a culture as a whole to embark on ambitious enterprises and achieve great military feats. In human evolution and history until fairly recent times slavery, as an industrial system, has played a conspicuous part.

It is hardly necessary to point out that slavery as a legal system is at present not compatible with the democratic constitution of any nation or state. The general level of knowledge, the nationwide and world-wide system of communication and technique, have given a greatly increased power to the masses of man. The re-introduction of slavery and even the maintenance of strict caste discrimination demands now a large scale apparatus of control by force, as well as the acceptance of doctrines of human inequality which are not compatible with the fundamental doctrines of democratic culture. The caste system which existed for centuries, probably for millennia, in a country like India is breaking down. The policy of color-bar is being modified in the Southern States and in the parts of Africa where it has been well entrenched. The main reason for this is that slavery and caste, as well as serfdom, are based on principles incompatible with the fundamental tenets of Christianity and democracy. When public opinion spreads to all classes of humanity through universal education, journalism, and the radio, it is extremely difficult to bottle up the cumulative resentments, grievances, and natural disloyalties of the oppressed caste. It is equally demoralizing for the higher caste to cherish two opposing ideals, such as those of freedom and of bondage; those of justice and of discrimination; those of equality and of ruthless oppression. Dealing as we do now with enormous quantities of human beings, the only way in which slavery can be re-introduced is by constructing an enormous mechanism of secret police, espionage, preventive and restrictive measures in order to keep a large part, perhaps the majority, of human beings in permanent slavery. Today the democracies are gradually—perhaps too gradually— reducing and pulling down the remnants of racial discrimination and of class distinction. The totalitarian systems, on the other hand, are introducing a "new order" essentially akin to slavery. Without slavery totalitarianism would become meaningless to any "master nation" which has been made to accept it.

The main argument concerning education as a cultural process makes us realize that it is one of the most powerful instruments of democracy. Its cultural value consists in that, abolishing birthright, it supplies us with the greatest opportunities to mobilize real talent. In making education universal, democracy makes possible the participation of the people in the guidance of its own destinies. In extending the charter of citizenship to all those who, through the natural birthright of ability, physical strength and intellectual qualities, have been able to use an adequate system of training to its full advantage, democracy becomes the open road on which the pursuit of happiness is made possible.

On the opposite side of the ledger we find education of the totalitarian type as represented by the present German regime.

The racial doctrine which declares that only "Aryans" are full human beings, and among the Aryans the Germans are the chosen master nation, limits first class birthright to a small section of humanity. It introduces a rigid class and caste system, in which the lower ranks are destined either to inferior and subsidiary types of work or else condemned to banishment in some form of ghetto or other, or into the outlying parts of the world. Education follows suit. In Germany there are schools for leaders and schools for ordinary Germans. These also grade into a somewhat complex hierarchy. The main doctrine which pervades this education is that of the individual's submission to the political machine of the state. The whole system is a denial of man's natural birthright; it curtails and cripples all critical tendencies and all personal initiatives. It replaces spontaneous loyalties to such institutions as family, church, workshop, or professional group, by a dictated and powerfully sanctioned loyalty to the central authority of the gangster state. The charter of citizenship is primarily determined by a man's real or pretended adherence to the party.

Comparing the educational system of totalitarianism with those of democracies we see that the fundamental distinction hinges on the question of whether the individual is made into a cog within a human machinery, or else whether he is fashioned into a responsible personality with his initiatives, powers of purpose, loyalties, and creative contributions untrammeled. Totalitarianism makes the individual into a means to an end. Concretely and specifically, the average member of the master nation is made into a really efficient piece of gun fodder. He may be also made a really efficient spy, policeman or secret service agent. His personal contribution, however, is made always subservient to a complex machinery constructed for purposes of war, conquest, and the permanent oppressive domination over other peoples. All the arguments advanced in this essay prove that such a type of humanity is well suited for short range, highly disciplined, and highly mechanized performances of the type indispensable in total war. The type of humanity, however, in which all individuals become a means to an end and an end of destruction, subjugation, and oppression of others, is not best suited for the carrying out of the highly differential constructive tasks of peace. Nazi and other totalitarian education, as well as Nazi systems of religion, law, and economics, are not based upon those laws of cultural determinism which have grown up gradually through the age-long development of each differential institution. The Nazi system is based on principles of short-run, rapid, and effective success in the wielding of the military machine and instrumentalities for pervasive policing and control. This end is fundamentally different from that under which humanity lived under primitive conditions. These gradually developed into the various aspects of organized cultural life, under which until recently humanity was still advancing in conditions of peace and by constructing scientific theories, refining religious attitudes, and producing works of art in literature, painting and music.

5

Freedom Through Organization

WE HAVE now to supplement the above considerations which so far were facing the individual, groups, and the community at large, with the analysis of human action as it actually occurs, that is, within institutions. There is one point on which an important addition to the problem of freedom has to be made. Freedom is primarily related neither to the isolated individual, nor even to society, nor yet perhaps to the potentialities of freedom and slavery given to man by machine. The real instrument both of freedom and oppression is always the organized partial constituent of a community: the institution. We have already foreshadowed the importance of these organized systems of activities. We must now discuss them fully.

An ethnographer taking a rapid survey of various types of human culture, from the most primitive to highly developed ones, would make an interesting discovery. He would find that the work of culture is not done by any community as a whole, nor yet by individuals, but by smaller organized groups, that is, institutions, which are organized and integrated to form the community. The significance of this discovery is due to two facts, first, that an institution always presents the same structure, and

153

second, that institutions are of universal occurrence; thus the institution is the real isolate of culture. It is possible to indicate the structure of such a system of organized activities: they are always carried on by a group in a definite manner, using a certain type of material outfit, and obeying norms which bind the members of that group and that group only. Thus equipped with a material outfit, with specific norms of conduct, and with a social organization, including central authority, the members of the institution carry out a type of behavior through which they achieve a definite purpose and contribute in a definite manner to the work of the culture as a whole. In the family and the state, in an occupational group, a factory, a trade union, a church, or a gang, we have to study exactly the same main factors and the relations thereof.

The study of any culture must therefore be carried out in terms of institutions.* This means in other words that an object or artifact, a custom, an idea or an artistic product, is significant only when placed within the institution to which it belongs. Certain institutions are to be found in all human societies; other types of institutions, though less universal, can be found in many cultures although some of them are more characteristic of primitive levels; still other institutions are characteristic of highly developed societies. As culture advances we find that various organized activities, which on the primitive level were carried out as a by-product of other institutions, become organized in their own right. First and foremost perhaps appear military groups, administrative organizations and the political state. Later on courts of law, professional pleaders and judges become detached and organized. Economic institutions multiply into the various guilds of artisans and craftsmen. Since the Industrial

---

* This is more fully treated in *A Scientific Theory of Culture* by Bronislaw Malinowski. (Chapel Hill, 1944.) [ED.]

Revolution, factories, banking systems and large mercantile enterprises have multiplied almost indefinitely. It may be well to list first the main types of institutions in the following table.

Main Types of Institutional Organization

1. Family and derived kinship organizations
   (Extended family; kindred groups; clan).
2. Municipality
   (Local group; horde; village; township; city).
3. Tribe as the political organization based on territorial principle
   (Primitive tribe; polis; tribe-state; state; nation-state; empire).
4. Tribe as the culturally integrated unit
   (Primitive homogeneous tribe; tribe-nation; nation).
5. Age-group
   (Age-grades; age hierarchies; professional age distinctions).
6. Voluntary associations
   (Primitive: secret societies and clubs; advanced: benevolent, political, and ideological societies).
7. Occupational groups
   (Primitive: magical organizations; economic teams; artisan guilds; professional associations; religious congregations).
8. Status groups based on the principle of rank, caste, and economic class.

Let us now inquire more closely into the nature of institutions in their relation to implemented human action. Our sequence: the formation of purpose, its implementation into activities, and the distribution of benefits resulting from the activity, is in a sense applicable to the individual. If we, however, consider how the individual, who never acts alone nor yet without some material instruments, can make his personal purpose real and valid, we find that in all cultures, primitive or developed, an individual forms his purpose by adopting some choice among many already existing collective systems of value. He chooses a career, that is, joins a workshop, a primitive hunting or agricultural team, a modern factory, a liberal profession, or a religious hierarchy. To satisfy his need of companionship and carry out his reproductive drive, he marries. For recreation he becomes associated with some organization for dancing or tribal games, for football or cricket, for listening to music, or looking at pictures. In every society, the business of satisfying the primary needs of hunger, sex, protection from wind and weather, or safety against human encroachments, is transacted by such institutions as marriage and family, police organization, households, hostels and hotels, restaurants and the whole system of catering. Education takes place in schools. Legal differences, whether civil or criminal, are settled in courts and through the activities of the police.

Were we to take the daily existence of any individual or follow up his career, we would always find that the satisfaction of all needs, all interests, all desires, that is, of purposes, occurs in homes, in offices, in schools, in hospitals, on recreation grounds, in churches, in universities and research organizations. The career of an individual starts in the home of his parents and leads him through school, church, and workshop or factory in which he receives his apprenticeship, the professional man's organization and his business place, to the founding of a new home, and his becoming a member of a whole series of institutions, or groups organized for hard work, for recreation, for the carrying out of a political ideal, a creed, a fad or an idea.

In the rare cases where an individual makes a new invention, conceives of a new idea, becomes an inspired founder of a new religion, the individual purpose has to be realized through the process of organizing a group of people, finding the wherewithal to carry out the new cultural increment of knowledge, belief or principle, and establishing a system of norms on which the group can co-operate. Whatever might be the task, human beings have to organize. Why? Because the simplest technical device, if it is to be permanently incorporated into any productive process, requires rebuilding of the machinery, reforming of the habits and skills, advising of all those who co-operate, and a permanent modification of the tradition which underlies this activity.

This concept of the institutionalized realization of everything which makes life worth living has a clear bearing on the concept of freedom. The institution as the organized means of realizing the values, the techniques, or the contributions to human welfare embodied in its charter, is the very cultural instrument of freedom, if freedom be the realization of purpose and reaping the benefits thereof. Because, as we have been insisting throughout, no man ever achieves anything, new or old, fundamental or peripheral, sound or fantastic, through his own unaided efforts. It is clear that the freedom of his personal purpose and its pragmatic success is always a by-product of the freedom of institutionalized activities.

This forces us to look more closely into the nature of these cultural units of actual behavior. The accompanying chart shows us the universal structure of an institution. In discussing our definition of freedom, we have already seen that institutions correspond structurally and functionally to the tripartite character of human action. In other words, each institution has its charter or collective purpose; its system of organized activity, which includes the personnel, the specific rules and norms and the material apparatus or special instruments defined by the charter; and its function or the enjoyment of the results of the activity, which is the fulfillment and achievement of the collective charter or purpose. Translating our concept of purpose into its cultural, that is, real equivalent, we find that every institution is based on a system of needs, biological or derived, which are rephrased in every culture into a specific doctrine. I propose to use the term "charter" as a label for such a doctrine on which an institution is based.

The charter therefore defines first and foremost the specific purpose and value, and the organization on which a group of

Diagram of an Institution

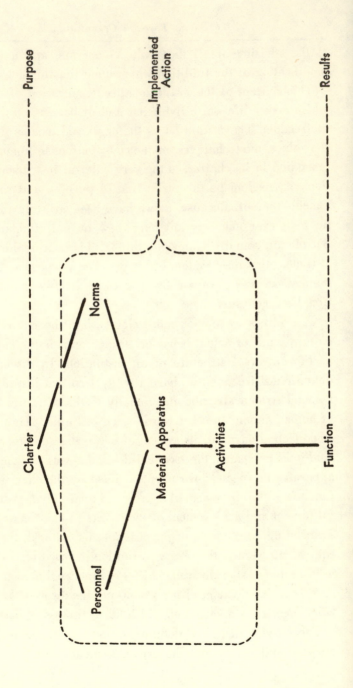

Purpose

Implemented
Action

Results

Charter

Norms

Personnel

Material Apparatus

Activities

Function

people agree to co-operate, that is, to carry out a system of purposeful activities subject to certain rules of conduct and implemented by a specific material apparatus. The charter of an institution therefore comprises its real and mythological history, and the statement of the ideals, aims and principles of organization and of conduct, which result from this past history or mythology. The charter of the family is to be found in the cultural reformulation of the biological drive of sex and all that it implies physiologically, emotionally, economically and legally. This definition holds good for all human societies. Everywhere we find that the fundamental need of sex and reproduction is reformulated into a doctrine which declares that reproductive activities, that is, the right to cohabit and to produce children, depend on a body of legal rules; that only permanent unions contracted under these rules and through a clearly defined contract which validates the union, are considered legitimate. The law of marriage and kinship defines first and foremost the eligibility of the partners, it determines the nature of courtship, and the act, customary, legal and ritual, which publicly validates the union. Such a contractual act involves a body of mutual obligations as between the partners and as parents of the offspring to come. Over and above the contract of marriage there occurs a body of physiological and spiritual interpretations of the act of reproduction. We have societies which are matrilineal and others based on father right. This legal ruling is generally related to a reinterpretation of the reproductive act in which the contribution of the mother or of the father are emphasized respectively. The charter of marriage and the family is the concern not only of the two partners, but it involves their respective families, kinship groups, and the community in which they live as a whole.

The charter of an institution is invariably related to the mythologies, religious doctrines, and moral principles of the tribe, or of the nation in which we find it. When it comes to the founding of a new religion, we always discover the drafting of a charter, based on the revelation experienced by the founder. A new movement of racialism like that in Germany becomes translated in its charter into a whole set of institutions and their organized by-products, such as the formation of a new ghetto for the Jews, family changes, new marriage laws, the abolition of religious sanctions. The gospel of racialism of the totalitarian states seeks not merely a revelation, but also scientific backgrounds.

In the same way we could analyze the charter of a modern state. There also we would find that, over and above the legal constitution and constitutional law, we have to include in the charter a mythological reinterpretation of history and geography for the whole body of sentiments, nationalistic and imperialistic, associated with the symbol of the state, the flag, the constitution or the crown. Taking a more prosaic institution like a factory or a workshop or a whole industry insofar as this is institutionalized, that is, socially organized, implemented, and normed; we would discover that law, applied science, professional honor, the folklore of capitalism or of Marxism enter into its make-up.*

It is clear that we can quite briefly indicate where the charter of each type of institution would be found and what it looks like. It must be remembered, however, that in each concrete case

---

*Cf. Thurman Arnold's book, *The Folklore of Capitalism,* which fits very well in its main argument into the present analysis. In my little book, *Myth in Primitive Psychology,* I have tried to point out that in some primitive cultures mythology can be defined as the body of specific charters buttressing, validating, and controlling the values, laws, and ethical principles on which institutions are founded in collective psychology. The whole system of Sumner and Keller is closely related to the present argument. Sumner and Keller speak of institutions being based on a "concept" and having a "structure." This corresponds in our terminology to the charter as a collectively formulated purpose, and its traditional reinterpretation in doctrine, mythology and law; while structure means to us the social organization, the material outfit, and the detailed rules which are followed more or less adequately in the activities of a group.

the definition of a charter would require a rather full scrutiny of documents and data. The importance of this concept lies in the fact that we include in charter a reference to the past, the emotional elements surrounding an institution, and that we definitely indicate that the charter must be studied in conjunction with other aspects of the institution. Thus as we have said, the charter invariably contains on the one hand the definition, the structure and the purpose of a group which composes an institution, and on the other hand the rules which this group has to obey. Charters must and do cover integral needs.

From our definition of charter as collective purpose it results that such a purpose has to be translated into activities. Structurally this means that at a primitive level, such activities as hunting, fishing and herding are carried out by a group, with the aid of its tools or implements and the rules necessary to the carrying out of the activity. In more advanced cultures, in order to manufacture certain goods or to carry out a religious revelation as in Christian Science or Mormonism or the Quaker faith, it is necessary to mobilize a group of followers, proselytes or converts. Such a group then becomes organized for the execution of its tasks. A factory implies commercial management, controlling engineers, foremen, and labor, skilled or unskilled. A new sect has to have its prophet and his apostolic successors. It has to have its churches, devise its liturgical instruments, define its ritual, and lay down its ethics. A new scientific discovery must be embodied into a laboratory where it is demonstrated by a staff of research workers who in their scientific technique follow the norms corresponding to the new discovery, which then becomes part of science when and insofar as it is embodied in the teaching and research activities of organized universities and laboratories. When the discovery leads to applications, it becomes an invention, and has once more to be embodied in engineering, industry, or systems of communication; in each case a personnel is necessary for the carrying out of the activity.

By personnel we understand not merely the numerical membership of a group, but also the way in which the various members are placed into a hierarchy, the manner in which authority, technical and specialized skills, and the division of tasks are apportioned. Obviously the technical aspects of personnel require a much fuller study of details than the general values and fundamental rules contained in the charter. Specifically, in a modern community the charter would be found in the codified or customary laws as well as in the religious and moral values. The full analysis of structure and personnel would require careful statistical field work, with the inclusion of such studies as the house in reference to its family members, and their occupations and economic activities.

This brings us directly to one or two other aspects of the institution. Thus the charter obviously contains the fundamental rules, but under norms we would have to enumerate a whole realm of regularized behavior which does not exist in the charter. In an occupational group such as a factory, the charter consists in the rules defining its ownership, its business organization, the various labor laws, and the legal rules concerning the relation between organization, labor and employer. The knowledge of the full rules would go far beyond this, and would force us to enter into the technicalities of the work done and into problems of industrial psychology, into customary divisions of labor and consideration of how the efficiency of work is induced by wage, recreation or other stimuli. These aspects of the rules of behavior which are not defined by the charter we call norms.

We know, however, that human beings not only organize into a definite co-operative structure, not only obey rules, but that in their cultural activities they have to manipulate some sort of material apparatus or other. Here again we see that in each case the material apparatus can be briefly defined and that it is different for each type of grouping. The family manipulates the house and homestead, the family lands, and the implements of domesticity insofar as it is a group of consumers and producers. The local group in its material aspect operates a conjoint territory, the public buildings, and means of transit, the places of communal worship, and municipal services. The state deals with its territory, with military force, and with public funds. Each voluntary association must have at least its seat, and each modern occupational group is required by law to have an address in order to become a legal personality. Status groups are also invariably distinguished by some material paraphernalia, and insofar as they are organized into orders of nobility, into guilds or crafts, they have the equipment of their calling, some of it joint, some of it owned and used by every member of the group. Thus we can see that in each case we have a specific type of material apparatus including a portion of environmental setting and a body of artifacts. It is only through and with this apparatus that the group can carry out their activities.

We are making in our diagram a distinction between activities and norms, because human life never completely adjusts to any prescription or ideal. Through action, the purpose of an institution is carried to a successful conclusion; and to achieve this, the personnel of the institution engages in the activities, obeying the norms of the institution and using its material apparatus. Thus we see that these four aspects of an institution—personnel, norms, material apparatus, activities—together form the "implemented action" of our tripartite sequence.

One more concept which has been implicit in all we have been saying is that of function. We have been constantly aware that every group is organized for the satisfaction of one main need, to which all the other activities are subsidiary. It is for the satisfaction of this need that its material equipment, technical or otherwise, is developed. It is around this need that the organization of the personnel centers, to this end the rules are always carried out; and the charter is connected with function, though it is never identical with it. The function of an institution therefore is the satisfaction of the need or needs for which that institution was organized. In other words, the function of an institution is equivalent to the enjoyment of the results of the activity by the group or personnel who performed it.

We see therefore how closely the institutional structure is related to the structure of implemented cultural action. In discussing freedom we referred it to three phases of individual action: the formation of purpose; its implementation into activities; and the distribution of benefits reaped through the activity. Passing to a collective, organized, and implemented system of activities, that is, to an institution, we find the same phases. We find a standardized purpose or a charter; the constitution of a group fitted out with a portion of material wealth, and submitted to rules of conduct; thus working, they produce results which we may define as the function of such an institution. We can demonstrate this more clearly by means of a diagram:

Purpose ⟶ Implemented ⟶ Results
Action
Charter ⟶ Activities   ⟶ Function

We could discuss every part of cultural production and achievement, and we would find everywhere that when a purpose, culturally relevant, is formed, it has then to become embodied into an institution; through this it is realized. If we apply the institutional analysis to any culture, to all primitive cultures, and, with certain reservations, to more advanced cultures, we find the widest common measure of the most relevant and most essential types of organized human activities. The institutions satisfy the basic needs of man and his fundamental drives and develop his independence with respect to nutrition, the need of defense, the further development of kinship, of blood-bond, and of sex. All these become gradually translated into permanent organized types of human activities with a definite system of law, a definite purpose, and a very clear intention of continuity.

We might say that culture is exercised not by any vast conglomeration of human beings, nor yet by individuals, but by the humble, unexciting, prosaic groups which we call institutions. They are differentiated to a large extent, autonomous and yet co-ordinated, working together and fitting into each other. Thus in order to achieve any determined end, human beings have to organize on some traditional principle or agreement, which is always tantamount to the development of the instruments necessary for the work to be performed, of rules, and of personnel.

Having analyzed the structure of an institution and seen its relation to our sequence of human action, we must now look more closely into the problem of freedom as existing within institutions. What interests us in this context is the element of authority; our institutional analysis is helpful here in revealing an important characteristic of the process of training. In studying any primitive tribe or directing our attention to any higher culture, we find that the processes of training are not carried out by one authority within one institutional setting, which would take over the control of the whole development of the personality.

The earliest stages in physiological development, in the learning of language and elementary skills, happen in the family. At primitive levels we often find specific initiation ceremonies at puberty in which frequently a specific effort is made to wean the young man or woman from the authority, the outlook and the restraints of the domestic institution. In any primitive society, the individual has to enter at various stages of his development more or less ritually and formally into the membership of the clan, the local community, a specific economic team and the religious congregation. In each case he undergoes an apprenticeship in which he has to learn the rules of behavior, of ethics, of technique, as well as the mythological, dogmatic, or historical traditions of the new institution of which he becomes a member. In each case also, he submits to a new authority which does not cover his whole life or control all his activities, but only that part through which he co-operates with the new organization. The home, the play group, the school, the church, the workshop, the factory, or the university represent to the individual each a new authority, a new type of training, a new orientation in which he lives a part of his existence.

What does it all mean for our particular problem of human nature, culture, and freedom? We have discovered here the principle of multiple authority, multiple training, and multiple cultural functions which control the existence of an individual, primitive or civilized. Discipline such as we find is directed towards the development of physical habits and skills, and towards the inculcation of certain strong social rules. This discipline, however, is stage by stage reformulated: the growing individual is submitted to new authorities and new rules; his outlook, his abilities, his modes of behavior are diversified. Although his range of choice at primitive levels is limited, he is not denied the possibility of making choices, deciding in this or that matter upon the course of his career, and identifying his interest with one institution or another.

Thus we find that the essential freedom of an individual depends on that multiple, diversified, and differentiated constitution of society which we find in many cultures. We have found that everywhere the business of life is carried on by a number of institutions. The greater the autonomy within each of them, the more opportunities there are for an individual to choose his adherence and his loyalties to this or that organized activity, occupation, or profession; that is, the more integral freedom he enjoys. Obviously, too, the greater the autonomy of each institution, the more freedom it has to carry out its activities independently of any centralized constraint.

We must first point out that some of the rules which a man or woman have to obey in entering an institution—whether through birth, when it is a family or local group; or by a deliberate act, when it is an industrial guild, a secret society or marriage—are determined by the impersonal authority of cultural determinism. Since human beings also never organize for the sake of organizing, but always in order to carry out concerted activities, and since these are directed towards a definite end and implemented by technical devices ranging from purely pragmatic tools to instruments of worship, the rules of conduct, especially the fundamental authority of purposive, related action, must never be lost sight of in discussing freedom at large. The partial surrender of freedom in the fragmentary phases of human behavior is an ineluctable quality of the cultural process.

All this had to be stated in order to bring into relief the other aspect of authority, the authority of power and organized physical coercion. This, once more, is an inherent necessity due to the character of human beings and to the nature of human action. Were we to take the rules of any technological behavior, in the production of primitive implements, in the skill of artisans and craftsmen, or at a higher stage of industrial workers, we would see that there is scope for control by authority over and above the determinism of material and the laws of material, and that this control is essential to the successful run of any activity. Integral freedom implies the submission to determinisms of mechanism, rule, co-operation, command and authority. There are however dangers in such submission. As we have seen, an artifact both as wealth and weapon leads to the exercise of force. Constraint occurs, for it must occur, both in the training for co-operation and in its exercise. In all these restraints we may see an abrogation of freedom. This however would be false; an artifact, rules, co-operation and the constraint of authority are indispensable to the effective action of a group.

We must therefore distinguish more precisely between the degree of authority necessary for the successful run of an activity, assuring freedom within the institution; and the abuse of authority, coercive in its action, which results in a denial of freedom. To find the criteria of due or undue restraint, we must remember two principles. First, all action consists in aiming at a desired result, and the enjoyment of results. It is based on purpose, that is, the acceptance of a task; on access to implements; and on consumption of the resulting commodities or the enjoyment of the spiritual values produced. The second point is to understand the inception and growth of the restrictions and denials of freedom. These denials lie in the institutionalized modes of oppression which change man into a mere means to an end, and deprive him of initiative, property and results by means of a legally sanctioned and fully implemented system of force. This grows out of an abuse of authority. The ultimate element of authority is always a personal, man-to-man act of coercion; coercion by force, by wealth or by the constraint of belief. The elementary form thereof again is physical force or skill in its use, hence authority in this form is instilled into each individual. If and when one individual or one group holds the concentration of power, whether this be political, legal, economic or technical, and uses this power to gain the advantages of an activity, we find an abuse of authority. In the individual sense, the freedom of one is achieved at the expense of others, and through discipline imposed on others.

The real battleground between freedom and its negations must be studied with reference to the constitution of cultures; to the scope of organized groups within the culture; and of individuals within the institution. In this however we shall have to inquire how far within a culture, primitive or developed, the individuals have a certain range of choice, and what opportunities they have for the formation of their personal purposes; we shall have to inquire into the distribution of the means, social and cultural, for the achievement of purposes; and finally, into the freedom as regards the distribution of benefits. Taking slavery in any of its manifold forms as an index, we can see that the slave enjoys the full freedom of working, and working hard, but that this benefit is a negation of freedom in that his work—that is, all his activities—is not related to his own purpose nor yet to his benefits. The disruption of a traditional primitive culture by the impact of any outside influence which prevents people from following their own tribal customs is an abrogation of freedom in the fullest sense, exactly in terms of our definition, since in this case the people or groups are no longer able to frame their purposes, carry them out through their own cultural instrumentalities, or enjoy the benefits of their effort.

Whenever there is a concentration and manipulation of power, freedom is threatened. Each institution and all institutions hold a certain amount of power: political, economic, or moral power through pressure on opinion. I submit therefore that on the nature of an institution depends freedom. When we consider the tripartite character of our definition of freedom—the conditions necessary and sufficient for the formation of a purpose, its translation into effective action through organized cultural instrumentalities, and the full enjoyment of the results of such activity —and relate this to an institution, we can formulate clearly the conditions which give freedom within the institution and those which result in a denial of freedom. When the purpose is chosen by the group as a whole; when the action is taken by autonomous responsibility; and when the results are shared among all the members of the group, we find freedom within that institution. When the purpose is accepted by command or instilled by indoctrination; when the action is controlled by coercive authority; and when the results of the activity are doled out for the advantage of those in authority, we find a denial of freedom. We can see this even more clearly in diagrammatic form:

	Freedom	*Denial of Freedom*
Purpose	chosen by individual or group	instilled by indoctrination; accepted by command
Implemented Action	taken by autonomous responsibility	controlled by coercive authority
Results	shared	doled out

The denial of freedom within an institution occurs therefore through an abuse of the authority held by those who organize and control the institution. For without an abuse of authority or coercive power, the other members of the institution could not be deprived of initiative, of autonomous action and of a fair share of the results. Thus a denial of freedom in each phase of our sequence is finally determined by the abuse of authority or power, for the enjoyment of all the advantages by the few in authority. This, as we have already seen, can occur as between individuals, within institutions and within cultures. In every case, the middle factor of our sequence, implemented action, is the one where freedom grows and where it receives its restrictions. Freedom is born there and freedom is killed there. For it is through implemented action, that gross quantum which means success, efficiency, mobility, wealth and moral control, that power is developed. There always exists the plus or minus of freedom as the abuse of force and constraint, as opposed to the use of persuasion and reward. The real abuse of authority, however, begins when discipline has to be made chronic, permanent, and pervasive.

We have analyzed here the structure of an institution and seen that freedom within the institution is dependent on the legitimate use of authority, while a denial of freedom occurs through an abuse of power for the benefit of the few in control. We shall now have to analyze authority, and trace its growth and development. We shall also have to examine the sources of power, the use of discipline and the abuses of power in a wider setting, that is, within a culture and between cultures. And we must distinguish clearly between the rules of cultural determinism which give freedom, and rules which result in the abrogation of freedom.

6

The Nature of Cultural Determinism

To GAIN a still fuller understanding of this argument, we now turn to the problem of cultural determinism, as this is embodied in the various rules which guarantee order and security, and which foster co-operation and concerted action under conditions of peace and progress. We were made already to realize that culture is based on the existence of rules, on their recognition, and their acceptance. Such rules by and large are the essential instruments of freedom. Certain of the rules, however, may be used for discrimination and oppression and thus become inimical to freedom, and at times annihilate it completely.

The rules of natural process must be obeyed by man and animal alike. If our concept of cultural determinism is valid, man has also to obey the rules of this determinism. We shall have now to establish with greater precision and clarity the distinction between the intrinsic rules of cultural determinism, and rules of tyranny which are an abuse of certain cultural mechanisms, in the interests of some at the expense of others.

To anticipate the essential principle in our distinction, rules which are accepted through education, in which reference is made to the learner's experience, and rules which grow up in

172

a long tradition, controlled primarily by experience of technique, co-operation, and ethical action and reaction between individuals, are rules of freedom. We shall see that such rules may produce at times the highest degree in discipline and performance, without becoming in any way rules of tyranny or oppression. Rules, on the other hand, which are based on doctrines outside the experience of the individuals who learn; doctrines which dictate considerable claims of superiority, power, and privilege to certain chosen individuals, are rules of oppression. We shall be able to see that false, mystical, or social doctrines of hierarchy and discrimination are invariably associated with organized mechanisms of physical violence. It is impossible for any group or any culture to pervert the rules of freedom without the instruments of violence to back up this perversion. There never is, and never can be, an abuse in the domain of ideas without the abuse in the domain of constraint. The opposite is also true in the sense that a community socially organized on principles of inequality, that is, of differential distribution of freedom, always develops mythologies, doctrines, and dogmas which serve spiritually to mold the oppressed groups and persons so that they might passively submit to oppression.

Turning now to our analysis it is well first to face two difficulties connected with the concept of rule, norm, and law. The first difficulty is semantic. We use the word law in the sense of a rule of intrinsic determinism of a process, Law (1). We use also the term law as a promulgated command of authority sanctioned by force, Law (2). The term law in the first sense is outside the perversion of whether might is right. No political power can change the laws of natural process, nor yet punish them for their misbehavior. Xerxes may order the sea to be flagellated and King Canute may try to stave off the waves; the savage magician curses the wind, and exorcises earthquakes, tidal waves, and volcanic eruptions—yet the power of majesty or of magic acts only on men and not on nature.

The word law in this sense means that through scientific research we construct an exact and empirical formula of a process which describes it, establishes its uniformity, and allows us to foresee and to predict the course of events within an isolated system. A law of nature means, therefore, that given certain conditions we can state with more or less precision what will happen provided no outside interference occurs. Nothing which is not given in a law of nature can occur, except through outside disturbances. Law in this sense means the prediction of events, the possibility of application, and the isolation of relevant variables. Such are the laws of mathematics, astronomy, physics and biology. Their essential character is the same although the degree of precision varies considerably. It is maintained here that laws of this type are to be found also in the processes of culture, though in this domain they are even less definite and precise than in biology. When we say that man must obey all the laws to which he is submitted by determinism, we mean therefore that he has to walk, swim, eat, and digest according to laws of mathematics, physics, and biology. We mean, also, that in all technical processes, from the making of a stick to a skyscraper, and from fire by friction to a power-plant, he has to obey rules of technique, of co-operation, of economics, and of certain inherent legal determinisms which cannot be evaded if the enterprise is to succeed. It is clear that into the make-up of such cultural determinism there enter certain laws of nature.

Over and above this, when two or more people are engaged in concerted action, when they pull together a heavy weight, or paddle a canoe, adjust the rigging of their sailing boat, or else man and manipulate a bombing plane, they obey the rules of concerted action which are based upon the habits and skills acquired by them; upon their knowledge and conscientiousness; upon their wisdom and honesty. Imagine a surgeon with his staff in an operating room, an experimental team in a laboratory, or the control of some complex technical device of modern industry or transport. All the people engaged in such activity are, as it were, in the grip of the material apparatus which they handle, and of the problem which they are solving. They must be fully cognizant of, and fully adapted in their bodily behavior to this mechanism. The quality of human behavior with regard to the mechanism, but also with regard to each other, determines the success or the failure of the performance quite as much as the quality of the material in the machine and its component parts. A defect in knowledge, in endurance, in the moral stamina of the actors, is as damaging or dangerous as a physical defect in some part of the machine. Freedom in the naive sense of a free floating quality obviously becomes meaningless when applied to such a process controlled by cultural determinism.

Let us turn to the other meaning of the homonym of law. By law in the sense of a socially established rule we mean a command or rule of conduct sanctioned by organized constraints. Here belongs obviously modern law in the lawyer's sense. All the rules of morals, manner, etiquette, ceremonial, and custom, as these are taught to children at all stages of civilization, also belong to this class. In the study of law socially established we have to consider always the manner in which it is inculcated; the manner in which it is made permanently known, that is, codified; the manner in which it is affirmed and contested respectively by the interested parties, that is, the problem of litigation; and the manner in which it made valid, that is, its sanctions.

The difficulties in the distinction between Law (1) and Law (2) are related to the second source of confusion which we must here clarify. Law (1) and Law (2) are not independent in the manner in which they appear as control in forces of human behavior. We have to submit to Law (1) whether we are aware of it or not. Primitive people have never formulated the law of gravitation yet they can neither levitate, nor fly through space, and when they fall or jump from a higher to a lower level they may be hurt or killed. Fire burns them as badly as it does a modern physicist or chemist, while water drowns them irrespective of whether they know the need of oxygen for their lungs. They explain disease by sorcery and not by microbes, yet smallpox and cholera attack them in the same way as they do a modern bacteriologist. In making their fire by friction they follow the first principle of thermo-dynamics, and they use temperature according to the second principle. In all their economic activities they have to obey the rules controlling the fertility of soil, its moisture, and the incidence of rain and sunshine, as well as to study the behavior of animals and the growth of plants.

The code of the law of nature is primarily written in the behavior of natural forces and entities. Yet this code becomes from the very beginning of culture at least partly embodied into the significant and symbolic responses of human behavior. In order to organize his own behavior and to transmit it to his children, primitive man is compelled to distinguish the beneficent from the dangerous in nature, the useful from that which is harming, the important from that which is irrelevant. His theories are piecemeal and sporadic. They are bound together by consistent behavior rather than by long verbal arguments. They appear as rules of conduct, and not as extensive verbal texts. The fact however remains that the translation of Law (1) into Law (2), that is, the formulation of certain natural determinisms into precepts, piecemeal explanations and technical rules, does exist and must exist from the very beginning of human culture.

Only through such knowledge, essentially scientific in that

it is based on experience and logical in its nature, can man succeed as far as his instrumentalities and his organization allow him to succeed. Where these fail, as they do in illness, in death, in natural catastrophes, man supplements empirical knowledge with revealed truth in his magical and religious doctrines. Yet here also the revealed truths of religion, primitive as well as civilized, are never completely outside experience, nor are they non-functional or anti-functional. They do not contain fundamental denials of freedom, in that they would be inimical to successful action, except when magic, sorcery, and religious bigotry lead to spiritual oppression, related as it always is to political power. On the contrary, we have demonstrated that both magic and religion exercise an integrative and organizing influence, and thus are indispensable to the formation of moral attitudes in the face of adversity, and of organized action in cases of real danger.

At this point it is well to realize that the derived need of rules of correct knowledge, empirical and consistent, arises from the fundamental need of survival, and that it begins to act even under the most primitive conditions. Scientific curiosity, at first used to manipulate knowledge and to build it up into more and more extensive and constructive systems, becomes later on one of the most powerful driving forces in forming more and more complicated devices of civilization. It has its roots in the simple biological necessity to utilize the earliest teachings of experience in order to foresee the useful as well as the dangerous, to select the important and harness it to one's own uses, and to reject the adventitious and irrelevant.

We see also throughout our arguments that all the messages from nature to man are embodied in human tradition. The realization of natural determinism is thus received by each generation from culture. We see here the foundations of the confusion from which even now as users of words we are suffering—the confusion between law as a phase of natural determinism and law as a human precept. This confusion comes from the fact that although Law (1) is embodied in the outer reality, it comes into the hands of man invariably as Law (2). The commands of nature or of the supernatural are, therefore, easily confused with commands of man.

In our analysis of education we have seen that the social fact of authority enters from infancy and appears even at the earliest stages of development. The parents use their authority of dictating precepts, rules of behavior, and rules of value in the child's own interest. Their authority is so much bound up with real devotion to the child's interest and with the mutual affection between parent and child that no suspicion attaches to what they say and teach, as well as to what they enforce. The child soon learns to realize that many of the at first sight oppressive prohibitions—not to play with fire, not to climb, not to handle sharp and pointed objects—are really promulgated in his own interests. He thus finds that the commands of parents are also commands of nature. Thus social learning acquires the initial force of objectively founded validity. The punishment by parents becomes synonymous with the punishment by experience—and so are the rewards. Their authority is chronically confirmed and becomes permanently accepted. Its foundations are a compound of reverence, of dependence, of experience and of knowledge. Their right to exercise force becomes gradually, perhaps grudgingly, recognized as something indispensable because it is vital.

The social rules of manner, etiquette, and behavior learned at home are also soon verified as being valid when the child finds that non-compliance brings about social punishment from other members of the community. In learning language the child realizes that the word and the sentence are instruments of power.

In the measure that he can handle language correctly he is able to influence others and to obtain what he wants. All religious and ethical teachings receive their confirmation through the impressive ritual to which everyone in the tribe submits, and which carries the confirmation of its truth in the occurrence of miracles, handed on by tradition, or even at times witnessed. In all this an immediate or delayed punishment teaches the developing organism that the tradition learned is true in the sense that conformity leads to success, and disobedience to punishment and to the thwarting of purposes.

The authority of playmates, usually much more rigid and directly expressed than that of the parents, brings in another installment of conviction that social law must be obeyed so that freedom in the social sense can be enjoyed. Later on the authority in economic enterprise or in the workshop receives once more the sanction of successful performance by adherence to the verbal rules and demonstrations which the growing man or woman receives from those already experienced.

The gradual building up of reliance on tradition in which the rules and commands of technique, of ethics, and manners are integrated, develops a respect for the social authority which teaches us tradition, wields the sanctions and the distribution of rewards and punishments. The established tribal authority which is distributed among the father, the elder sibling, clan elders, the village headman, the magician and tribal chief, becomes thus the integral source of wisdom, of experience, and of goodness. The main ethical principle of all primitive tribes is that conformity to tradition is good and deviation bad.

We can understand this in reflecting that the degree of knowledge, as well as the strength of social coercion, are the mainstay and basis in the chances of survival. A primitive culture is an integral and coherent instrumentality. It is limited in its material and instrumental outfit. It is thus fragile and it depends in its working on the generally established intellectual and ethical attitudes as well as social relations of its members. Disrupt any part of it and you may destroy the whole. The rapid and pernicious collapse of primitive cultures when they come in contact with Western civilization establishes this only too cogently.

In primitive cultures, as we know already and will perceive even more fully, oppression and exploitation do not occur except in minor matters and on rare occasions. Yet it is important to show, as we have done in our last argument, that from the very beginning authority is a principle with many potentialities and temptations of being abused and misused. Its abuse is technically not feasible under simple conditions of life. Supply it, however, with instruments of violence and possibilities for coercion, and it is liable to flare up into that whole range of forms of tyranny, of monopoly, and of exploitation which we can observe throughout the course of evolution and history and which we now see once again organized and made active by the worst tyranny ever known to the human species.

7

Rules of Freedom and Rules of Servitude

IN ORDER to establish clearly how authority as the wielder and guardian of tradition becomes tyranny, changing human beings into means to other people's ends, it will be well to make a brief survey of the various types of law and rule found in culture.

1. Rules of nature as they control the behavior of an organism as a whole, that is, insofar as man as a piece of matter has to submit to them. These rules are taught early in life. The infant has to learn how to walk, how to use his limbs, how to avoid the dangers of gravitation and impact, of fire and water, of hurting, poisonous, or noxious substances. In the teaching of language, primitive or civilized, this is implemented into prohibitions and discriminatve nouns and adjectives.

2. Rules of biology, that is, of the functioning of the human organism. Here enter all those interactions between the organism and the environment which we have described as the specific needs of man and which we find expressed in the primary drives of the individual. Here enters the need for air and oxygen, food, suitable temperature, rest and sleep, reproduction, and also for the elimination of organic waste matters. Culture standardizes

human responses to such needs into the system of regular meals, times for waking and sleeping, rules of cleanliness and hygiene, and arrangements for protection against cold, heat, wind and weather. Such rules and arrangements are taught to the young in the code of manners, in the principles of bodily behavior and in the various taboos of food and sex. Here also the positive activities and habits of daily life and the satisfaction of natural functions are inculcated. The close-range common existence of man obviously demands that both the routine and regulation of these functions should be implanted firmly and early in life, so that all members of the group can live together without giving offense to each other and co-operate in joint feeding and in the privacy of certain activities.

3. The laws of nature which man utilizes in his technique must be distinguished from those which affect the organism as a whole. Human knowledge is here embodied into various precepts and demonstrative rules which are partly taught in the family, partly in workshops and other productive organizations.

4. A number of rules of common life are necessary for the safety and order of all the members. They do not refer to the formation of habits and the regulation of bodily functions, but are protective rules as regards life and limb, property, and the prerogatives of such institutions as marriage and kinship. The rules or laws which aim at the prevention of crime are indispensable to ordered life. There exist always strong temptations as regards sex and property, while anger, greed, and ambition readily lead to the use of violence. It is well to realize that wherever there is a strong temptation or inducement to an act of violence, there must be a law which prevents this act. The opposite would mean that the act is positively sanctioned, in other words that it will be universally carried out since, being tempting, its execution has a premium put on it. Hence criminal law must be

universal in its occurrence. Such a law does not affect human freedom when its incidence is equal for all members of the community. We have here the freedom of order as opposed to the freedom of crime. Only under conditions where the temptations for crime are socially and culturally manufactured; when economic conditions impose hunger on some and plenty on others; when political oppression makes hate inevitable—only under such conditions is criminal law a denial of freedom, because it obviously must have an uneven incidence affecting some and leaving others outside the temptations of crime, that is, the penalty of law.

5. The rules of give and take in co-operation, in concerted action, and in the concatenated routine of long-range enterprise. Were we to consider any organized enterprise, we would find that each actor in the performance has to play a role. The rules which define this role must be learned by the actor, and they must also be known by all the others. Foreknowledge, reliance of one on all, and of all on each, and dependability are necessary factors in such performance. They are, indeed, essential parts of this cultural determinism which we are analyzing. The earliest forms of transport are often made possible through the handling of heavy objects by a number of people, each contributing according to his strength and training. The building of primitive canoes or houses, the conjoint hunting of large or dangerous animals; the carrying out of a tribal ceremony, or of joint deliberations imply a differential regulated contribution of every actor. One and each has to play his part in the game, and unless the rules are observed by everybody the game will be lost by one and all. Here we see the principle of cultural determinism acting clearly.

We can see it also when there occurs a chain of mutual contributions. The exchange of goods or services may be at times simultaneous. In primitive forms of trade or of ceremonial exchange on early market places, and in activities of communal labor, people exchange objects or services directly. They do it because of the differential utility of the object or of the service. In order to make this differential utility real, there must exist rules determining the common measure in exchange, there must be means of assessing the quality and quantity of material supplied, or of effort developed. Here again we see that all the rules defining measure, value and form, in service or artifact or raw material, are parts of cultural determinism. Beyond a certain measure, cheating, evasion, non-compliance are destructive to the activity as a whole. The rules are necessary on the principle of the mutual long-run benefit of any organizations in which people exchange services and goods.

The same refers to such partnerships as between husband and wife, between two or more hunters, fishermen, builders, or craftsmen. In all such activities we may trace the beginnings of a differential taking of advantage when through physical strength, superior rank, or the power of mystical or personal intimidation, one of the participants takes advantage of another. Here once more under primitive conditions there are powerful limiting factors as against the possibility of abuse. They consist once more in certain physiologically founded elements of consideration and affection as between husband and wife, parents and children, siblings and kinsmen. Most transactions at a primitive level are so simple, so directly concatenated, and so easily assessed that meanness and cheating are difficult to conceal. The general importance of equity, that is, freedom, is embodied in the fact that no virtue is rated higher in primitive communities than that of generosity. We have here in the organization of co-operative exchange of services and in the exchange of goods certain rules dictated by cultural determinism and leaving little room for abuse under primitive conditions of culture.

So far we have listed norms of conduct which lead to the freedom of safety from danger, of safety from crime, and to the freedom of efficient action. We pass now to certain types of rules where the problem of a denial of freedom presents itself in a definitely tangible form.

6. Rules and laws imposed by authority constitute the class to which we will have to devote most of our attention. In one way, as we have seen, all rules are thus promulgated in the process of teaching and learning. It is from this process that authority gains its psychological and social basis in human behavior. We have, however, to distinguish between authority inevitable and indispensable to all social organization, and political authority based on the use of brute force.

The distinction is not easy to make because the element of force, as well as that of dependence and of spontaneous submission, enters into the make-up of legitimate authority. In our analysis of the raw material of authority as it becomes established in education, we have seen that the parent, the elder sibling, the stronger member of a play group have to use force occasionally and that they invariably do it. We have also seen that a number of special methods, typified in initiation ceremonies, with a purpose, and by definite methods, implant respect and the authority of socially established power. It is thus the combined effect of physical force, dependence, and actual reliance upon the judgment, ability, and wisdom which enters into the attitude of those who follow the orders of the master or mistress in a household, of the chief, and of the leader of any enterprise. Their commands are obeyed, their approval cherished, and their judgment valued.

We are also aware that all the real business of human culture goes on in the organized systems of activities, that is, institutions carried on by groups formed for a definite purpose. In each such group there is a man or woman who, sometimes by birth, sometimes by personal merits and qualities, is the real wielder of authority. Even when we have councils or committees there is invariably one who assumes the lead. A close scrutiny would reveal first of all that certain personal qualities are expected from such a leader. Succession under primitive conditions of life is very frequently elastic, and if the legitimate heir is not up to his task he will be replaced by the next in line whose physical, intellectual and moral qualities are superior. We would also find that under primitive conditions authority is largely formal. The chief, the headman, the *entrepreneur* in an organized hunting, or fishing, or commercial expedition, act according to very well-defined traditionally established rules of procedure. The leader is often merely the master of ceremonies. He opens the proceedings, delivers the initial words, formally asks for the opinions of others, and then the activity as prescribed by old, established custom runs its habitual course.

Only when some difficulty arises, a hitch in a ceremony, or a dangerous episode in sailing or hunting, has the leader to assume his lead and the other members behave in a disciplined manner. On such occasions, discipline need not, indeed cannot, be sanctioned by force. Such configuration also sets in when a major disaster threatens the tribe, such as a drought, a famine, an epidemic, or an attack from neighbors. On such occasions we find, first, that the mystical order of reality comes to the fore. When a hurricane sweeps over some islands in the South West Pacific the magic of wind is performed and the magician assumes control. When excessive drought or else rain and floods threaten a region, magic again disciplines people psychologically and socially. The magic of rain and sunshine, incidentally, is often associated with tribal chieftainship or kingship. This will be realized by anyone who has read Frazer's *Golden Bough* and wades through the innumerable examples of early political power through the magic of basic natural fertility. Epidemics associated with sorcery recrystallize the tribe into a number of groups, vigilant, armed, and on the alert against the mystical enemies who have scattered illness throughout the tribe. Any serious quarrel between families, local groups, or clans may give rise to a killing and start a more or less drawn out vendetta. Under such conditions each group becomes disciplined, and the authority of the master comes into play.

Thus as soon as danger, or panic, or disorganization disturbs the normal course of life, we find that through fear of natural or supernatural forces mysticism is mobilized. It never occurs in any behavior of man which is perfectly under the control of primitive knowledge and technique. Yet with this, authority and submission to it, that is, discipline, come into play. Organization, close-knit and well-disciplined, is always indispensable for the protection and defense of any threatened community. All human action in a crisis implies a temporary abrogation of freedom in the real sense of the word. When a group of primitives— or for that matter, a community, or an organized body of men engaged in an enterprise at any level of culture—is going through a crisis, facing serious danger and mobilizing for effective action in the face of a natural or human enemy, there is no room for deliberation, for independent action, or for the discussion of what ought to be done, and for what reasons. If the group is disorganized, or badly organized, it will be overwhelmed by panic, by chaos, and will so far fail in its active response to the situation. If the group is organized and under competent leadership, its only chances of success is to submit to leadership, hierarchy, and all the differential orders of when and how to act.

This brings us to the fundamental point bearing on freedom in human life. Our argument leads us to the conclusion that authority or the raw material thereof is a natural and indispensable by-product of education, of organized life, and of the normal, ordinary carrying out of all concerted and purposeful activities. We see also that at certain stages of human endeavor there arise conditions of crisis where authority, and its counterpart of discipline, enter to an extent which, for the time being, abrogates freedom. This is in essence the political factor in culture. We define here the concept of politics as the use of force and the organization of force for the enforcement of discipline in the carrying out of a task. From our previous analyses we see that such a disciplined action occurs often under conditions where we usually do not employ the word politics. The operating room, a scientific laboratory, a factory of precision tools, are one and all examples of highly disciplined activities. The circumstantial process of freedom has to be eliminated from such activities. They are free in the sense that human beings accept the discipline of the moment since this is an essential part of their purpose. The process of choice as regards the end, the instrumentalities, and the equitable distribution of the result must occur before the critical phase of action. Free decisions, free and spontaneous acceptances, not only of the rules, but also of the necessary process in training, in the establishment of necessary knowledge, skills, and responses, fall within the fundamental categories of free action. But these categories have to be completely eliminated from the actual execution of the critical activity.

Now the thesis which is being here presented is that no human culture, however democratic, constructive, peaceful, and liberal, as well as libertarian, can exist without the political factor, that is, the factor of discipline established by drill and ultimately sanctioned by force. Let us remember that criminal neglect in an operating room is an act of manslaughter, hence subject to all the stringencies of criminal law.

The real difference between free cultures and cultures pervaded by serfdom and bondage, lies in whether they are constituted for the avoidance of crises and their reduction to a minimum; or else whether they are constituted on preparing crises, thriving through crises, and using the creation of crises as the main means to the end of establishing more slavery. There is only one type of crisis which has beset humanity, which, starting at a late stage of evolution, has lasted throughout recorded historical times, and which has survived as the fountainhead of all present evils. This is the crisis of war. As regards other disasters to mankind such as earthquakes and droughts, volcanic eruptions, and floods, man cannot produce them. Indeed, civilization has been aimed gradually and consistently at preventing any such natural cataclysm. Civilization also has worked continually so as to prevent epidemics, reduce infection, and build up the resistance of the human organism against its main enemies, disease, disability, and accident.

War, and war alone, is that principle of collective abrogation of law and of substitution of crime for constructive behavior with which we have not been able yet to come to grips. War and all that it means in preparedness and aftermath creates conditions under which political force, that is, the use of violence in regulating all human motives, resources, and endeavors, becomes the dominant regulating force of humanity.

Let us once more sum up some of the results so far obtained so as to define the distinction between political authority which is legitimate, and that which consists in, and must constantly generate, abuse and oppression. To change this wording which may smack of "value judgment" into a more objective one, we define as legitimate those uses of authority which are founded in the intrinsic determinism of a critical performance. Authority abusive and oppressive we find wherever it is carried out in the partial interest of the vested monopolies of power, wealth, and prestige. We can sum up the distinctive marks of the indispensable use of political influence as opposed to the abuse of violence under three headings.

1. *The Teaching of Tradition v. Spiritual Indoctrination*

All the rules of conduct, including those which imply submission to authority, are acquired by teaching. Teaching at the earliest levels of development implies constant reference to experience, scientific, that is, technical, or else mystic. Mystic experience at primitive levels is not mobilized and all tribesmen form a congregation or a number of congregations in which there is no legitimate hierarchy and no exclusive access to revelation. Authority is based primarily on age and status, and one of its strongest supports comes from greater wisdom, wider experience, and fuller pragmatic skills. Primitive education is essentially scientific, in that all knowledge gained is immediately tested in technical applications. It is obviously scientific in the sense of being logical, since effective action is fully subject to the principles of identity and contradiction. Primitive knowledge is not scientific in the sense that the learners are not encouraged to criticize, to strike out along new lines, or to indulge in independent inventions. The gradual, infinitesimal improvement in technique and knowledge develops *pari passu* by accidental increments in skill, device, and empirical principle, probably due to the wielding of tradition by outstanding individuals.

This general attitude to the scientific and mystical doctrine gives full access for one and all to the range of general knowledge and skills. It also, at a certain age, provides opportunities for most to become acquainted with the mysteries and esoteric doctrines of early mysticism.

As opposed to that, we find at higher levels of development and in historic times monopoly and centralization of spiritual truth.

When the divine king or chieftain has an exclusive mystical control of natural fertility, and at times also of the health and prosperity of his subjects, we say that spiritual truth is made to support political authority. When astronomy, mathematics, and physics, rudimentary yet powerful instruments of spiritual influence, become a monopoly of a priestly caste and a monopoly of its highest ranks, we see again that knowledge, scientific and mystical, becomes an exclusive and centralized power which can be used for oppression. We could quote the Spanish Inquisition, certain sects or phases of Islam, as well as of Christianity, Protestant and Catholic, as examples of monopoly in spiritual truth. Today this is represented in the religions of totalitarian systems which make the leader practically omnipotent, omniscient, and ubiquitous.

Education in such cultures inculcates above all the attitude of submission, intellectual and spiritual. From ethnographic evidence we know that the regimented drill of such African tribes and races as the Ngumi, Masai, and Chagga, as well as the submission to West African monarchs, and to the secret societies of that region, are implanted in the mind and character of a growing man or woman. In historic times we find the worship of authority and of the book in Scholasticism, in the schools where the spiritual authority of the Koran, the Talmud or the Bible were taught, as the main sources of spiritual authority, very often combined with established political authority. The modern schooling and indoctrination of all totalitarian regimes is the last word in an education which kills initiative and criticism, induces complete submission to dictated truth, and thus establishes the psychological background for a complete integration of the individual into an obedient human machinery, ready to accept any order or command from those above.

In such cultures the main point with reference to freedom is that the individual is made to accept all his differential purposes as well as the purpose of his life and his career as dependent upon the centralized authority. How much mysticism and the belief in value is essential to freedom we see in the mushroom growth of the various mythologies, pseudo-religious ritual, and prayer which have been produced to order by the totalitarians.

2. *The Full Access to Organized and Implemented Activities v. Artificial Hierarchy and Rank*

Under primitive conditions as well as in the very constitution of a democracy, the principle of free access to any institution and opportunities for advancement are an essential element of freedom. This certainly is the case in primitive communities where hierarchy, except that of age, experience, and personal quality, is almost completely absent. The limited amount of wealth and its rudimentary character allows practically everybody to produce his own instruments of action. Provided that he is personally equipped to act as a magician or as the leader of an enterprise, he has considerable chances of making headway in any organized type of work. That no modern democracy is completely equal to the ideal here stipulated needs only to be mentioned. The American will undoubtedly think of the British stratification into classes. He might forget that it was in England that the freedom to rise from the ranks and through the ranks supplied some of the best leaders England has had. The stratification into the various classes has worked in Great Britain so well because adequate opportunities were given for rising from a lower to a higher social status. The medieval forms remain, but the personnel has changed profoundly. The Britisher would think of the American negro problem, the influence of wealth, pressure groups and city bosses, and similar obstacles to democracy in the United States. Admitting all this as regards both countries, and any other deficiencies, the charter of democracy still declares that opportunity for intrinsic merit is one of its fundamental principles. This principle and the whole charter of democracies leaves ample scope for improvement. Any improvement, however, is impossible if the essential principle of a charter is based on the theory that race, nationality, and the place in a more or less arbitrary hierarchy determine the value, the position, and the essential purpose of an individual.

This is the principle which we find today as the fundamental doctrine of all totalitarian countries. The hierarchy of totalitarianism is even more destructive in that it is not established by tradition or by birth, still less by personal merit, but rather by a purely arbitrary principle, that of party loyalties, of a parrot-like adherence to its doctrine, a personal allegiance to the man immediately above. This dissociation from really intrinsic value as regards a piece of work to be done, and the power of control and decision, is probably one of the main danger spots of totalitarianism for its own nation and its own culture. If carried out consistently it would lower the standard of every activity whether this be inspired by artistic genius, scientific ability, or mere technical efficiency. If the principle of placing party allegiance above personal merit be abandoned, then totalitarianism would die a natural death. Totalitarianism as a constitution of culture on party principles is not compatible with the exercise of culture. Yet it is the very essence and the very life blood of the system, that it has to place party advantages over and above the values of cultural performance.

We could give a whole set of antecedents to this present day example. As soon as military power becomes the main concern of a tribal culture—and this occurs only at fairly high levels of development—and the tribe becomes transformed into a striking force, full submission to leadership, hierarchy, and discipline must become the highest virtues. Once more we see that there is a profound clash between a culture based on the principle of military efficiency, and one which is constituted for the invention, maintenance, and advancement of the peaceful arts and crafts of moral human existence.

3. *The Pursuit of Happiness.*

In primitive cultures and, to a large extent, in democracies the standard of living tends to be equal for most persons. This is fully so in what we called a proto-democracy. Luxuries do not yet exist. A plentiful crop, catch, or haul have to be distributed equally since they cannot be preserved. There are only a few objects of value and they can, as a rule, be made by each individual for himself, or else acquired from the specialist. In the modern democracy we are faced by a problem rather than a perfect solution. Yet once more we can say here that no democratic spokesman or supporter of this type of cultural constitution would disagree that a certain level of prosperity is indispensable to the full exercise of a democratic constitution.

Inequality in wealth, in the distribution of valuables, of privileges and enjoyments, starts in human evolution with the first advent of war. For a planned and instituted inequality in wealth and privileges can only be achieved through the use of force, and force within a tribe cannot exist unless there is a group of people organized and disciplined. Such an institution again arises only in the face of external enemies. Thus here once more, powerful, discriminative principles in the standard of living and level of enjoyment are brought about by the factor of politically founded authority in communities who practice war.

In this comparative analysis we have pointed out the three main, distinctive differences in the establishment of purpose, in the access to instrumentalities and in the enjoyment of results.

In this there are two points which still require a fuller discussion. One of them refers to that aspect of culture which we have labelled as knowledge and mysticism. It will be necessary to show their place in the integration of primitive and advanced cultures. It will be well however first to show even more fully the place of discipline under conditions of crisis.

8

Freedom and Discipline

WE MUST now scrutinize more closely the use of discipline and drill, since we have come to the conclusion that no human culture can exist without the factor of discipline, with force as its ultimate sanction. And we must give special attention to the use of discipline in a crisis, in view of the fact that this plays an important role in the processes of freedom and in its abrogation. We shall try first to show that it is not the quantity of constraint or discipline which matters; human behavior within the freest of free communities demands under circumstances the extremes of discipline. In the second place we shall discuss more fully the perfectly simple, clear, and empirical criteria which allow us to determine which discipline is compatible with freedom and which is destructive.

The rigid discipline of primitive tradition is due to the danger of trial and error experimenting by small groups living on a narrow margin of survival and achievement. Within primitive communities people have also to obey the rules of distributing the benefits of what has been achieved. The whole organization of family and kinship is based on a number of rules, restrictions, privileges and duties. The wisdom of the ages is achieved through the fact that rules of long-run give and take are developed through trial and error. The best cultural arrangements survive, and whether they are appreciated or not, they work. Deviation from these rules brings direct penalties. Thus the existence of norms, rules and laws, and their effective sanctions are embodied in the very fact that organization means a long range of concatenated services, or reciprocal privileges and duties; and that all such rules, laws and discipline are clearly recognized as essential to the system of activities. Once more we come to recognize that freedom is a quality of more or less simple or complex systems of organized activity, in which a degree of discipline is necessary for effective action.

Under primitive conditions, however, in all dangerous and chance-ridden activity, we find a good deal of preparatory drill. It is characteristic that the strongest development of special processes and institutions for the instilling of discipline occurs among tribes who are notoriously good fighters, such as the Zulu, and their neighboring Hamitic and Nilotic neighbors; the North American Indians; and some of the head-hunting tribes of New Guinea and Indonesia. Thus, indoctrination and drill are associated with the preparation of man for a crisis. The drill is also inevitably backed by the use of physical force as well as by other coercive measures, related often to food taboos and other dependencies on wealth. Elements of a rude and rough discipline are often inculcated at initiation ceremonies, which determine the entry of an individual into an age grade or a secret society. As humanity advances, discipline enters with the growth of military institutions.

Leaping across the ages, let us see what part discipline plays in the ordered activities of contemporary mankind. Here once more we find that obedience to rule in its various aspects is indispensable. Think of a ship's company, the organization of a modern factory, or the carrying out of a large scale engineering enterprise. You will see that discipline and submission to the rules of technique, of organization, and of certain ethical principles, above all, honesty and faithfulness in the execution of each man's task, are indispensable. Without such a submission to rules no enterprise can succeed.

Discipline is indispensable under all critical conditions, and whenever a very delicate, important and highly skilled task has to be accomplished in concerted action. Discipline however under such conditions is not an abrogation of freedom. During that phase of activity, the circumstantial processes of freedom— deliberation, the gradual framing of purpose, the choice of adequate instrumentalities—obviously cannot occur. These prerequisites of freedom take place in the choice of a profession, in the training for it, and in the acceptance of the professional codes of honor, responsibility and ethics. When, in a scientific laboratory, an important experiment is conducted, the self-imposed discipline of the workers must be at the maximum. Unless they obey the rules of the performance, the results will be worthless. The surgeon in the operating room is one of the most complete autocrats during his performance.

In all cultures, our own included, all these difficult, dangerous, highly skilled activities, momentous in their consequences, involve specific drill which is associated with indoctrination, coercion and reward. The physician, the surgeon, the lawyer, the colonel, the ship's master, and all their associates and dependents, accept the codes of honor and professional ethics. They submit to stringent rules of discipline, partly dictated by their work but also by the laws of the land. They are drilled into this acceptance as well as into the skills which go into it. They can be prosecuted for criminal negligence if they fail in any essential matter. They have to be well equipped with the material apparatus of their trade and be rewarded economically according to the quality of the work done.

Discipline reaches its highest level when any such complicated, highpowered, and fully organized type of activity is faced by a crisis. A ship's company when storm breaks out, when shipwreck threatens, or when a U-boat is sighted, cannot enjoy any freedom of thought, deliberation, or discussion. One and all have to obey the orders of the ship's master. Each has to carry out his differential task with supreme submission to the rules of skill, of division of functions, as well as of conscience and morale. They have to fall back on discipline, unquestioning and mechanical. The same is true when a factory or a house is on fire and this has to be extinguished or localized by a fire brigade, volunteer or professional. Once more, strict discipline is the condition indispensable for any successful effort. When a large engineering project is threatened by a flood or a landslide, a rigid and hierarchical discipline sets in. In all such crises an almost dictatorial constitution of the group in action must be mobilized for the time being. Dictatorship here, of course, is temporary. The more effectively it sets in, that is, the more clear-sighted and authoritative the leader, and the more fully his orders are observed, the greater are the chances of success.

We are dwelling on this point in some detail because it implies a very important lesson for the crises through which we are now passing. A democracy threatened with annihilation by totalitarian aggression is the supreme case of an organized group passing through a crisis on which life and death depend. Here also we must submit to a temporary dictatorship-of-the-occasion. This undoubtedly implies certain dangers. It must however be recognized, not as an equivalent of a permanent and culturally destructive totalitarian organization of culture, but as a phenomenon inevitable in all crises of human existence, whether these crises come from natural catastrophes or from man-made upheaval.

Let us once more envisage the temporary dictatorship of a ship's master, or the captain of a fire brigade. Such a type of dictatorship of the moment does not imply any profound and permanent changes in the minds of those who submit to it. They have to recognize the existence of the crisis and the fact that unless they co-operate to the fullest extent of their ability and moral submission, the crisis may overpower and destroy all that they are working for, and in the case of shipwreck, one and all of the participants. Such a potential and proleptic discipline is a state of affairs for which definite preparations are made in every well-planned and well-ordered undertaking. A seaman, a soldier, a fireman are taught what they have to do under conditions of danger. They are drilled into it. They have to be prepared for such an occasion. Their preparedness to accept such a temporary dictatorship of circumstance is thus imposed by the real conditions of the moment. It is pre-ordained by external events and not by some process of mystical indoctrination. When the ship is sinking, the realization of danger is clearly present to all those who have to act in lowering the boats and organizing all that can be done to save their lives. For this the crew as well as the passengers are made to submit to occasional drills. To speak here about any freedom of choice, of deliberation, or of action for any individual is obviously beside the point. From ship's master to cabin boy the behavior of everyone is determined. Any deviation from the straight path of duty can result only in the freedom to be drowned—one and all.

Compare this with the dictatorship which results from a systematic establishment of the totalitarian principle as a permanent regime.

Looking at any totalitarian system of today, we find first and foremost that the mind of each member of the nation has to be indoctrinated. This includes all education, all distribution of news through newspapers, radio, and public harangue. Such indoctrination centers round the dogma of the omniscience, omnipotence, and ubiquity of the leaders, the state, and its agents. Right through Germany, the child, the boy and the adolescent are impressed with the wisdom, the power, and the supreme authority of Hitler. This is embodied in the formula of greeting, in the oath administered by every teacher and every official, in the daily hymns and prayers, and in the public ceremonial of procession, demonstration, and collective national worship.

This whole mystical and metaphysical doctrine of leadership is associated with the affirmations of racial superiority, of a world mission, and of the blood and soil theory of Nazism. The dogmas are connected with the ethical code of unlimited and universal submission in all matters of faith, conscience, and behavior. Belief and ethics alike pervade the totality of an individual's life, of all human actions and of all human groupings. Doctrine and ethics preach the value of violence as a supreme realization of the German nation and of each individual German.

There is no doubt that all systems, religious or political, which instill in the individual a firm belief that death on the battlefield leads to Valhalla or to Mohammed's paradise, are a great asset in military discipline. Here therefore we find a type of "freedom" which refers directly to cultural training and cultural results. This problem is important, since it plays a considerable part in the ability of present militaristic powers to develop a suicidal type of bravery, especially in the armies of the Mikado. It is a great tribute to the intellectual qualities of the Italian nation that Fascism was not able to make the Italian armies invincible. The German people are now born and bred to die heroically on the battlefields, but above all to enslave other people, or to kill those who refuse to be enslaved. Any promptings of humanity, kindliness, or decency are considered as weaknesses unworthy of a true German. The value of agreements, the binding force of a word given, the very foundations of law, national and international, have been destroyed.

Here we have not the discipline in a crisis due to misfortune or catastrophe. We have instead a gang of people preparing carefully and scientifically a crisis to be imposed upon humanity, by the creation of an arrogant, self-centered mysticism and by the fullest scientific implementation of this arrogance. In the willful and open preparation of such a crisis, the toll taken of human freedom is complete. Here we have the systematic and scientifically thought out preparation of artificial disaster for humanity as a whole, so that a small section shall retain a permanent control over mankind through scientifically organized violence. In this lies the real, the gigantic crime of totalitarianism. It means the denial of freedom even to the average member of the master nation. It is the negation of all economic freedom so as to create national autarchy. It is the negation of political freedom for the creation of full national discipline. It is the denial of spiritual independence so as to produce a community with a single purpose. The system thus aims at enslaving the world and also its "master-nation", so as to establish the exclusive privilege of a party, its centralized executive and finally one leader. Let us remember always that the destruction of real and integral liberty is not conceived here as a temporary measure during the crisis, but as a permanent establishment of human civilization.

We find here the criterion which allows us to distinguish between discipline as an inevitable quality of human action in crises, and that pervasive discipline which prevents the formation of purpose, the carrying out of independent activities, and the enjoyment of chosen results. The coefficient of freedom as against bondage depends upon the aims for which power is being mobilized. It also depends upon the circumstances under which discipline occurs. When discipline is brought into being by a temporary inevitable crisis it must be accepted or else the group may perish. When discipline is imposed upon a community and the culture as a whole, transforming thus the whole group into a passive instrument of power politics, it destroys the very core of civilization.

The concept of freedom here as elsewhere has thus to be discussed with reference to the context of such a large scale enterprise as war. The democracies are now fighting a war of self-preservation. Each democratic nation has to submit to discipline, to leadership, and to the temporary renunciation of certain aspects of freedom. When there is one single purpose imposed by circumstances, the deliberation as to this purpose cannot remain open. When the guidance of military affairs has to be entrusted to a general staff which cannot be replaced in a hurry, their decisions have to be submitted to. Full democratic criticism, deliberation, and doubting may result in an irreparable chaos of public opinion. The situation is closely analogous to that of a ship's company overwhelmed by shipwreck.

The fundamental difference between discipline in a democracy at war on the one hand, and totalitarian discipline on the other, is to be found in the fact that for us discipline is a means to an end, while to the Nazis it is an end in itself. Returning now to' the theoretical aspect of our problem, we see that freedom under such circumstances has to be considered with reference to the end of a disciplined activity. The context of the cases we have previously discussed is that of a crisis resulting from circumstances. The end is to put environmental disasters as much under control as is humanly possible. To mobilize discipline which must lead to disasters instead of preventing them is the capital crime against freedom. Once more we see that freedom can be defined only with reference to cultural processes taken integrally. To cut up human action into fragments, especially choosing irrelevant and insignificant forms of action, must lead to futility. It is only when activities based on discipline result in a planned destruction, mass murder, violence, and the destruction of moral values that we can register a total and integral, as well as a partial and differential, loss of freedom.

9

The Role of Religion and Magic

THE main reservoir of all values, that is, of all motivations and formative forces in culture, is tradition. By tradition we mean the body of symbolic texts mostly incorporated in language, in which the collective values of a community, economic, legal, and spiritual, are incorporated. This is not the moment to enter into the nature and origins of symbolism. Suffice it to say that the roots of symbolism are probably to be found in human gesture, demonstrative act, and pre-articulate sound such as a grunt of approbation or disapproval associated with a non-symbolic act of bodily reward or punishment. Were we to think over the earliest incorporation of an artifact, or of such a device as fire, into the permanent possession of a human group, we would have to posit some means by which this invention became transmissible as well as defined. This probably was made possible by a combined demonstration, manual and bodily, and certain signs corresponding to the yes and no, to approval and disapproval, by which the inventor or inventors instructed others and made such instructions standardized.

However language might have originated, we find it fully developed among the earliest surviving primitives. It is a system of articulate sounds, symbolic, that is, directive and pragmatically instructive. Language developed step by step with the invention of artifacts and with the formation of habits, skills, and values. Each new object was named, techniques required the formation of verbs, possession and social rule were described. It is an integral part of the conditioning of the human organism to responses which are determined not by nature but by culture. Language and value are thus intrinsically related.

The primary function of language was to embody the rudiments of primitive knowledge, as one of the vehicles of freedom. From the very beginnings man must have acquired real, that is, truly scientific, knowledge in order to transmit his earliest technological inventions. Submission to knowledge is a diagrammatic case which demonstrates where submission is not bondage but freedom. Such knowledge became embodied into symbols referring to useful raw materials, to technical procedures, and to description of uses and fundamental legal principles of ownership. We have to assume elementary theories concerning the nature, the technology, and the uses of fire, of stone implements, of shaped wood, and the construction of primitive shelters. There must have existed theories of the useful as well as the dangerous aspects of the environment, and theories how to approach it for exploitation, and how to avoid its hostile aspects.

In this it is important not to lose sight of the fact that all primitive knowledge was fundamentally pragmatic, and that all pragmatic concerns combine physiological drive and emotional response with intellectual interest. Knowledge, primitive and developed, refers to matters vital to man. These are as definitely pervaded by hope and fear, by desire and despondency, as by elements of calculation, prevision, and intellectual insight. Man thus could not have developed in primitive times any systems of thinking, of foresight, of retrospective reflection, which were completely detached from his personal concerns about his safety and well-being, about his health and the prospects of his desires, sentiments and emotional anticipations. Through knowledge man acquires freedom—the freedom to do what he desires by planning, production of tools, and organization for work according to that tradition in which his practical experience and knowledge are embodied. But knowledge alone is not enough; not everything is known, and there remains the unforeseeable.

Thus we have to assume that the emotional contents of primitive thought brought man immediately into that rude impact with realities which every individual at every stage of development must experience. This essential conflict of human destiny has dogged human feeling and thought from the very beginning, even as it nowadays imposes on us with an unprecedented tragic magnitude the problems of the very survival of culture and humanity.

Human beings always and everywhere are threatened by ill health, by ill luck, by natural catastrophes, and by the interference of human conflicts. The occurrence of such hostile acts of ill luck, destiny, and mismanagement affect not merely man's reflection and his theories, but also his emotional responses. They force the human group and the individual to take action. The occurrence of disease or epidemic, or a natural catastrophe such as drought, earthquake, or hurricane, disorganize the ordinary, commonplace, and normal texture of human theories of knowledge. They demand a new type of explanation, a new system of reference, and a new guidance practiced. Here we come to the very source and origin of the supernatural, as we find it in the beliefs of magic and of religion. Acting within a world of uncertain calculations, living as he does in a universe where from beyond the rim of the ordinary and well-controlled, there emerge forces of evil as well as acts of supererogatory assistance and benefaction, man is led to assume the existence of another world. His needs of controlling luck and destiny lead him to the assumption of entities benign or malignant, helpful or dangerous. Freedom in this world therefore is not enough. The wall of the unknowable exists which is not experienced in physical tasks and is not to be harnessed and managed with eyes, hands and implements.

Another type of human experience suggests the concrete nature of these entities. They emerge out of the human world of dreams and visions. They crystallize from the contacts of man with the environment, where he co-operates or fights with vegetable and animal fertility. All this allows us to understand why man comes to affirm that vegetable and animal species have a supernatural relation to his existence. Ghosts of the dead which visit man in dreams and which haunt him in his longings, become helpful or hostile as ancestor spirits or as inmates of the second world. Finally the integral beneficence and hostility of the environment lead to certain monistic beliefs either in a pervasive force of magic, or in a tribal All-father, or else in a cultural-hero.

In all this the beliefs of man do not remain idle. Indeed, his beliefs arise out of the need to act beyond what simple, manageable experience dictates. They become expressed in ritual which is an attempt at reaching the supernatural and communing with it. The supernatural also imposes its demands upon man in the form of ritual observances, taboos, and ethical rules. Both religion and magic again produce systems of organized activities, that is, institutions. Where is the contribution of magic and religion to human freedom? The answer can be briefly given. Every dogma, every religious or magical affirmation give to man the freedom that springs from confidence in his own value and of reliance on the powers beyond but not alien to him. This is an addition to the strength of man in facing illness, misfortune, and even death.

Any system of mystical belief arises as a cultural response to the disorganizing fear of adversity and disaster. Every such system consists first and foremost in a dogmatic affirmation, mythologically founded. The affirmation declares: "There is a God, who is a source of strength to those who obey his words. There is a Providence which can be induced to co-operate with man and make his efforts effective and successful. There are ancestor spirits, who demand sacrifice and prayer, but who free man from the hindrances of ill-luck and the schemings of his enemies. There is another world, where those who have been oppressed, ill-treated and persecuted here will exist in the glory of strength and pleasure, hence of freedom. There is a force which man can capture and use to master and harness luck and chance through magical rite and spell".

Such affirmations are invariably based on a long pedigree of previous events which prove the truth of each dogma. We have Holy Scriptures and holy traditions in which we learn how God created the world, how the laws of nature and the laws of ethics were established. We have long pedigrees of miracles, of magic, and religious ritual. We have narratives in which the good, that is, those who obeyed the Divinity or the spirit, were rewarded, and the bad, those who went against the dogma, were punished.

All religions are essentially pragmatic. In all revealed dogma there is always one pragmatic truth: it not only tells us that totems, spirits, saints and gods exist, it also demonstrates how by prayer, sacrifice, sacrament and moral communion we can reach the Divinity. Religion or magic taken as a system of belief, practice, and rules of conduct is, as a rule, the central or focal point of all cultural values. We have shown that it pervades human life by the sacrilization of all crises and that it endorses and standardizes most of the basically important activities and rules of conduct. Thus religion and magic on the one hand give man freedom from fear, from despondency, from spiritual and social disorganization. On the other hand they cement and integrate the partial and specific values of conduct and of achievement into one system or several systems, each converging on the central value with its focus of efficiency placed in a world sacred, firm and powerful, just because it remains outside the normal, ordinary experience of man. The freedom of religion and magic resides, therefore, in its general integrative contribution to all the partial activities of man. In this, religion and magic like knowledge subserve the need for permanent and standardized systems, embodied in tradition, that is, in language, guiding and instructing human actions and based on the affirmation of an order, natural or supernatural.

In some of the previous sections we already analyzed one aspect of human belief, that which seems to contradict the general conception of freedom as here established, that is, the freedom of order and determinism. Both religion and magic essentially contain in one way the occurrence of miracle, that is, of an event brought about through the contravention of natural determinism, with a minimum of miraculous rapport with the supernatural. Even Quakers, the most sober of all Christians, are moved by the Spirit. The Buddhist in the more refined atheistic form of that religion experiences the miracle of escape from the world. In magic this seems to be even more blatantly an affirmation of free-floating-freedom, since to a superficial view the magician, the wizard, or the sorcerer create phenomena and events through their own mystical power. Magic even has been affirmed to be in its essence the declaration of "omnipotence of thought" by man.

In reality both magic and religion are not the denial of determinism. They are only the affirmation of a new order, mystical and supernatural. This, however, is not free in the sense that it would allow man to attain any results without obedience to rules, and in contravention of established principles. On the contrary, man can obtain results by prayer, sacrifice, sacrament or rite only by the acceptance of the fully revealed commands of God or of other traditionally defined realities of the supernatural. God himself may be free, though even this is not at all the view of most theologies; but man can only pray to God, try to move Him, try to induce Him through gifts and sacrifices, or to constrain Him by exemplary conduct to fulfill his prayers. With God man is never allowed to take the slightest liberties. He may be able to bind God with prayer and virtue, with sacrifice or sacrament. Such instruments of divine bondage, however, are always produced by God himself. We could say that to the determinism of nature there is added another determinism of the sacred, the magical, the divine or the spiritual. Exactly as man has to obey the rules of natural determinism in order to pursue the path of freedom, that is, of effective action; so also in the realm of the supernatural he has to obey slavishly and devoutly the rules of divine commands and instructions, that is, the rules of supernatural determinism, in order to have his prayers answered, that is, his ritual or his ethical conduct rewarded.

The same refers to magic. Magic, primitive and contemporary, is not a system of daydreaming, not a spontaneous outburst of hate or despair, or wave of hope or despondency without purpose or efficiency. It is a form of action. In the magic of agriculture, hunting, or fishing, primitive people carry out complex ritual and they believe that through this they do actually achieve a surplus of favorable luck. Hate, when translated into acts of sorcery, becomes a verbal and manual act believed to produce disease, accident, ill luck and death. In war magic or the magic of dangerous enterprise, primitives and barbarians, ancient and modern believe that chance is being manipulated through ritual. Thus here also we find that freedom refers to a purpose which is believed translatable into action. Magic implies at times very elaborate but invariably pragmatic action in speech and ritual. The results of such culturally standardized behavior are rewarding. People believe that something has been achieved, that luck and chance have been harnessed, that victory is secured, fertility guaranteed, or else that the enemy, personal or tribal, has been smitten. The sociologist or anthropologist can show that this belief is not altogether idle.

Another reason why we have to distinguish active magic from mere daydreaming is because all magic is traditionally standardized. The primitive or the sophisticated magician does not improvise his magic. He carries it out on very well-defined lines of traditionally formulated spell, rite, and taboo. Magic has to be learned. It can be carried out only by specialists, and in order to be effective it has to run on strictly prescribed patterns. Thus, far from a free-floating-freedom of untrammelled improvisation, man here once more becomes bound by tradition. This is here indeed as minutely prescriptive as in any other form of manual and verbal technique. The underlying magical belief is that very strict determinism makes certain words, substances, gestures, and artifacts the only effective implements of the magical ceremony.

From our rationalistic point of view we reject magic as a fallacious form of action. In spite of this we can assign to it a positive and constructive function in human culture. Psychologically magic represents the efficiency of standardized optimism. The belief that by magical action dangers are averted and luck ensnared gives people confidence, endurance and determination. War magic instilling a belief in victory makes people fight well. In a dangerous enterprise those who are convinced that they will overcome circumstances, work better and keep better control of their organic forces of resistance. Magic thus means morale.

Sociologically speaking, magic adds to the force of solidarity and to the power of leadership. In primitive communities the magician—who occasionally is the leader himself—always inspires the community with a consciousness of discipline and with the faith in leadership.

It would be tempting here to analyze the structure and functions of Nazi and other totalitarian mysticisms with the insight gained by our analysis of primitive magic. The whole doctrine of Aryan superiority in race, and of the right to world domination by the master race, is essentially mystical. So is the belief in the infallibility, mystical omnipotence, and ubiquitous power of the Fuehrer, the Duce, or the Head of the Soviet State. Those who have studied the techniques of real propaganda, as this has been developed in the totalitarian countries, will realize that the thrilling promises, the affirmations of power and efficiency, as well as the canalizing of hatreds and passions, are built up essentially on the technique of a magical spell. The binding function of this magic for the followers is clear and it has been demonstrated by the efficiency of totalitarian military aggression. This is one of those truths which we have to recognize even though they lead to melancholy reflections on the impotence of democracies as against totalitarian creeds. Indeed, we have to recognize this truth because of all its depressing consequences.

The magic of totalitarian propaganda has been capable not merely of producing a mystical integration within their own nations, but also of sapping the spiritual energies among the victims. For this we also could find precedence in primitive magic. But the real contemporary lesson to be learned might lead us well to think whether democratic thought could not and should not also be as firmly integrated into a constructive faith, as has been accomplished by the totalitarians. Is truth incapable of the same vital dynamism which error can accomplish? Are we who believe in scientific truth, in religions of charity, consideration and justice, as well as in social codes of decency, honor and kindness, not able to answer mystical cohesion by spiritual unity? Are we doomed just because we respect the rights of the individual, the claims of minorities, and the value of spiritual truths? If this be so, if error is stronger than truth, and brutality more powerful than right, then indeed not only democracy but also humanity is doomed. I firmly believe however that our democratic ideals are stronger than the destructive faith of totalitarianism. All the arguments of the present essay hinge round a simple proposition: freedom is the essence of civilization because freedom is neither more nor less than obedience to the rules of science, of social justice, and of ethics. These rules are not arbitrary. They are founded in the order of material process, of organic reality, and of cultural structure.

The spectacular military successes of the totalitarians are possible only because in the short run you can use or abuse the power and efficiency of your culture. You can translate the constructive drives into one enormous effort of violence and destruction. In doing this, however, the very fountainheads of creative and constructive work are killed. Totalitarianism in the long run means not merely the submission of the world to political units based on principles which we reject emotionally. Totalitarianism also means the destruction of national, that is, cultural efficiency within the nation organized on such a system, and through this, the destruction of all other cultures if these become submitted to totalitarian rule.

10

Man's Dependence on Mechanical Device

THERE is one aspect of freedom which we have still not sufficiently considered. Looking at culture as a set of mechanical devices which intrinsically imply tradition and co-operation, we have seen that the artifact submits man to its direct technological determinisms. It also makes man more dependent on others, both in the fact that he has to assimilate the tradition of previous generations and inherit their wealth; and also in that he must handle all mechanisms co-operatively.

We have seen that freedom is achieved by an increase in efficiency of organized and implemented acts. Without this there would be no freedom in the integral sense of a widened and increased control by man over his bodily needs and environmental conditions; but this freedom is achieved by men's submission to all the rulings, technical, mechanical, legal and moral, which implemented co-operation implies.

The integral freedom of a co-operative group can be in this context identified with power. Yet since power is vested both in machine and in man, the distribution of power within co-operative groups opens the problem of freedom as an inquiry into the cultural structure of the collective activity in its purpose, its execution and the distribution of results. Here perhaps we find the most essential problem of freedom.

The more fully and concretely we study the nature of human action, the more we find that integrally it opens up ever-increasing vistas of possibilities, of efficiencies, of controls. Thus it gives integral freedom. At the same time, the very essence of action lies in the submission of all actors to the constraints of knowledge, of skill, of co-operation, of joint response and joint claims to the goods, values and enjoyments produced.

In this we see that the constraint may turn in two ways against human beings, and exact too high a price in individual or in group restrictions for any benefits given. The first types of danger from machine turning on man are when man's mechanisms become an end in themselves. The speed in modern means of locomotion, with all the toll in human life and limb, with the senseless distortion of time tables in human existence, and the useless wastage of energies and purposes which do not very often lead to any appreciable end, is an example of machine oppressing man. I do not know whether a sociological analysis in terms of value obtained for time wasted has ever been made. Such a study would be a real inquiry into freedom as a concrete factor in our civilization.

Machines and mass production methods as factors in the standardization of taste, desire, appetite and ambition, produced through the syndicated standardized agencies of public opinion, the newspapers, the radio and the advertisement, raise also the question how far the control of means within a big organization can enslave the ends of individual decision. All this, as has been pointed out already, is a question of the organization of power within a community, especially within a democratic community.

The second great problem in the relation of man to machine is the very specific organization of violence which we have produced through science and its application in technique. The modern material apparatus of a culture implies an enormous concentration of power in the hands of a small group or of one man. Essentially, this cannot be prevented. Compare the sailing boat with its complicated apparatus of mast, rigging, canvas and steering to a small canoe manned by a dozen people. The canoe is democratic in the sense that no very definite hierarchy is needed except perhaps at critical moments. The square rigged boat or any large wind-propelled vessel implies division of functions, discipline and in some cases the most despotic management of decisions and orders by the master. The gigantic modern steamer brings this even to a higher pitch in social organization, which has to follow the mechanical centralization of control.

In the same way, an intertribal battle fought by a small military band very often dissolves into a series of single combats. Strategy and tactics are rudimentary if they exist at all. As arms and protective armor develop, as differential tactics of single combat have to be translated into coordinated movements of attack and defense by small detachments, discipline and centralization of tactics and strategy make their appearance. All additions to the effectiveness in weapons of attack and in armaments for defense—mounds, palisades, walls, moats—impose the necessity of organizing human beings with the gradual expanding apparatus of attack and defense. The armed band is gradually formed into detachments; the open line of defense becomes a walled fortress; the technique which uses a variety of tactics related to an integral strategy supplants the hand-to-hand, man-to-man fighting of primitive times. Ideologies related to good luck and the help of spiritual powers, war magic and the protective guidance of divinities, ancestors, gods and prophets, enter as integrative psychological elements. In all this we see that the gradual development in the material apparatus of fighting imposes a progressive increase in military organization and in spiritual discipline. The freedom of violence, that is, the efficiency of enforcing political issues by the appeal to armed force, grows. With its growth, however, there runs parallel the ever-increasing submission in military discipline, in spiritual indoctrination, and in the submission of groups and individuals to machine, organization, rules and beliefs, alike. Here again totalitarianism is the last word in military efficiency on the one hand, and in a pervading tyranny of military means over any ends of private existence and the differential interests of groups and individuals.

The same arguments would show us that the transition from tribe to city-state, to a historical sovereign state, an empire and a totalitarian world empire is very largely based on technique. Political development has been dependent in its evolution on the power of effective technique, radiating from the center to the whole territory and the whole tribe, state, confederacy or empire. Ethnographic and historical evidence shows that the quality of roads, the dispatch of messengers, the possibility of rapid aggregation of large numbers, or dissemination of orders or instructions over a distant territory, were the material prerequisites of extensive control. Were we to study the structure of political control in the Persian Empire, in China, in the Aztec or Peruvian State; or again in the Roman Empire or the Europe of the Middle Ages, we would find everywhere that roads, communication, the organization of some form of police control, combined with the service of information from the periphery to the center, and decisions radiating from the center to the outlying regions, have always been the sinews of political and administrative control.

In our present world, the techniques of road-building, of railways, telephone communication and radio, supply an apparatus of unlimited control by a centralized group, of gigantic size and distributed over a wide territory. An effective new service, the spiritual mastery by a well-organized propaganda service, and the indirect exercise of violence by intimidation, are being used by the totalitarian powers on a world-wide scale. Fifth columns have been organized by Germany in every part of the world where news can be distributed by short-wave radio. Thus technology gives now an extremely dangerous two-bladed instrumentality of spiritual aggression to well-organized systems of monopoly in indoctrination and violence.

If we mean by freedom in one of its aspects the ability of groups and individuals to form opinions on the basis of fact, of real experience and of well-considered self-interest, there is nowadays perhaps the greatest danger to this first prerequisite of freedom, that of independent maturing of opinions, through a bondage which machine once more has imposed on man. This danger can only be counterbalanced by the same mechanism of impartial all-round distribution of initiatives. The problem of propaganda has been badly mismanaged in theory and in practice by many of our contemporary approaches to the subject. The expression of opinion—any opinion and all opinions—is not in itself propaganda, in the sense in which this word must be applied to the subversive, fifth column breeding activities of totalitarianism. Propaganda starts with monopoly in the dissemination of truth, a monopoly based on force. Each totalitarian system, including Russia, has already established such a monopoly at home. As soon as the power of the machine gun and the effective organization of the Gestapo reach any region, propaganda follows.

In democratic countries, there has always been and there still exists the only remedy for that evil. This is usually labelled freedom of speech, and it is necessary to a democratic constitution for many reasons. Language and symbolism play an important role in the framing of purposes for all the values, that is, all purposes, are collectively and individually laid down in doctrines, by means of verbal statements. Traditional knowledge is thus transmitted in speech, is received through question and answer and is memorized by the recipient. It has at times to be applied or adapted to particular problems, and on these occasions, such applications are made by means of discussion and debate. At all stages of development, from primitive cultures up to modern times, we find deliberative councils meeting to discuss and decide upon some proposed course of action which is then translated into instructions and orders. In all this, freedom of speech is essential, so that the individual or group can have access to all the funds of knowledge, and therefore be able to make his choice and to reach a decision through unimpeded discussion of the possibilities open. Freedom of speech is also of great value for the successful adjustment of a collective purpose to each particular individual case.

We can easily understand the role of speech, thought, deliberation and discussion in the development of freedom. Thought really is speech, for culturally effective thought has to be translated into teaching, discovery or empirical proof before it emerges as matured purpose. It is through speech, as a part of the process of training, that individuals mature their personal purposes. Through deliberation and reform, charters, that is, collective purposes are changed. A new idea, expressed and conveyed in speech, may lead to a new charter. Thus freedom of speech is essential in culture for the formation of purposes, individual or collective. Without freedom of speech, a new idea cannot be developed, nor can a collective purpose be autonomously formed in discussion and deliberation. Beside this, public utterance is essential to the development of scientific thought, political criticism and religious liberty. Freedom of speech therefore is the prerequisite of the freedom of action. And the science of semantics is that vigilance which is the price of freedom of thought.

Language is primarily an instrument of action and influences profoundly human behavior. It is essentially inadequate in its hypostatizing function. It also plays an important role as a means of coercion. The pragmatic power of words is found chiefly in the dynamism of words in magic, in the systems of disciplinary drill, and in the orders and instructions given in the carrying out of organized activities. In magic, the spoken word is a verbal act by which the force of magic is called into action and through which a powerful influence is exercised on human behavior. The utterance of magical words acts also as a strong organizing force, and, through fear of the consequences, can be used as a means of coercion. This pragmatic power of words is found as well in sacramental utterances, exorcisms, curses and blessings.

In words of command, the power of language affects profoundly the course of action. The word is as powerful as any manual grip, and is above all a stimulus to action. In all organized undertakings the control of action is in the hands of those who give the commands. Authority is exercised by means of the spoken word, and the success or failure of an undertaking depends on the correct use of speech. When we consider systems of disciplinary drill, we see that control and manipulation of action is again achieved by means of spoken commands and orders. Thus language plays an important role as a means of coercion and affects profoundly the freedom of action.

We must therefore register that two main limitations are necessary in the freedom of speech to preserve the freedom of the group or the culture. For any liberty which endangers the freedom of others is a decrease in liberty as regards the group as a whole, that is, of every individual in it.

The principles of this limitation are perfectly clear. In any case where speech is direct incitement to action which is dangerous to the freedom of others, rather than freedom of debate and submission of principles, we should exclude every statement which leads to activities forbidden by what we have defined as the constitutional, civil and criminal laws prevalent in a democracy. Since in most matters however it is possible to implement and institutionalize public debate so that its pragmatic execution can be deferred until a public decision is reached, a democracy under normal peaceful conditions can still afford to give an enormous leeway to free speech. Some subjects, such as pornography and obscenity, the advertising and procuring of dangerous substances on which there is a medical agreement and a justified legal ban, can be submitted to an enlightened and liberal preliminary scrutiny before they can be put on the intellectual market.

The other perfectly clear and sociologically sound limitation consists in the fundamental veto of coupling political views with organization for their enactment by violence. It is hardly necessary to prove here by a detailed analysis of facts that growing Fascism in Italy and Nazism in Germany were not merely movements of opinion, but also organizations of violence. A state which under the charter of sovereignty ought to have the monopoly of all armed force, and which at the same time allows a determined minority to preach its own gospel and to constitute itself an army for the overthrow of the state, obviously signs its own death warrant. This happened in every community in which, by a *coup d'état* of a prepared, carefully organized and determined revolutionary army, the constitutional government was overthrown—in Germany, Italy and Russia, and at the birth of Pétainism. Hence Hitlers and Mussolinis may be allowed to speak. They must not be allowed to organize armed private police forces.

In other words, we are on the one hand fully justified in demanding that the elaboration of truth should be embodied into the constitution of every democratic country. We must however also demand that institutional, municipal or central authority should watch over monopolies in opinion, over the tyranny of a syndicated factory of public opinion, or any one-sided power politics in civic totalitarianism. It is the relation between opinion and the possible acts of a criminal nature to which it may lead that has to be considered every time we grant full freedom of conscience, thought and speech.

In all this we see that the determinism of every advancing technique places the problem of freedom on a basis which is very concrete and real, and reaches to its very core. We see that freedom, as the scope given to subordinate groups, to spiritual movements, to legal, economic and educational agencies within the sovereign state, can now be completely annihilated by the technique of the *coup d'état*, and by the concentration of all means of violence, of expropriation, of control and of persuasion.

If we claim that our concept of freedom, one and indivisible, valid for the whole body politic, for its component institutions and for individuals, consists in the ability to cultivate traditional ideals; to formulate new goals; to mobilize the means or devise new means for the execution of their purposes; and to control the results—then we see that freedom is threatened under present conditions to the point of a mortal ailment or of total extinction. The only remedy is to devise means, technical, detailed and carefully thought out, so as to counterbalance the supreme dangers of monopoly in power, wealth and indoctrination. Exactly as the Founding Fathers of this Republic thought out, carefully and pedantically, and planned, with fullest consideration of the details of the political mechanism, such a division of powers as would make tyranny impossible; so also under present conditions those who realize that the future of mankind is threatened by an infinitely greater and more pervading tyranny must think out a constitution for the federated and united nations of the world, in which the new and graver danger of the technical centralization of all means of control has to be regarded as a central danger spot.

Part V

THE REAL BATTLEFIELDS
OF FREEDOM

1

Democracy and Proto-Democracy

WE CANNOT imagine the earliest beginnings of culture without at least two social groupings, the family and the horde. The gradual early progress of humanity was connected with the formation of other groups or institutions, differentiated by function, by activities, and by social organization. Among the modern representatives of paleolithic man, we find such institutions as the family, the clan, the local group, the various teams of food producers, that is, groups of food collectors, of hunters, of fishermen, and of craftsmen, as well as institutionalized magic, totemism, and ancestor worship.

The constitution of a primitive tribal culture consists of a number of largely independent, yet co-operatively related institutions which conjointly work out and maintain their culture. They constitute an integral cultural whole, and between them they carry on the business of food supply and reproduction, of the earliest industries and primitive ritual and ethics.

We could coin the concept of proto-democracy to define the constitution of such primitive groups. They are essentially democratic, each group enjoying local government, the decentralization of authority and education, and the self-determination of the component groups, institutions and to a large extent, of individuals. This definition applies to democracy, not merely in respect to the political, economic or educational organization, but in an integrally cultural sense. Democracy as a cultural system is the constitution of a community which is composed of collaborating groups. Each such group is an institution, which is itself built on democratic principles, and in which initiatives, purposes and constraints are well distributed. The democracy of the whole group lies in the relations of institutions to one another, and in the relations of individuals within each institution.

Democracy is usually regarded as a rather evolutionary development, emerging at the time of the Athenian Republic, since the American War of Independence, or the French Revolution. Democracy means in the widest sense government by the people, the control of government by those governed, and it incorporates the republican form of government, that is, representative government, ballot and executive legislation. A wider and more elastic, more fundamental definition of the concept of democracy implies the maximum of discipline with the least amount of coercion. It implies obedience to law without the need of physical enforcement. Discipline must not occur except where concerted action demands it.

The realization of democracy under present-day conditions consists in types of political government where, through the ballot, the citizens delegate legislative and administrative powers to their representatives. This aspect, very important in higher cultures, is not relevant at very primitive levels. In these, such centralized influence as occurs takes the form of tribal councils of elders, some of whom achieve greater influence through the general acknowledgment of wisdom, traditional lore and personal competence. In such primitive groups there is no ballot, no vote, yet a general public approval and acceptance. There is very little centralized power, which gives results as good if not better than when such power is placed in the hands of authorities elected and controlled by the people.

There are, however, other aspects perhaps more important than Parliaments or ballot, if we consider democracy as a principle of cultural constitution rather than political organization. Democracy, in our modern free commonwealths and right through evolution and history, implies always a considerable amount of self-determination or autonomy. The most important cultural aspect of democracy, the autonomy of institutions, is seldom, if ever, considered in theoretical argument or practical application. This autonomy of institutions really contains and embodies all the other principles of democracy. Functional autonomy is found both in primitive cultures and in fully developed ones, for in a democracy or proto-democracy no central power exists which controls all aspects of the culture. This functional autonomy is realized in the independence of institutions, and makes possible the organization and combination of any groups where co-operation is necessary and interests divergent.

The separation of powers or functional autonomy implies that administration, the framing of laws, and the system of administering justice should not all be in the hands of the same individuals. It also implies independence of specific combines, or institutional autonomy. The delegation of powers is controlled. Powers are granted which assure the continuity of government; but this continuity cannot be abused, for there is no permanent election of those in power. The principle of separation of powers has been clearly recognized by those who prepared and carried out the American War of Independence, and drew up the Constitution of this Republic. It had also been clearly formulated by the English and French forerunners of modern democracies. In reality, modern democracies carry this principle of functional autonomy or separation of powers even further. The separation of Church and State, or more correctly the freedom of conscience and of religious organization, which exists in Great Britain as well as in other democracies; the independence of economic organizations and of artistic production, are one and all embodied in the cultural ideals of a democracy.

Local autonomy, in the sense that component states, dominions, regions, municipalities, and even smaller local units have the right to govern themselves with a large degree of self-determination, is as important to cultural democracy as is the delegation of powers through representation and functional autonomy. The Federal principle, that is, the decentralization in the territorial sense of the many legislative, administrative and police functions, is also worthy of very precise clarification to all of us who believe that a Federal Union of commonwealths is the only mechanism for the attainment of collective security. Federalism, far from being dangerous to democracy, is essential even within homogeneous units. When a democracy, like that of Switzerland, the British Empire or the United States, consists of peoples whose regional character is different, and whose environmental conditions demand a differential wielding of authority, federalism becomes the very core of a sound democratic constitution.

Democracy gives, first, freedom and scope for the formation of purposes; the freedom of forming opinions, that is, educational freedom and freedom of conscience; freedom of speech, or the right to decide by resort to experience, to deliberate in public and to combine. Democracy secondly gives freedom of opportunities, of instrumentalities and of action, for the translation of collective purposes into organized collective behavior. Here freedom is political and economic; it is the means of action, the exercise of authority necessary to action and the delegation of such authority. For effective action, instrumentalities are necessary, in the sense of securing means, apparatus and the access to raw material. Thirdly, democracy gives the freedom of enjoyment, through an equitable distribution of tasks, of rewards, and of rights to power, wealth and privilege.

Thus democracy can be defined as a cultural system devised so as to allow the fullest opportunities to the individual and to the group to determine its purposes, to organize and implement them, and to carry out the activities upon which they are intent. A modern democracy has also the duty to guarantee to its members an equitable distribution of rewards, the full enjoyment of recreation, the privileges of knowledge and of the arts, and of all that constitutes the spiritual prerogatives of contemporary man. These at least are the main principles of the charter of democracy; and it is with the charter, that is, the avowed intentions of a cultural system, that we are now concerned. Democracy therefore is a political system which we believe to be the real guarantee against coercion and oppression.

We can sum up the main aspects of democracy as follows:

(1) No centralized power which dictates all aspects of life

(2) Distribution of influence to those who do the work

(3) No accumulated monopolies

(4) No secret or open centers of oppression by violence, blatantly illegal or camouflaged, from which there is no redress and no appeal

(5) Access by one and all to most avenues of influence and self-expression.

The earliest human cultures known to anthropology fully conform to these aspects of democracy. Yet for reasons which will be indicated, these earliest cultures are not fully democratic in the highest sense of the term.

Let us approach our survey of primitive humanity from this point of view. It is clear from the facts briefly surveyed that the

cultural constitution of humanity in its early stages of development was founded on principles closely akin to what we call
cultural democracy. The fact that their central forms of government have a surface resemblance to our representative system is
of little importance. Centralization of any control hardly occurs
under those conditions of life, for political power is distributive,
and institutions are autonomous. Such proto-democracies correspond very largely to what we call nations today in the cultural
sense, that is, groups whose identity is defined by the use of the
same language, and occurrence of the same economic institutions,
customs, law, and religion, that is, by the same culture.

Freedom in such proto-democracies can be studied with reference to culture as an integral change in human adaptation, an
increment in efficiency in the control of human impulses and environmental factors, in the greater range of purpose, of achievement, and of pursuit of happiness, that is, the standard of living
in the widest sense. This greater range gives thus a new freedom
to the species. In this context also we must consider the problem
of increasing wants with regard to the means of their satisfaction,
and to the relation of demand to supply. Integrally speaking, a
primitive culture presents a low level of expectancy. The alternative choices are limited; the wants, material and spiritual; the
satisfactions of ambition; and the diversity in loyalties are all
restricted. Within this range, however, the institutions are more
or less well adapted. A man, as regards economic freedom, may
be occupied more in fishing than in hunting; or he may be a
specialist in a skilled work, such as stone-chipping, bow and
arrow making, or spear production; or a specialist in magic or
sorcery. As regards freedom of association, he often has the
possibility of changing his household; he always has the choice
of founding a new one at maturity. The existence of kindred
groups, clans and age-grades may allow him to throw his loyalties

more definitely with one group rather than with the other. The bent of each occupational organization, the evolutionary advent of each new pursuit, skill or trade add to the range on the economic, social and technological side.

The most remarkable characteristic of primitive communities is that the political element in the form of centralized power and violence is absent. In relation to this, war as a purposeful instrumentality of transacting intertribal business does not exist. The political element, that is, any administrative influence, any decisions, any enforcement and, in fact, any wielding of authority, is definitely distributed among the various institutions. Freedom, as we know, depends on authority within the institutions and as exercised between them. This institutional authority is the most important form, since the life-needs of the group and the individual are fulfilled through the work of the institutions, in which authority is distributive. It is vested in the heads of the various families, it is wielded by the headman of the local group, the head of the clan, or by the organizer of a productive team or of a religious ceremony. Institutional autonomy is one of the most conspicuous factors in primitive organization. The institutions are the real carriers of culture, which they exercise.

To this is also related the fact that most educational activities are distributed among the various institutions. As we have seen, the household is the first school in which the young primitive learns his language, his bodily skills, the rudiments of tribal tradition, of manners and ethics, and of course the foundations of tribal kinship law. When he passes through his initiation ceremonies, or, where these do not exist, when he enters the play-group of his contemporaries, he acquires a number of new, independently formed attitudes to social relations in the rules of co-operation and submission to new authorities. His participation in clan life and his apprenticeship to acquire clan status develop in him another side of his tribal personality. Marriage and maturity—and for both of these he or she receives as a rule a special training and a special induction into new duties, responsibilities and privileges—are once more an independent installment of tribal training. At each stage he acquires new status, he submits to a new authority and takes up a new role in life. We see therefore that if we conceive of democracy in its cultural sense as implying varying types of submission to rules, to authority, to wealth and to ideas, there is in primitive cultures a considerable amount of such democracy.

The principle of authority comes into being from the beginnings of mankind. In disciplining the individual, authority is an indispensable factor of the process of training at any level of culture. In the enforcement of criminal law it is at all stages and in all societies a *conditio sine qua non*. When authority occurs in a crisis which demands complete discipline, it is once more fundamental both to the safety of human beings and to the success of the enterprise.

The relations between various institutions, the quarrels between families, clans and local groups, are often settled by legal principles of deliberation and agreement. There is no one institution which tyrannizes over others. Occasionally we find that fighting between component sub-groups occurs, either as a spontaneous and unregulated hand-to-hand melée, or else it assumes the form of more or less ritual duels, single combats, or collective fights. Such fighting has a distinctly legal character, and is comparable to the phenomena of God's judgment or trial by ordeal or vendetta.

Only gradually there emerges a centralized authority within the tribe, such as the council of elders which fulfills the function of moderator. It carries out judicial decisions, and in the course of evolution it also takes up the military functions of protection and later of aggression. With the development of such centralized political institutions, with the beginnings of real political wars, the problem of freedom, political, economic and legal, takes a more real and acute form. As humanity advances, discipline enters with the growth of military institutions.

In the peaceful phases of constructive existence, customary law and ethics supply measures which limit and mitigate personal tyranny. Our modern democracies have developed a whole set of general measures to prevent any surreptitious and occasional or else permanent abuse of personal authority. The separation of powers, which is one of the constitutional principles of democracy, is a case in point. The limitation of tyranny by police is another problem which has been solved in England by depriving them of firearms, while in other democracies it is a matter of constant, and more or less successful vigilance. In sharp contrast to this, totalitarian regimes allow and encourage every form of police tyranny.

As soon as organized violence can be used to subjugate other tribes or nations, to enslave individuals, and to exploit them economically, we face that specific denial of freedom which is the leitmotif of human evolution and history, and which the present world, far from solving, has rendered even more acute through the technical perfection in the means of enslavement of the human body, labor, and spirit.

Culture, which is the organization of human abilities, muscular faculties, and instruments for effective action, can thus be used for destructive as well as constructive ends. It can be transformed into an instrumentality of power for power's sake. Constraint and war are developments of culture, even as are art, religion, and economics. The molding of the human spirit to make it receptive through falsehood, indoctrination, and the greeds, ambitions and hatreds of war-mindedness, is an element which at every stage of evolution and history was inherent in militarism.

Freedom is closely related to the proto-democratic, and in historical times, to the democratic constitution of culture. Cultural democracy we have defined as the existence of a number of independent, yet related institutions. Proto-democracies enjoy a measure of freedom which, on this low level of development, is limited in the way that all other cultural goods, actions and achievements, such as wealth, power, initiative and knowledge, are limited. But in the sense that control is restricted and diffused and that the individual can determine his personal allegiance and his choice, this freedom is very real. The individual in proto-democracy is free because he can make his choice in what he wishes to do and how he does it. This is made possible to the individual through the diversity of institutional settings which he can join. Exploitation does not yet exist, and the individual is not deprived of the fruits of his activity and can do what he wants with what he has achieved. Whether in proto-democracy or one of our modern communities, man or woman enjoys his personal freedom insofar as he can join the institution of his choice, and insofar as that institution allows him to develop and to realize his own personality.

In this outline we see that proto-democracy implies certain negative qualities. There is no privilege connected with any class or group. There is hardly any concentration or centralization of power and control. There are no monopolies in wealth, in spiritual control, or in power. Nor is there any legal oppression, for since law is administered within each institution and between institutions, it is usually a matter of private litigation. Education is not used for a one-sided indoctrination. There is indeed very little indoctrination, for each group trains every one of its members to do his work according to traditional norms.

Such organization of life means obviously that everyone can make his choices, frame his purposes, and take the initiative according to his inclinations. The access to the means of production as well as to the enjoyment of consumers' goods is open to all. There are no patents, no secret technological processes, nor yet does there exist any hoarding or appropriation of instrumentalities. Everyone can make a pointed stick, or produce or acquire shaped stone. Young people are usually equipped by elders with implements necessary for work. There is a wide and generous scope for anyone who wishes to work a piece of land, to grow food on it, or to hunt animals. The social relations of such early groups are a network of friendly and neighborly give-and-take. In primitive cultures there are no rich people and paupers; no people of great power; nor yet people who are oppressed; no unemployed, and no unmarried.

In saying all this we imply that such primeval freedom in a proto-democracy is a necessity rather than a virtue. Our sober and exact statement must not be taken as a paean in praise of proto-democracy. We could go over our list of primeval freedoms and point by point show that riches do not exist because there are no means for producing them. Man cannot be used as a means to an end when the ends are so limited that they do not extend beyond the elementary necessities of the human organism.

In order however to make our argument relevant in the pragmatic sense, it is not enough to establish the fact of primitive freedom; it is necessary to show that this early freedom played a dynamic part in the processes of culture. Freedom in fact is essential to the survival of culture at its earliest stages. Culture, let us repeat, is a gift of this early freedom. All means, technical and intellectual, and social achievements are at the very primitive levels embodied in the members of the group. Culture lives in their memories, in their acts, in their forms of organization. When the groups of culture carriers are excessively limited in numbers as they are at this stage of evolution, the greatest necessity is to maintain the survival of culture. There is always the danger of forgetting a technique, a code of rules, a piece of useful knowledge, natural or supernatural. The maximum of guardianship is necessary.

We need not assume that any such primitive group should be aware of this truth and practice freedom in order to comply with that law of cultural continuity. We can apply in all evolutionary arguments the principle of survival of the fittest cultural constitution, as a counterpart of the principle that a culture built upon a fundamental flaw must have perished in early human history. Were we to imagine a primitive community where the making of fire, the shaping of stones, the techniques of food collecting and hunting, had become a monopoly of one or a few lineages, such a culture would have become wiped out within a few generations. The first time that an incompetent individual received any piece of traditional knowledge into his exclusive safe-keeping, that part of culture would have dropped out. Thus the determinism of cultural continuity, that is, the safe-guarding of cultural values, demands that freedom, that is, full, equally distributed opportunities to learn, to know, to practice, and to enjoy results, should obtain at a primitive level. The importance of equitable and full enjoyment of the results is clear. Only the personal motive of a strong reward makes for the retention of rules or habits in the human organism. Slaves can be coerced into learning; they reject this as soon as the coercion ends, that is, unless they can enjoy what they have acquired under slavery also in their freedom.

We can even refine upon this principle that full membership in tradition is necessary at primitive levels of development. Even at such a level there exists already a certain differentiation or specialization as regards skills, pursuits and types of knowledge. This requires differential ability. Some people, through physical fitness and strength, are better at hunting or fishing or fighting. There are others who excel in intelligence and memory and those can play their part as wizards, magicians, and carriers of verbal tradition. Others, again, have greater manual skills and there are also born dancers, actors, and entertainers. To give this process of specialization by ability the best chance, freedom, as the access to culture equally distributed, is necessary. Within a very small group we have to give opportunities to everyone so that the few really suitable may take up their real vocation.

We can make one more addition. We generally assume that the earliest types of rude men were essentially conservative. Undoubtedly there exists a great premium on retention and little encouragement is given to change or improvement. Nevertheless, just because at each generation culture is carried on by relatively few people, its exercise shows always both infinitesimal increments of individual contribution, and also definite deterioration when an incumbent is not up to the mark. The observant field worker registers always certain ups and downs in the level of each concrete aspect of his culture. He learns, for instance, that two or three generations ago tribal magic was in the hands of an exceptionally powerful wizard. He may discover that the present incumbent is a limited and stupid man with a poor memory and hardly any personality. Similar ups and downs occur in art, in construction, in the technical skills and in the organization of enterprises. Even when tribal history does not go back more than two or three generations, it is possible to register an ebb and flow, a rise and a fall, some substantial increments here and deteriorations there.

Here once more, the greater the free mobilization of effective man power and woman power into the service of tradition, the greater the chances of talent being found in every walk of life, and of degeneration being prevented. Yet here as elsewhere, freedom must consist in the full access to the whole range of tribal tradition. It must mean also the freedom to exercise it and to enjoy the privileges and benefits resulting. We are able thus to state why freedom has to be maintained at a low level and obtains so fully, so universally, and dominantly. Its denial would impair, gradually and slowly perhaps, but inevitably and fundamentally, the maintenance of any primitive culture. Probably such a process would be very rapid and fatal except for the fact that even the most primitive culture disposes of a certain amount of symbolism, that is, of signs which direct human behavior by being embodied into outward material objects of the natural and artificial environment. The very structure and outward disposition of dwellings and other buildings within the settlement and upon tribal territory insures a certain continuity in the mode of living; and the mold of the physical framework reminds people in each generation of certain rules of conduct. All artifacts, either tools or consumers' goods or implements of ritual, are both instrumental and symbolic. Their instrumental aspect is defined by the pragmatic use which they subserve. They are symbolic in that each such shaped piece of matter is an embodiment of a piece of human knowledge. As culture advances, decorations, symbolic paintings, objects which function as diagrams, plans, and *aide-memoirs*, multiply. The discovery of symbolic writing is the final step in this and the end of preliterate humanity. Once this is achieved, the need of embodying tradition and every part of it within the minds of a large quantity of carriers diminishes. A scientific formula, practical instructions concerning a technical device, a sacred text or a piece of folklore, can be written out and preserved. Knowledge lives enshrined in that material aspect of our culture without which contemporary intellectual life would not be possible: the archives, the libraries, and the laboratories of today preserve human experience in a condensed symbolic manner. They allow also of a degree of specialization and concentration of intellectual knowledge which would be impossible at early stages without impairing the continuity of tradition.

Yet when this stage of development begins, perhaps some ten thousand years ago, the need of freedom is not extinguished. It becomes necessary not so much for the retention of culture but for its progress. Progress consists in the modification of human ideas through discovery, invention, and new technical applications. It is a constant and gradual raising of our level of knowledge. The freedom of thought, which is equivalent in our terminology to the range of choice of individuals as regards the freedom of collective purposes and of the social appreciation of the best means and the most valuable ends, is thus one aspect of the advance in freedom. Philosophers and moralists have perhaps concentrated too much upon the freedom of thought. To a certain extent, however, they are justified. The essence of action within the cultural context is that it is planned, prepared, based on well-founded knowledge and on adequate skills.

It is necessary also to stress the constitution and integral freedom of proto-democracies, for we find so frequently that primitive peoples are referred to as "savages" with blind passions, who are slaves to custom, warlike and cruel. Totalitarianism itself is often described as a relapse to savagery. This misses the point, for totalitarianism lives by the misuse of power in its modern technological developments, through the use of brute force, indoctrination and communication. The elimination of totalitarianism is not a problem of individual psychology or psycho-analysis, such as the elimination of aggressiveness, sadism or pugnacity. The end of totalitarianism can only be achieved through the elimination and prevention of the use of violence and the technique of the *coup d' état*, of the irresponsible armament of partial groups of humanity, and of lawlessness where law must play an active role.

We have studied evolution in terms of an increase in crystallized institutions, and throughout the institutional analysis of the beginnings and development of culture, we reiterated the problem of freedom and bondage—freedom in scope, mobility and control, and bondage in submission to rule. As institutions rise, multiply, and develop, there is constantly the bondage of law; the law or rule of technique; the law or rule of group organization; the law and rule of property, and restraint in many physiological functions. This bondage to law is vested in institutions, which are the seat of authority and control. An increase in freedom lies in the gradual development of institutional differentiation. At the same time, the increasing diversity in institutional organization adds new avenues of specialized activity, of variety in occupational self-expression, of choice in allegiances, obligations, duties, and privileges. Freedom, therefore, is a positive attribute of culture, as it develops in the Spencerian sense of differentiation into institutions and integration of the various efforts. It can still better be predicated with reference to a culture as a whole, that is, the organization of a society.

Metaphorically, freedom in its essence is the acceptance of the chains which suit you and for which you are suited, and of the harness in which you pull towards an end chosen and valued by yourself, and not imposed. It is not, and never can be, the absence of restrictions, obligations of law and of duty. In this form it becomes the extreme despotism of an African chief, of an Oriental despot. Even then once he starts an enterprise he is a slave to that enterprise.

Freedom is the possibility of "self-realization" based on personal choice, on free contract and spontaneous endeavor, or individual initiative. This self-realization consists in the building up of a career which, however limited, has a certain choice of privileges and scope for specializing; the possibility of entering one occupational group rather than the other. The greater the opportunities of self-realization there are for more people, the more freedom there is. However free a political constitution, and however diversified a culture, the individual is obliged, stage to stage and step by step, to renounce certain freedoms; in choosing his vocation; in choosing his mate; in the acceptance of certain decisions and commands. Man therefore undoubtedly loses at each step of his career some of his possibilities of choice. He never loses his freedom, if freedom is to be defined in terms of a chosen task accomplished, of a chosen mate cherished and occasionally obeyed, of a creative impulse realized through the terrific strain and effort of that sequence in taking infinite pains which turns potential ability into real talent—because these activities were undertaken not from constraint, but under the dictates of preference, ambition, affection, or inspiration.

Freedom in individual existence is this selection of specific differential bondage. Freedom however is very real; it is the range in molding the individual's existence, in choice of mate, career, hobby, creed and art; it is the organization of opportunities, the supply of wherewithal, the range of initiative in creative change. This is the treasure-house of freedom in democratic cultures.

2

Power, Its Birth and Development

IN THE course of our analysis, we have found that culture—the complex instrumentality of social organization, mechanical invention, habits and customs, and spiritual values—is the real context which determines human freedom and which also is capable of limiting it.

We must, however, hark back to the beginnings of power at the very origins of the human career, and examine the rudiments and potentialities of oppression. We have already seen that in each pursuit and in each institution—since all activities become in time integrated into institutions—the element of authority and its hierarchical delegation are indispensable. Discipline and some means of enforcing this submission are essential to authority; these however are not necessarily a denial of freedom. It is the nature of authority, the way in which rules are enforced and the conditions of discipline which determine the presence or absence of freedom. Authority becomes oppressive and abusive when it is exercised for the one-sided benefit of the few in power, at the expense of the many.

The three principal sources of power are moral, economic and political; and these can be abused through the use of fear, wealth and violence respectively. We must therefore examine more closely the various methods of abuse of power, since while the legitimate use of authority gives freedom, its abuse results in the denial of freedom.

Ethnographically we find that the earliest abuse of power occurs through the manipulation of fear, in which magic, sorcery and mystical fear are the chief instruments. Magic in its very essence is the belief that man, by virtue of his tribal lore, traditional spells and ritual gestures, can conquer accident and overcome disaster through the assertion of his mystically founded power; and thus secure success in human enterprise. It is the belief in a man-made, infallible force to achieve practical ends. Man becomes God in order to dictate his own will to his followers, or to impose the collective will on nature, on circumstances, or on destiny.

Scientifically, the persistence and fundamental importance of magical systems lie in the affirmation of value when action is taken under stress of danger, fear or desires. Magic brings about the spiritual mobilization of all values, the affirmation of faith in the issue, the organization of all resources, and a system of mental and social discipline. It instils an *esprit de corps* in the group, with a discipline of spirit and body which supplies one of the strongest forces of primitive organization. The drill and the solidarity organized into economic pursuits are one of the most important functions of magic, in that they strengthen the social texture and develop economic virtues in man. The moral and social force of magic, not only in primitive cultures but also in our modern states, lies in the crystallized sense of power. Magic is a powerful tool for good and for evil, and can be a dangerous tool.

The power and sanctity of the magician is founded in his control of chance and destiny by means of magic. Magic is therefore a technique of ritual, both manual and verbal, by which leadership is established, a man-made power which is also man-wielded. The belief in magic thus creates a spiritually hallowed leader; his verbal and ritual performance mobilizes the psychological forces of all and organizes the group. Thus we find an agency, spiritual, social and pragmatic, which fulfills an important cultural function; it produces a body of men better prepared to fight and endure, to struggle and to co-operate, to have a single mind and a clear purpose, and to pool their efforts for the task in hand. It produces also a leader who can control the actions of his fellow tribesmen by means of his magical power.

Magical beliefs are invariably associated with an important by-product: the belief in black magic or sorcery. Beneficent magic has as its counterpart the conviction that misfortune can be manufactured by the spells and rites of ill-intentioned, nefarious sorcerers. Even though it is performed secretly, sorcery produces powerful social results of a negative character, for in primitive communities, ill-health and death are often attributed to the evil spells of sorcery. In everything which affects health and survival, the belief in and fear of sorcery is dominant.

Thus we can see that magic and sorcery are powerful factors in controlling human destiny, since magical belief mobilizes a specific type of mysticism associated with a mythology of power and human self assertion. Here we can clearly recognize the potentialities for abuse, since magic integrates morale and organizes human groups for effective action; and since within the situation of magic there is complete submission to the leadership of the magician.

The constraining factor of mystical fear lies in the threat of punishment in the other-world. The power of fear is also effectively used through fear of this-worldly consequences which result from a curse, excommunication, sin, and divine or sacred displeasure of a permanent nature. All such moral authority is wielded by charysmatic personalities, such as magicians, witch doctors, sorcerers or priests. This point—the abuse of authority through the use of fear and mystical power—is important and must be emphasized in relation to freedom, since both the formation of purpose as well as human action can be imposed and controlled through fear and indoctrination. The present system of centralized indoctrination through propaganda and education in Nazi Germany is evidence of the power of fear and mysticism to determine human action for the abrogation of freedom.

The beginnings of economic power are founded on wealth in the widest sense of that term. This brings us to the forms of economic oppression and curtailment of freedom. These are few and far between on primitive levels. Within the family, the withholding of food and its use as reward to children is used rather as an educational device than as a form of arbitrary oppression. Before the advent of military pursuits and political power, which appear late in human evolution, there occurred no taxation, no confiscation of private property by chiefs or other tribal potentates. The earliest ways of using wealth as power are related to magic and religion. We find frequently that a tribal magician is regarded as responsible for the surplus in fertility of animals or plants. Another form in which partial oppression exists is related to differential food taboos. The best food is sometimes monopolized by the old men of the tribe at the expense of the younger, or by the men to the disadvantage of the women. Since however we deal with but small advantages, and with rules which are inelastic and hence do not lend themselves to an additional exercise of pressure, it would be difficult to find in them a serious abrogation of freedom.

As regards the concentration of wealth, this is hardly possible under primitive conditions. Food cannot be preserved in any large quantities, still less accumulated. There are very few objects of value, and these are individually distributed and used as ornamentation. The only monopoly which occurs is in objects of a magical or religious character.

At a somewhat higher level, the power of wealth begins to be used in the form of bribery or reward, but the special privilege of wealth is the power it gives over the control and use of tools. Wealth makes possible the production of tools of coercion, such as spears, clubs, shields, blowpipes and bows and arrows, which become the monopoly of the group who uses them. Such groups in primitive cultures are formed for the purpose of policing, of carrying on vendettas, and for types of fighting, such as head-hunting, cannibalism and raids. The members of the group are organized under a leader who wields the central authority; they undergo a period of training; they have exclusive access to the instruments produced for the carrying out of the activity; and they have a common ideology and purpose. Thus through control of the weapons or implements, and since they are organized, the group is able to impose its will on the other members of the community. We see therefore that oppression occurs through artifacts used both as wealth and as weapons.

These aspects of the abuse of wealth are closely linked with the abuse of political power. Political authority as we know is indispensable even at primitive levels; we have defined it as the legally vested power to establish norms, to take decisions and to enforce them through the use of sanction by coercion. We must however once more emphasize that at primitive levels the political element is definitely distributed among the various institutions; and that there is no centralized and organized authority. Such primitive groups are for this reason essentially democratic. Freedom, which we have found to be dependent on the autonomy of institutions, is a very real attribute of primitive groups.

The magical and religious control of nature is one of the

earliest foundations of political power. This, however, does not seem ever to be used in the extortion of wealth or other abuses except at much higher levels, when the magic of fertility becomes associated with military might. Abuse of political power occurs when the elements of discrimination and of institutionalized one-sided political power and monopoly of advantages come into being, with the development of the principles of rank and caste and the beginning of slavery. This was only possible when the accumulation of wealth had begun, and with it, large constructions needing the work of many men; when work was organized industrially; and with the pursuit of military tasks. The abuse of political force thus occurs when doctrines of inequality by birth or function, and of wealth as a means of reward or bribe, are developed. It takes place as soon as hostilities offensive or defensive are undertaken. Experience and force together become concentrated in the hands of a leader, who exacts submission from those who work for him, and who is surrounded by loyal and self-interested henchmen, sometimes armed. In this way force becomes oriented centrifugally.

Authority gradually had to widen its scope, and become extended to function between institutions, as well as between individuals. If we look at the formation of a primitive tribe, we find that families become grouped together to form municipalities; that a group of municipalities forms a district; and that a number of districts form the tribe. Thus authority becomes extended to function also in the relations between families, municipalities or districts within the tribe.

Now the growth of authority was slow, piecemeal and erratic; it was rather the development of inter-institutional law based on gradually extended institutions. As soon as there emerges a more or less centralized authority in the tribe, we have the first sketchy outlines of budding political statehood. Yet it is only when such a central authority becomes endowed with a small armed force that we can speak of centralized political organization within a primitive tribe.

In this process of institutional crystallization, the three principles of power begin to exercise an increasing amount of control over human behavior. The rise and development of political institutions, of which the state in its various stages and types is the most important, is related to the organization of force and constraint. On the economic side, the use of human beings for compulsory labor becomes at times translated into slavery, serfdom and cognate institutions. A religious doctrine and dogma achieves also a degree of centralization and authority which at certain stages of development makes the church, the congregation, or the sect a powerful institution able to impose its opinions on its followers. It must be stated at once that political, economic and spiritual influence or constraint are, as a rule, interdependent. Extreme forms of coercive control occur in connection with military activities and become incorporated into institutions which combine the use of physical force, the pressure of wealth, and the power of doctrine for the control of people.

The formation of authority and constraint within institutions and the occurrence of coercion in this process is of special interest in the study 'of freedom. Democracy in its cultural sense is primarily determined by the independence of institutions from central power; and by the establishment of freedom within each institution. Servitude, oppression and coercion come into being with the rise of institutions based on the principle that human beings can be turned into means to ends. Under conditions of slavery, serfdom, military tyranny and other forms of political, economic and spiritual oppression, we find large sections of a community who have neither the right to decide on the purposes of their work, nor to enjoy any benefits from their toils, except those granted to them by their masters.

Wherever therefore we find the development of institutions based on violence and organized power, in which there is embodied a principle of discrimination as well as compulsory membership, we face an abrogation of freedom culturally established. The denial of freedom occurs at the point when violence and the principle of "might is right" enter the charter of an institution. We see therefore that authority is the raw material of servitude, through the abuse of force, through indoctrination for submission, and through monopolies. The line of distinction between freedom and bondage runs along the incidence of concentrations of force and of wealth. Insofar as property means an exclusive access to the use of certain instruments and the ability to deprive others of the use of such instruments or of the benefits derived from such a use, we have potentialities of slavery in the economic sense. When the instruments in question are weapons and other means of coercion, we have potentialities of slavery in the political sense. It is therefore always round the distribution and organization of authority, violence, and wealth that the problem of freedom hinges. In our modern culture we can establish checks on tyranny. This always occurs through the distribution of powers. A society based on the division of political authority, on a large measure of independence given to administrative groups, but also of control of such groups especially by courts of justice, autonomous and independent, puts considerable check on abuse of power. Such institutions as the family, the municipality, the province must also have large measures of local autonomy. Above all, education, justice, religion, and economic enterprise must remain largely independent while they also remain open to inspection. Totalitarianism denies all these principles. Its main principle is a complete, pervasive, and unquestioned centralization of all initiative, all dependence, and all executive and administrative activities.

3

Tribe-Nation and Tribe-State

HUMANITY, primitive and at every stage of evolution, does not consist of one culture. We shall have to consider the widest group united by the same type of culture; we shall have to define it, as well as to study the relation between such an integral community of carriers of the same culture and its subdivisions. This will lead us to the problem of the beginnings of centralized authority and its further development.

We find that in our analysis of culture we have left out one important fact. We spoke perhaps somewhat vaguely about the community, the group, or society in an indefinite sense; we have left out, in short, the question as to the nature of the integral group which carries on its culture and exercises it as a whole, that is, the tribe-nation. In reality the modern ethnographer finds primitive surviving humanity divided into very definite groups by clearly marked off cultural boundaries. Were we to take the map of any continent, Australia, Africa, Asia, or America, we would be able to divide it neatly into ethnographic tribal boundaries. Within each such ethnographic area we would find people of "the same" tribe. On the other side of the boundary another tribe would be found, distinguishable from the first by a different language, different technologies and material objects, different customs and forms of grouping. Besides these it would be also distinguishable by different tradition, that is, myths, legends and histories; different law, economics, educational system and social organization, in fact, by different institutions. In the terminology here adopted, we could say that the dividing line separates two different types of institutions, that is, two cultures, since for us a culture is the related system of institutions. The tribe therefore can be defined as a federation of partly independent and also co-ordinated component institutions.

We would find for instance that the institution of the family shows the same structure and the same character over a clearly defined area. Within this area intermarriage occurs, the rules of kinship are the same, and the adoption of children may take place as between one family and another within the area, but not outside it. Indeed, the whole texture of kinship and the organization of clans implies the tribe, which is subdivided into a system of clans, and where practically everybody is related, really or fictitiously, to everybody else. Those outside the tribe are not regarded as full human beings. Over the tribal area or within well-marked boundaries we would find that the constitutions of the local group, of the age grades, of secret societies and economic teams do not vary. Indeed, members of the tribe concur in tribal meetings, public ceremonies, and for acts of collective worship, magical or religious. Local performances on a minor scale are open to any tribesman and every tribesman who wishes to attend.

On the adjoining diagram is shown the structure of the tribe as a cultural unit, the tribe-nation. The tribe-nation thus is the widest group which exercises the same culture conjointly. It is a system of inter-related, interdependent institutions, each one enjoying a high degree of autonomy, but all

Tribe-Nation Diagram
(The Tribe as a Cultural Unit)

Provinces

Local Groups

Tribe

Magical & Religious Congregations

Age-Grades & Stratification by Rank

Family and Domestic Groups

Organized Economic Pursuit Groups

Clans

Extended Kinship Groups

united when an enterprise on a larger scale is undertaken. The tribesmen are able to co-operate, to interchange services and goods, and to communicate with each other. This is possible because united by the same culture they use the same tools and goods, they have the same habits and customs and, most important of all, they speak the same language. This also means that the whole body of tradition, of customary law, of religious and social values, is common to all the tribesmen. The tribe-nation is the real carrier of culture and the guardian of traditional values. The unity and cohesion of such a tribe consists in the homogeneity of its culture. The tribesmen are bound by the same system of customs, and since custom is king, the tribal realm extends as far as the writ of king-custom runs.

Each tribe in short has its own way of life, that is, its own nationality. I have called this form of tribal unity or integration the tribe-nation, because it is necessary to recognize the concept of nationhood as the cultural principle of integration, in contra-distinction to the political principle on which the tribe-state is founded. The tribe-nation is thus the prototype of what we define today as the nation, that is, a large group unified by a common language, a common tradition and a common culture. Nation-hood is thus a primeval and fundamental fact in human evolution.

We can therefore define nationhood as Unity of Culture, cul-ture being the way of life of the nation, with its ideals, traditions and language. Cultural unity however goes deeper than this and embraces the whole range of day-by-day contacts in family life, friendship, social intercourse, recreations, institutions and schools. It includes also the national concepts of freedom, justice, efficiency, honor and values. Sub-nations, with their regional cul-tures, are in one way the bedrock of nationhood. The creative side of nationhood lies in the activity of the nation as a workshop of culture and progress.

The national differentiation of primitive humanity has probably been the main creative force of progress. Each tribe was working on its way of life, on its religion, and on its economic development with a considerable measure of peace and tranquillity. Yet the diversity of cultures achieved by this national independence of our primitive ancestors was a creative element. The protective isolation of primitive tribes was never an absolute isolation. Through trade, through occasional contacts along the frontiers, the achievements of civilization would cross the dividing bar and thus cross-fertilize, stimulate and lead to greater things. We can speak of primitive nations which were the real workshops in the creation, in the maintenance and in the transmission of cultures. We can also speak of the dynamic element in early civilization which resulted from contacts, impacts, and clashes between the early nations.

The breakdown of the cultural machinery would imply at least gradual extinction. This is clear when we look at the evidence of historical facts. A serious breakdown in the economic, political or legal order, which usually also implies deterioration in the systems of knowledge and ethics, leads human groups to disorganization and to the sinking of the cultural level. The breakdown of many simpler cultures under the impact of western civilization and the extinction of many racial groups supply one example. The ever-recurrent decay of once flourishing cultures, which are then replaced by others, or else enter a period of Dark Ages, is another case in point. Even today we are faced with a serious threat to culture, that of total war, which is waged not merely in terms of destruction and physical aggression, but also as economic war against the systems of production and, above all, of nutritive maintenance. Through propaganda, it aims at the breaking down of moral and social resistance through the sapping of the constitutional principles of organization, both as regards defense and the normal working of institutions.

The exercise of culture and the continuity of tradition have been throughout the long ages of human development, and are still, the work of that group which we call the tribe-nation, through its autonomous decentralized institutions. The value of this institutional diversity and autonomy and the varying educational influences of such groups as the family, the municipality, the church, and the guild of craftsmen, is obvious. It has created a diversity of groupings, a multiplicity of social ties, and it has led human development to create individuals who acquire their skills, their intelligence and their civic attitudes through the association with these groups, with whom they were co-operating for the continuity of civilization. The tribe-nation or nation therefore is essentially democratic in its constitution; indeed, it is inevitably democratic.

By reason of the multiplicity of institutions, and hence also of differential seats of authority, the tribe-nation implies a variety of systems of influencing the individual. Democracy therefore is to be found in the community, in the relations of institutions and within each institution. Humanity thus achieved its earliest, most heroic and most fundamental development under a regime of proto-democracy. Freedom, as the scope for group and personal self-determination, flourishes among primitives and flourished at the beginnings of culture.

We see therefore that the tribe-nation or nation is the very instrument of freedom, constituted as it is for the peaceful exercise of culture. This point is of great importance to us in our analysis of freedom. Throughout the development of humanity, there have always existed two principles of integration or unification: the principle of unification by national culture, embodied in the tribe-nation or nation; and that of unification by political force, embodied in the tribe-state or state. This fact has been observed by anthropologists, both in evolutionary times and throughout history. The two principles are not independent; they are closely related and mutually subordinated in a free culture. But they are very far from being identical, and are not co-extensive. They are two different mechanisms, each of which has its own system of instrumentalities, social organization, ideas, sentiments and values.

From the outset, the national cultural unit has worked for production, construction and creating; it is inevitably democratic and is the real source of freedom. The real carriers of culture from the beginning of evolution right up to our times are the nations, or the culturally unified peoples of the world, defining nation as a culturally homogeneous group unified by a common language, tradition and organization. The distinction between tribe-nation and tribe-state is important for us because the principle of nationhood is bound up essentially with the normal, peaceful, and hence also free exercise of culture. The tribe-state we define as the unit based on political force as the integrating principle, with a centralized authority and the corresponding organization of armed force. Political force as the integrating principle is associated with all the manifestations of servitude and bondage, when the political organization engages in one of its functions, that is, war.

In order to substantiate these statements let us survey, in evolutionary perspective, the formation and the development of statehood, that is, of the political principle in human organization. In its simplest and crudest definition, the political principle always means the use of physical force as the executive backing of authority. We have defined political authority as the legally vested power to establish norms, to take decisions and to enforce them through the use of sanction by force.

The political principle has always been the use of the "big stick" in human relations. In this sense, as we have seen, political authority as embodied in institutions has existed probably from the very outset of human collaboration, albeit in a diffuse and diversified form. A number of families living together in the same local group are usually subject to the authority of the local chief or head man. When quarrels occur between the component households, or even when illegal acts of violence are perpetrated within a household, the authorities of the local group have as a rule the right to intervene. They can also use force in sanctioning their decisions. We can say therefore that the local group has a political over-right as regards its component parts, whether these be households, local teams, local age-grades or religious bodies. It is important to realize that at the level of development usually designated as "lowest savagery", the local group seems to be the widest unit with political prerogatives. In other words, it is autonomous as regards any interference from larger groups and it fulfills the only administrative, that is, co-ordinating functions between its component institutions; it is the only group which can use unchallenged force within. Again, most organized fighting at this level occurs either between clans within the local group or between local groups.

The beginnings of the tribe-state indeed probably took place through the formation of a local group within the tribe-nation, for the purpose of the co-ordination of institutional interests, policing, defense and aggression. This formation implied a centralized authority, the formation of a military group with possession of weapons, and above all, the development of a policy, which aimed at the gradual extension of political influ-

ence to other local groups—that is, the extension of the tribe-
state to the tribe-nation.

The formation of the tribe-state brought about the effective
abolition of internal discord, replacing internal feuds by the
decisions of organized authority; it was probably the result of a
long evolutionary process, through the working of internal forces
within the small groups in the tribe.

Thus, as we progress along the line of development, we find
that the instruments of political force are at times used to enlarge
the sphere of influence of one local community over others. A
careful scrutiny of the evidence referring to Melanesia and
Polynesia, for instance, indicates the probability of such a historical hypothesis. We find there conditions which are best in-
terpreted as statehood in the process of formation. The same
picture could be also substantiated from the political history of
the Maori of New Zealand, the Fijians, or the Samoans, or again
from the formation of political groups among the Bantu of southeastern Africa, or in the case of the League of the Iroquois.

In the Trobriand Islands we have a large cultural unit which
in 1914 numbered about eight thousand people. They were one
tribe in the cultural sense of the term. Politically, that is, as
regards the exercise of force and the administrative authority,
they are subdivided into numerous districts. In other words, the
tribe-nation in this area was composed of a number of tribe-states,
each one with its own centralized authority. Each had a capital,
that is, a village which exercised control over several of its
neighbors. The historical tradition ranging over several generations past indicated that such districts are the results of fights
between villages, and of a partial submission of several of these
to a stronger village, thus bringing about the formation of larger
political units or tribe-states. The fighting there occurred between
politically organized districts within the same culture. In times

of peace, all the natives of this archipelago were united by a number of cultural interrelations. During occasional outbreaks of war, there was a political recrystallization within the tribe. It would not be correct to say, however, that wars of conquest occurred at that stage. In other words, the victors did not annex the territory of the vanquished.

These facts have been adduced to show that cultural unity and political unification do not run parallel at the beginnings of human civilization. At times the cultural group, the tribe-nation, is wider than the political group, the tribe-state. At times again, where we find two or several cultures living under the same authority, we can say that the tribe-state embraces several tribe-nations. This refers invariably to higher stages of civilization. In the recent history of Europe we can find examples of the overlapping of these principles. Switzerland is a political entity embracing four nationalities: French, German, Italian and Romansch. The old Austro-Hungarian empire was a monarchy in which some fourteen or fifteen nationalities were federated. On the other hand, Italy was divided and partly subjected to foreign rule until its unification in 1870. Poland is a nation which for one hundred and twenty years was partitioned among three large states: Germany, Austria and Russia. Germany before 1918 is an example of the united nation-state, for it consisted of one nation and one empire which was a federation of some twenty-three component states. Before 1871, it was a nation divided into states.

When the political control extends to the boundaries of the cultural unit, the tribe-state and tribe-nation coincide, and form a primitive tribal nation-state. In the long run, inter-tribal fighting would probably have led to the unification of a whole tribe into one political unit. These facts show that the two principles of nationhood and statehood are independent of each other in their beginnings and during a long stage of evolution; it also shows that the tendency towards an overlapping of these two principles is inherent in the cultural character of a tribe-nation and in that function of the state which we define as protective isolation.

The natural unit of collaboration and interchange in goods, ideas, and services is the unified cultural group, that is, the nation, primitive or developed. When the boundaries of centralized administration, policing, and isolating protection which are provided by the state, primitive or civilized, are extended to the limits of one culture, so that the tribe-state and tribe-nation coincide, this adds substantially to the working of the culture as a whole and produces no inherent conflicts. The tribe-nation, by being organized into a tribe-state, is better protected against outside disturbances; while the strongest tribe-state is the one which coincides with the tribe-nation, for the political organization is based on a more solid foundation when it embraces a group who are united by the exercise of a single culture. When tribe-state and tribe-nation thus coincide to form the nation-state, we find that the same legal principles can be applied within the same domain of linguistic, traditional, religious and customary unity. The co-operation of the group is facilitated through possession of one economic system and one type of military equipment.

When a nation is divided into political sub-divisions which fight against each other, we find a process which always contributes towards the attrition of a group of culture carriers and which, pushed beyond certain quantitative limits, would lead to the extinction of the whole group, hence of its culture. Intra-tribal fighting however occurs usually on a small scale in highly conventionalized and regulated forms, and does not generally approach a quantitatively disruptive limit.

The distinct nature of the two principles, the tribe-state and the tribe-nation, is as essential for the appreciation of the political and cultural troubles of the modern world as it is important for the understanding of the nature of democracy and of freedom. For it is the freedom of nationhood and the oppression of nationalities which since the French Revolution has been the dominant principle of political unrest, agitation, and warfare in our western world. All our contemporary political problems of nationalism, imperialism, the status of minorities and of irredentist groups are covered by the principle of national self-determination. These problems obviously hinge on the relation between nation and state. We see now in the present world events the same divergence of function on a gigantic scale. We are witnessing the last great struggle of culture versus force, and the severest blow by force to civilization. Culture must be protected from force and must tame force, for culture also produces force.

4

The State, Arbiter or Aggressor

THE political aspect of human culture has been defined as that use of physical force which is accepted by a group or community as a part of its institutional order. The words "politics", "government" and "the state" have in our thinking and talking almost a magical virtue. The state is a reality which rouses in men the responses of awe and abhorrence, of holiness and hate, of reverence and contempt respectively. Most historians up to the present time have chosen the state and its affairs as the main theme of their interests, praise and abuse. While the philosophers from Plato to Hegel regarded the state as a God-like reality, others, the anarchists and nihilists, regard it as an evil spirit.

The omnipotence, the omniscience and the ubiquity of the state is implied in all those arguments which blame the state for all evils or praise it for all the good which humanity has enjoyed. Recently, socialism came once more to regard the state as a vehicle of omni-competence in economic matters. The totalitarians unashamedly proclaim the divinity of the state, incarnate in the person of the leader. This however is not so much of an invention, since any reader of Frazer's *Golden Bough* can find

for himself that the divinity of early chiefs and kings has been
the normal doctrine of all barbarians.

In reality, the state and government are one among many
institutions. The fundamental difference, however, which contributes to all the mystic attitudes towards the state is that it is
the only historic institution which has the monopoly of force. This
is the main source of all our present-day troubles. Statesmanship
nowadays does not seem to have been divine either in foresight
or in knowledge or in any form of preventive wisdom. Totalitarian
statesmanship has brought us back to the combination of the
crudest mysticism, such as would be repugnant even to cannibals
or head-hunters, with the most refined technique in the use of
violence such as might bring us once more into the dark ages of a
new savagery. Democratic statesmanship failed to realize that if
other states are allowed to grow almost omnipotent in brute
physical force and in doctrines of aggression, one must oneself
prepare or else use force at the right moment to prevent the
preparedness of others. Even this, however, would not be wisdom
enough. Democratic statesmanship ought to have recognized long
ago that starting from a surrender of its own sovereignty, it must
compel all others to follow suit, and to create a superstate with
a monopoly of armed force. Such a superstate could not be
tyrannical, for tyranny is bred only and exclusively by preparedness for war, threats and the possibility of carrying them out.

The birth of the tribe-state is the danger signal in the history
of humanity, for with it occurred the birth of militarism. The
tribe-nation as we have already seen is the unit of cultural co-
operation, and must not be confused with the tribe-state, which is
the political unit, based on centralized authoritative power and
the organization of armed force. The tribe-state in its earliest
forms was a small executive committee of the group, with arms,

political organization and a military class as instruments of power.

Insofar as the armed band was there to enforce the decisions of the council, we find the beginnings of a police force within the group. Again, since such armed bands would protect the group to which they belong and occasionally attack other groups, we see the beginnings of the military function of such a miniature state. We can assume that in the course of ages or aeons the politically formless hordes or agglomerates of groups, in which resort was made to more or less regulated violence, developed into groups where an executive committee—a tribal council of elders, a chief and his councillors, an assembly of local headmen —was formed, a committee which could lay down rules of conduct or interpret the traditional ones, which had the right to frame decisions and enforce them by physical coercion. Thus politics or statehood in the socially relevant form were born out of earlier forms of violence.

In a primitive tribe-state the chief or tribal council perform a rudimentary administrative role and act as the moderating factor. They interpret tribal law, prevent conflicts or precipitate their solution. Such political organization can, at the stage when there is some armed force centrally manipulated, act as protector of the whole tribe. It can act also as aggressor. The existence of such a centralized authority at primitive levels however never supersedes or displaces the differential authority within the component institutions.

The primitive state is not tyrannical to its own subjects for two reasons. First and foremost, we know that a primitive tribe is always a body of people related by bonds of kinship and relationship, by clanship and age-grade. The initial dependence of its members and the power of the component institutions is considerable and it does not allow of any serious encroachments upon institutional autonomy. The second reason is that the instruments of coercion are still very rudimentary, and that neither physical force, nor the dependence upon wealth can lead to actual bondage. At this stage also, there are no instruments of propaganda. Politics in human evolution start when hunting spears are sharpened into weapons of aggression and defense; when the bow, the arrow, the shield and military formation are developed; when the hunting band is organized into a military band and submitted to the authority of the tribal council transformed into an administrative unit.

The tribe-state at its beginnings and throughout history has three main functions; its power is used to establish the equipoise, the golden mean, between the various groups, institutions and interests within the nation or tribe-nation. The second function is that of policing and enforcing law and order within. The third function is defense and aggression. Later in evolution we find the rare and small incidence of war in primitive humanity. As long as these three functions are well-balanced, the state maintains its protecting and isolating role. In external policy this role is associated with defense and not with aggression; but human history and evolution demonstrate that aggression occurs, that there are whole periods where power politics dominate tribal or national existence, when spears are used for fighting and not for hunting which, translated into modern terms, means that guns are preferred to butter.

The state throughout history and in our modern times is the politically organized institution which controls the territory within its boundaries in the administrative, legal and coercive sense. The element of politically organized authority must enter into any competent definition of a sovereign administrative unit, that is, a state. By sovereignty we mean monopoly of organized force, where the use of violence is not controlled by any other authority. We do not find even the vestiges of such centralized political authority in the primitive tribe.

The state in its primitive or developed form is but one among many of its institutions. It is the only institution which has a monopoly of force. Insofar as it remains true to its primary function as arbiter, as moderator, as an agency for balancing and adjusting institutional interests, it is an essential prerequisite of freedom. The state, in short, in which new laws are framed or old customs made legal; in which an independent judiciary administers such laws without any extraneous pressures; in which family life, the school, the economic activities are controlled but not dictated, a state of such a type is a fountainhead of freedom. Freedom also depends on the degree to which the various institutions assist the individual and accept him, and also reward him for his contribution. It is only at high levels of development when the state assumes the command of effective force and armed force that we can say that freedom becomes almost exclusively a political problem. We see therefore that the state in certain of its forms becomes the best guarantor of freedom, and in others the worst enemy.

The state is a dynamic factor in civilization. The essence of statehood, that is, of political organization, lies in submission to pooled force, so as to achieve harmony and security. Herein lies the positive, constructive function of the state. Harmony within is achieved through execution of the law by means of police, coordination between individuals and institutions, and organization of security through defense. The state thus acts as an executive organ, with the function of protective isolation. In this role it is essentially peaceful in character.

The state however can also function destructively, when it begins to desire more power, and implements this desire by aggression against other states or nations. In primitive cultures we see the earliest development of aggression when tribal elders or councils decide upon a policy of aggression.

It is evident therefore that we must distinguish clearly between the two phases in the development of the state: the state as protector of its own culture, which produces normal peaceful conditions and gives freedom; and the state as mobilizer of its nation for aggressive action, which occurs through the development of power politics, and which results in the abrogation of freedom. This latter type of state, which organizes its own armed bands, regiments and cohorts by strict discipline and which thrives by military success, with taxation of men and wealth for military purposes and for efficiency in war, is a state whose constitution is based on hierarchy, submission and discipline. Preparedness, mobilization and striking power are of the greatest value to the state which lives on war, where the recognition of and desire for military virtue and soldierlike discipline are indispensable to success. The constitution of such a state is throughout based on an abuse of freedom. All negations of freedom come from a monopoly of the constitution of the state. For our analysis has shown that once the influence of violence and brute force predominates and is allowed to organize, there are chronic dangers to freedom.

The political history of mankind begins with the organization of military institutions within territorial groups, and with fighting between groups which do not submit to the rulings of the same tribal law and custom. The political function of early fighting is found in the formation of tribe-nations into tribe-states. We must not forget that the full military efficiency of even a primitive tribe depends on at least a partial control of its manpower, of its mobilization of man by force and its mobilization of wealth and weapons. It is only when wars begin and when political power becomes more important than the exercise of culture that we have the development of such phenomena as slavery, serfdom and caste systems.

Once a group has acquired military power and extended its sphere of influence to the boundaries of its culture, it seldom stops there, unless the culture is isolated on an island or by some other ecological barriers. Ethnographic evidence and history alike demonstrate that the united nation-state often embarks directly after its unification on a career of external wars. Here we meet for the first time in human development a new type of fighting, between two different cultures rather than between sections of the same culture. This I submit affects profoundly the significance of war in its influence upon civilization and its advancement. Both types are wars of history. The process of political unification however lacks one important ingredient of genuine war: its intertribal or international character. Only when aggressive or defensive military operations occur along the boundary of two cultures, that is, two nations, does fighting become an instrument of international rather than of internal policy, with a difference as regards political function and cultural results. The earlier fighting is related to civil war rather than full-fledged military warfare.

It is at this point in our argument that we are able to formulate the distinction between the legitimate claims of nationhood and the aggressive impositions of nationalism or imperialism. I mean the fact that a nation is in its very essence constituted in terms of cultural democracy, and is intrinsically democratic, pacific and libertarian. The nation therefore is actually related to both peace and freedom, in virtue of its democratic constitution. The state on the other hand is essentially different from the nation; and this difference is due to the fact that violence is an attribute of the state. The real origins of political organization are to be found in the fact that power is inevitably a part of any organized life, and that the sources of power are to be found in violence.

It is only the state which under certain conditions can, and under others is obliged, to abrogate or destroy the democratic methods by the use of excessive violence, through mobilization, control and discipline, always under the pressure of militaristic aims or as an aftermath of war. In a democratic culture, the state functions as guarantor of peace, as arbiter in internal disputes and as controller. We shall see that slavery and national oppression are invariably dependent upon and fomented by warfare. We shall also see—and here comes the moral implication of our argument—that war, collective hatred, and even oppression never come into action as between nations. The guilty party in all such transactions is invariably the state. This is not a paradox; it is rather a truism. For no nation as such, no nation as a whole, has ever in evolution or history been completely identified with an armed camp. Nor yet have the interests of one nation as a cultural agent ever been at variance with those of another. Only when a state, primitive or otherwise, mobilizes part of its resources for conquest and political expansion, which usually also implies economic exploitation, are such phenomena as war, slavery, oppression, and tyranny not only possible but as a rule inevitable.

Let us here define nationalism in terms borrowed from the widest experience of mankind, from its evolution and its history. Nationalism is the mobilization of the nation by the state for aggression and conquest. Nationalism means therefore the temporary transformation of a group who live for culture, and who peacefully and constructively exercise their own way of life as a nation, into an armed and aggressive instrument of power bent on conquest.

Nationalism today is one of the main curses of humanity.

Indeed, Mr. Hitler has labelled his own regime "National-Socialism", combining thus the principles of socialism and nationalism into the hodgepodge of racial doctrine, the principle of might is right and the enslavement of humanity for the benefit of his master nation. Nationalism indeed in some of its forms is one of the most pernicious tendencies of our present world. Yet nationalism as the legitimate aspiration to cultural independence is based on realities of human life as old as mankind and as fundamental.

It is only when the cultural forces of nationhood, that is, of cultural unity, become activated by the political principle of the state that danger arises. Nationhood in its essence is the "way of life" of a cultural group; the mode of conducting affairs; the body of their traditional values, customs, habits and social organization. There is nothing aggressive or destructive in the nation itself. Nor is there or ever has been any possible clash of interest between people living within their own boundaries and carrying on the business of their existence, as they have been made to by tradition, and as they like it. Only when the state, which is an institution like any other, but one based upon violence, is able to mobilize the cultural forces of the national unit and turn them into an instrument of aggression, can the nation, transformed into a political state, become a menace to all its neighbors.

The growth of a nationalistic policy therefore is one of the danger signals in history, since it later results in the preparation of crisis and war, and in the abrogation of freedom. We must therefore distinguish clearly between nationhood and nationalism.

Let us sum up briefly the principles of nationhood. Humanity from the very beginning is divided into units whose cohesion is determined by the fact that they exercise and maintain the same culture. At any time in human evolution it would be possible to

draw such national boundaries between the culturally differentiated portions of humanity. The development of culture does
not follow one single route. Humanity does not consist of one
culture which evolves, but of a large number of independent
cultures each working out its destiny. These cultures occasionally
come into contact, and the lease-lend system which anthropologists call diffusion must have played a considerable part in
the progress of mankind. The fact, however, that at the beginnings
of the last century whole continents were peopled by groups
differentiated not only by culture, but also by the level of development is proof that diffusion is not omnipotent.

Indeed, nationhood as we find it today and within the region
of western, mechanized civilization, is fundamentally the same
as nationhood at the level of unpolished stone. In Europe for instance we still find people separated by language, tradition, and
differences in custom, habit, taste and temperament. Today these
nations, equipped with unprecedented instruments of mobilization, concentration of wealth, and also with instruments of indoctrination and of violence, are carrying out a gigantic war,
mainly determined by aggressive nationalism. At the same
time and independently of any such nationalistic policies, the
same civilization which has given us the weapons of hatred and
the weapons of destruction has imposed on all branches of
humanity a number of common interests. It has also made diffusion, that is, the interpenetration of cultures, not merely a
matter of choice but a matter of necessity. Everywhere and insofar as economic resources allow, human beings can and do pur-
chase their goods on a world market. The advantages of western
civilization supply not only missionary services, education and
literature; they also implant habits of cleanliness and hygiene,
and they prevent native populations from the development of
certain vices from which we ourselves have to abstain, such as

the use of morphine and cocaine and also of certain excesses such as alcohol from which we ourselves abstain only occasionally and fitfully.

While therefore humanity is still divided by national barriers which, if separated from political instrumentalities, would do no harm to anyone, it is united in its fundamental interests of common security, prosperity, hygiene and the prevention of crime and disease, and in the spread of scientific knowledge, and of elementary legal and ethical principles.

We can therefore formulate the basic principles of post-war reconstruction or, better perhaps, the ideal towards which the future construction of humanity, political, economic and cultural must move, albeit gradually. The fullest cultural autonomy must be granted to all nationalities, races and other minorities. Political sovereignty must never be associated with nationhood, since this produces the dangerous explosive of nationalism. Indeed, political power, insofar as it is centralized, must be vested in a hierarchy of federal units. Starting from local autonomy, it must proceed through administrative provinces, states and regional federations to a world-wide superstate.

We claim therefore full national sovereignty for each cultural group. Each such group is entitled to the complete exercise of all the rights and privileges of nationhood. Live as you like, do what you want according to your own way of life, to the traditions, customs and habits inherited from your ancestors. Such liberty has no dangers to it. The only liberty which must be curtailed politically, that is, by centralized force, is the liberty of attacking others, of meddling with the affairs of neighbors and of imposing ethnocentric egoisms upon the outside world.

There is one more generalization to be stated. We have seen that the two principles of organization, that for peace and that for war, are largely independent. The peaceful phase and aspect of culture is embodied in the nation. The nation is the carrier of the culture. Nationhood as such is therefore synonymous with freedom. We can here take up our previous argument in which it was shown that freedom enters substantially into the maintenance and exercise of primitive cultures. As humanity advances, its need of freedom in cultural concerns increases rather than diminishes. At the higher stages of preliterate humanity, the need of mobilizing large numbers of culture carriers is still there. The placing of specialized and difficult activities in the hands of those best suited for them is as imperative as before. The higher the level of culture, the more this need obtains, hence the freedom of culture to one and all must exist.

When we come to cultures where the art of reading and writing allows culture to be embodied into durable documents and archives, the need of maintenance is less. The need of creative change is greater. Under such conditions, it is even more important to mobilize talent, to foster initiative, inspiration and criticism. Monopolies of education decrease, while teaching and access to learning become gradually universal. Talent again cannot be expressed by mere learning. It demands some scope for action, that is, access to the means of research, of craft, of production and of management. Once more, reward by participation in cultural benefits is the only means of enlisting the full loyalties of the individual. Neither talent nor inspiration nor intelligence will produce anything useful to humanity if contributions of value are penalized instead of being rewarded.

5

War Throughout the Ages

THE real difference between free cultures and cultures pervaded by the principle of servitude and bondage is determined by whether they are constituted for the avoidance of crises, their prevention, and their alleviation; or whether their charter aims at the preparation of crises. Such latter communities at times thrive through such self-prepared crises, and use them as the means to the end of establishing more power for the rulers through discipline, bondage and slavery.

There is only one type of crisis which, starting late in evolution, has lasted throughout recorded historical times and has now plunged humanity into the worst universal calamity ever known. This is war.

Humanity has never been able to produce earthquakes and droughts, volcanic eruptions and floods. Nor has it been able to eliminate them. As much as foresight, prevention, and organized resistance can do, civilization helps man in dealing with natural disasters. We also attempt to prevent accidents—although our modern worship of speed is contributing more than any other factor towards that scourge. We have gone far on the road of prevention as regards epidemics, infection, malnutrition and other organic calamity.

War and war alone among all human activities is the principle of the collective abrogation of law and of the substitution of organized crime. War, and all that goes with it in preparedness and aftermath, establishes conditions under which brute force becomes the final argument, the final determinant, of all human motives, resources, and endeavors. War therefore brings about the imposition of effectiveness by violence; the preparation of violence and the establishment of violence as morally right; and the implementation and organization for violence. We can therefore lay down the general principle that the serious and large-scale abrogations of freedom occur through war and for war.

The anthropologist is in a position to trace the phenomena of human strife and fighting throughout the ages; from the beginnings of civilization to that new type of savagery against which we are now fighting in the hope of abolishing war forever. War can only be defined as an armed contest between two independent political units carried out by means of organized military force in the pursuit of a tribal or national policy. This definition makes a clear distinction between genuine political and organized warfare, and other types of fighting not relevant politically or historically. With this definition in hand, we shall be able to see that war is one of the most destructive elements in human civilization, and has played but a small constructive and creative part in the history of culture. As an instrument of tribal and national policy, war has had an important, but short-lived span of real significance and effectiveness in human evolution.

Let me start with the lowest primitives, the living representatives of archaic man. The various pygmy tribes of Africa and Indonesia, the Negritos, the Firelanders, the Veddahs of Ceylon belong to this category. Such primitives live in small groups, roaming over a definite territory. Most of the time they are hard at work searching for food, producing their simple commodities; trying, in short, to eke out their existence from the meager supplies of their environment. Occasionally they foregather to debate, to hunt, to amuse themselves. These people have no centralized authority, nor any tribal policies. Consequently, they have no military force, no militia, no police; and they do not fight as between one tribe and another. Personal injuries are avenged by stealthy attacks on individuals, or by hand to hand fighting. The Australian Aborigines have an institution resembling a regulated duel. In other tribes anger and resentment lead to acts of sorcery and witchcraft. Thus we do not find among these lowest primitives any organized clash of armed forces aiming at the enforcement of tribal policy. War does not exist among them.

One or two important conclusions can be drawn. If war were really due to an innate biological urge, it would certainly occur at the earliest stages of development. For at these stages the biological needs of man are most clearly manifested in an outspoken undisguised manner. Such biological forces as hunger, sex appetite, even individual or personal pugnacity, manifest themselves most definitely at this stage. But pugnacity, as a natural reaction of anger, is directed only towards the individual guilty of violence or malice. It does not engender any collective organized fighting.

The simplest analysis of human behavior shows that aggression or pugnacity is a derived impulse. It arises from the thwarting of one of the basic physiological drives, or else from interference with culturally determined interests, appetites or desires. When sex, hunger, ambition or wealth are threatened, aggression occurs. Culture is an adaptive instrumentality which transforms and redefines even such biological imperatives as sex, hunger or the need of protection. The derived impulse of aggression is even more subject to redefinition in an infinite variety of ways. Human beings fight, not because they are biologically impelled, but because they are culturally induced, by trophies as in head-hunting, by wealth as in looting, by revenge as in primitive wars.

The ethnographer has first to register a striking fact. Aggressiveness, like charity, begins at home. At the lowest levels, we find quarrels, brawls and fighting only and exclusively among members of small, institutionally organized groups. The closer the bonds of co-operation, the greater the community of interests, the more opportunity there will be for disagreement, opposition, and hence, aggressiveness. At the same time, culture steps in at this point and produces an indispensable remedy by means of legally defined avoidance between strangers, or else by strictly determined rules of intertribal intercourse, which are typical of primitive foreign relations. If we insist that war is a fight between two independent and politically organized groups, war does not occur at a primitive level.

We see thus that there is a complete disjunction at the beginnings of human civilization between the psychological fact of aggression and the cultural fact of feuds and fights. The raw material of pugnacity certainly does exist. It is to be found primarily within the component institutions of every society. It is never a biologically determined link between an impulse of aggression and an act of organized violence.*

Hence war is not just fighting; it is not the direct expression of anger, the passion of violence, or man-to-man aggression. Fighting under the impulse of anger occurs at all levels of development in face-to-face relations, as the eternal argument by force. This aggressiveness is definitely tamed by the law of organized life.

* For a fuller analysis of pugnacity and aggressiveness, see my article, "An Anthropological Analysis of War," *American Journal of Sociology*, Vol. XLVI, No. 4, January 1941.

We conclude therefore that primitive man, past or present, never used fighting or combat as an instrument of intertribal policy. He never knew genuine war. He was not, however, without virility or even pugnacity. Thus we see that war is not the original or natural state of mankind.

When we move in our survey from the lowest primitives to a somewhat higher level, we are met by a complexity of forces and facts. We enter the world of real savagery. Here fighting is associated with cannibalism, head-hunting, human sacrifice or scalping.

War however is not a permanent state of affairs in any type of tribal culture. Even the most pugnacious head-hunters and cannibals do not live by and on fighting exclusively. They have first and foremost to solve their own problems of life, that is, produce, distribute and consume; maintain their numbers; perpetuate the forms of their organization; and pay respect to their tribal ghosts or divinities. The earliest intertribal fighting—and we must remember that this starts only at the end of the paleolithic or the beginnings of the neolithic stage—is only an occasional affair and occurs on a relatively small scale. We have therefore to register the two-phase principle of human evolution and history, even under conditions of greatest military intensity in culture. There are long periods of peaceful existence, and brief but acute crises of war. Even a tribe who live by military robbery, slave raiding and occasional conquest, have to allow their victims to replenish wealth, man-power and instrumentalities, or else war would cease to be profitable.

At the stage of polished stone, we find a number of tribes whose life does not differ essentially from that of the lowest primitives, except that they dispose of a more advanced material apparatus, are numerically stronger and are in possession of a more com-

plex social organization. In all such tribes we would find that
the same basic institutions, the family, the clan, the municipality
and economic, magical and ceremonial teams exist. We would
find among them some additional institutions related to the further development in arts and crafts and in food producing
activities. Voluntary associations such as secret societies and
men's clubs flourish and economic organizations, markets, trad-
ing expeditions and enterprises for the exploitation of the environment multiply.

Were we to visit a Papuan tribe, such as the Kiwai of Southern
New Guinea, or settle for a time among the Dyaks of Borneo, or
the Nagas of Assam, we would find that these people have a
whole set of values and interests which center round head-hunting. Among some tribes it is necessary to obtain the head of a
man, woman, or child from a neighboring community in order to
marry. Smoked or pickled heads of enemies are essential among
the Nagas for the carrying out of fertility rites in the agricultural
cycle. The head of a slain enemy represents among the Papuans
a valuable spiritual ally, who brings luck to the successful head-
hunter. The drives and motives for head-hunting are to be found
in very complicated and conventional systems of value, belief and
sociological symbolism. As regards any political or cultural constructiveness, such combats have no elements of statesmanship
nor creativeness. Economically, such fighting is as barren as our
modern wars have become. The head-hunters and cannibals cannot loot because there is no portable or accumulated wealth at
that stage. We at the present level of our civilization, on the
other hand, are unable any more to loot effectively.

The fights and raids of head-hunters and cannibals cannot, in
short, be regarded as real war. They lack the most important element of genuine warfare, the use of military power for the

attainment of some tribal or national goals. War begins only when some definite fruits of victory are garnered after military action.

War, however, is a cultural and political reality. In following human development, the anthropologist can show the stage at which genuine war comes into existence. War begins when local groups or regions within the same cultural unit fight for the establishment of political control. This type of warfare leads to the formation of the earliest forms of political state. Only at a much higher level do wars between two culturally differentiated groups occur, in which one exploits the other occasionally and establishes permanent political rule over those conquered. This last type introduces real war, that is, fighting as an instrument of policy between two tribe-states. War therefore begins when two independent groups fight each other with the motive of tribal enmity and with the purpose of tribal policy. Conquest, as the incorporation of one country, one tribe or one political system into another, makes war significant and profitable. Thus we can say that two elements differentiate the various forms of armed contest as this is found in human evolution; first of all, the cultural relationship between the combatants; and secondly, the integral result of victory, according to whether this leads merely to temporary exploitation or to permanent conquest.

We must here recognize war as the chartered license to engage in all criminal acts, that is, acts which would be considered criminal in times of peace and within a well-ordered community. War is the use of collective, purposive violence with the aim of imposing the rule of one political unit on another; yet history and human evolution have cried aloud the freedom of war as one of the prerogatives of independent political organizations. Indeed some contemporary writers in Nazi Germany and elsewhere try to teach us that the freedom of war is one of the inalienable rights of man.

The problem is real but it is not insoluble. Two tribes, two nations, or two states at war do not constitute an ordered community. There is as yet no criminal law which applies to that grouping which we could define as two political units engaging in a fight. Looking back in human history, we can see that here once more the collective activity of nations at war has to be analyzed with reference to the purpose, the acts of violence, and the results. As regards the acts, it is clear that war is as much a collective crime when it comes to nations, as murder is an individual crime when it comes to individuals. Again, as murder is at times an act of justice, as in vendetta or a judicial execution, so war can be an act of collective vengeance by one political unit over another. It is always a cultural catastrophe when the freedom of violence is supreme, and the concept of an ordered, co-operating community is absent.

The organization of violence, economic, physical and spiritual, has led to innumerable wars: wars of class, wars of ideas, and wars of loot. We can formulate the principle that the power of the state increases in crises of disorder, of revolution, of dangerous wars, and of conquest. All such historical crises either lead to cultural reconstruction, in which the state again renounces some of its powers, and resumes its role of protective isolation, when the institutional organizations come again to the fore. Or else the state retains its power, and continues on a course of conquest which plunges humanity into a long period of international anarchy and dark ages.

War in its essence is also an institution, that is, war occurs only when a group of people unite on the charter of collective aggression against another group; when they accept a doctrine of value for which they fight; when they are fitted out with the material apparatus of weapons of offense and defense; and when in this they follow the rules of tactics and strategy. The purpose or charter of a military band or army is therefore killing, destruction, and paralyzing the enemy by means of propaganda. These give all the possible advantages which can be obtained by war: scalps, heads, cadavers and trophies, slavery, wealth and conquest. War thus teaches that the sanction of force is the means of obtaining definite results and also of the integral control of the vanquished and disarmed community, tribe or nation. Let us keep in mind that war is a crisis made by man and directed against man. The advantage of one, as has been already argued, means in the contest of war the misfortune of the other.

The charter of war from its very beginnings is founded on a basically discriminative conception between friend and foe as regards their essentially human rights. The primitive always considers that only he, himself, and his tribesmen are men. The others fall outside the scope of legitimate humanity. Linguistically, the word "man" is generally used for the tribe, and another word with an evil connotation applied to those outside. This even in our own language adheres to such words as "alien", "stranger", "foreigner". When war breaks out the word "alien" becomes synonymous with enemy and is used as a euphemism.

This discriminative principle enters into the charter of earliest warfare. The alien, that is, the enemy, becomes something outside the scope of humanity, and for him the laws which apply to the tribesmen are not valid. He becomes an animal fit to be killed as in hunting, to be eaten in a cannibal repast, to be deprived of his head or scalp or some other portion of anatomy which will be turned into a trophy. Later on in evolution when slavery becomes profitable, or when conquest can be implemented, the enemy population or those parts which are not killed, are often transformed into slaves, that is, men without human rights.

The charter of war and the charter of slavery are essentially cognate in principle. They are also related in actual occurrence. Slavery without war hardly ever occurs in human cultures. War without slavery would have been unprofitable and anomalous at a certain stage of development and might have died of inanition.

The common charter of both institutions is the doctrine that a relationship between two human beings or groups can be based on the abrogation of all human rights of one for the benefit of the other. This principle changes the foe into a non-human object fit for killing and destruction during the fight. After victory it changes him into an object to be used as the means for the master's ends.

In all activities of war and in the preparedness for it we find this charter "indoctrinated" into the minds of the military group. A tribe of warlike savages claims the intrinsic right of being the natural masters of their neighbors by virtue of superior force. They are taught and disciplined into a belief of invincibility, as well as of racial superiority. This is also accompanied by the indoctrination of unquestioning obedience to the leader and the belief in his magical or supernatural powers. Against the background of such convictions the military band are then instructed in the art of tactics and of killing, as well as in the practice of cruelty and destruction. A parallel between spiritual preparedness for war among cannibals and head-hunters, on the one side, and our modern totalitarian savages, on the other, would not be difficult to draw. The principle of "frightfulness" is also not new. Stone age savages even have magical devices to intimidate the enemy; they use war paint, drums, and other forms of noisy frightfulness.

The main activities of war, killing, destruction, paralyzing intimidation, rape and robbery, correspond strictly to the main principle of the war charter. War is the reversal of the normal constructive rules of human co-operation. Acts which are proscribed as criminal under normal conditions and within the tribe, become military virtues during war. In its preparation and in its execution, war consists in the reversal of most of the principles of human law and ethics.

The first really effective advantage derived by the conqueror from intertribal fighting is associated with an economic phenomenon as important in human evolution, as it is significant in the present argument. I mean the institution of slavery. Human material was, perhaps, the first type of wealth to be effectively looted. But it became of value only with a sufficient advancement in the arts of production. It is no good owning a hundred slaves, if these hundred slaves can produce nothing more but enough food to feed a hundred mouths. But the moment the food producing industries develop sufficiently, or additional arts and crafts make it possible to transform the food surplus into capital wealth, slavery becomes profitable.

Thus in the course of evolution, war becomes really profitable when it combines loot, slavery, territorial occupation and increase in political power. This is the war of conquest. We can define a war of conquest as one which takes place across a national boundary, when one nation, that is, one culture, overpowers another. As soon as conquest is possible, it becomes in the evolutionary stages of human development a powerful factor in political reorganization and cultural progress. It is possible to give anthropological evidence of this, as well as ample historical documentation. Thus, for instance, in West Africa, certain primitive monarchies, the Ashanti, the Dahomey, the Yoruba, came into being through the conquest of sedentary agricultural communities by powerful military nomads. In Eastern Africa, again, we still have a number of kingdoms where a clear stratification demonstrates that a powerful group of Hamites conquered a territory, organized it in a political and military sense, and continued to live on the wealth of the conquered. From the American continent we could quote the famous League of the Iroquois, as well as the monarchies of Mexico and Peru. History and archaeology furnish us with an unlimited wealth of examples.

What are the evolutionary conditions and prerequisites of conquest? We have to consider on the one hand, the appearance of economic efficiency in the production of wealth; and on the other, the military and political arts. The first is usually associated with agriculture and the beginnings of industry; the second, with cattle raising and the nomadic pastoral mode of life. The development of wealth and industry is favored by a benign and fertile environment. Economic virtues and efficiency develop in the large alluvial valleys, such as the Ganges, Euphrates, and the Nile. They also develop in well-favored parts of tropical and semi-tropical habitats. The desert and the steppe furnish conditions suitable for pastoralism and military efficiency. From the highlands and steppes hordes of conquerors descend into the fertile regions of the world, and occupy and organize the wealthy sedentary people. Under such conditions, war with a purpose, war as a profession, war leading to constructive conquest makes full entry on the evolutionary stage. Together with the conditions necessary for the phenomenon of war, we find also the development of a new technique of fighting, open attack and defense, entailing the virtues of military discipline and bravery. War ceases to be merely a cultural freak or disease, and becomes something with a consequence, a purpose, and a meaning. War always remains a destructive, cruel, and demoralizing mechanism, but it occasionally is also an effective and creative factor in cultural evolution.

Military conquest at certain evolutionary stages has given

rise to the early monarchies and commonwealths and it has been active in the creation of a whole range of military states. The creative contribution of military conquest has brought about the cross fertilization of cultures and the establishment of fuller political, administrative and legal efficiency. When a warlike, aggressive, nomadic population occupies the territory of sedentary agricultural tribes, we often find that the emergent commonwealth possesses a much higher type of culture than either of its component parts.

Fusion by conquest usually occurs between two fundamentally different types of culture. It can be said that, on the whole, tribes and nations who have developed within a relatively harsh and unproductive habitat, such as steppes, deserts, and highlands, are forced through their fight with the environment to acquire individual characteristics of hardihood, determination, courage, and the social characteristics of a closely knit political organization.

Discipline, as we have argued already, is always related to strenuous and exacting conditions of life, in which the group has occasionally to mobilize for catastrophic emergencies, and usually to fight its way with but a scanty food supply, and little protection against climate and animal or human enemies. Peoples living under such conditions lead as a rule a nomadic existence. Through this they acquire the ability to mobilize rapidly, to move about easily and to be independent of handicaps through large installments of material wealth.

Agricultural communities, on the other hand, living under relatively favorable conditions, develop the qualities of good husbandry, high technique, the attachment to that piece of soil to which they become bound by the sweat and toil of generations, and the appreciation of wealth, in the form of cumulative food supply, heirlooms, and tokens of value. This type of existence immobilizes, differentiates and leads to collective and individual characteristics, where we find the discipline of hard work, and the interest in technique, in craftsmanship and in property rather than in military or political virtues. Looking at the globe, we find that it was the impact of hordes descending from the steppes of inner Asia and its high plateaus, from the desert portions of North Africa, or Arabia; and in the New World, from the mountainous regions in Mexico and Peru, or from the steppes of North America, which gave rise to conquest through their impact upon the sedentary matriarchal groups of agricultural workers. The invaders therefore supply the political structure, the legal supervision and the administrative services. The conquered are the mainstay of the economic order and of many arts and crafts, as well as some aspects of religion and custom.

Thus the main positive function of war is its unifying, cross-fertilizing effects and the creation of larger sized units, which thus have a greater scope for development. Conquest under such conditions leads to a natural division of functions within the larger unit. After fusion between the two groups we find a new culture, a new nation, and a new state. From one of its components this new entity receives the elements of military and political efficiency; from the other its economic qualities, its wealth and its technological development. The impact of two cultures and the process of fusion invariably promote the clearer formulation of both tribal systems of customary law. We would be safe in assuming that it is through conquest that the earliest systems of formulated codes, of established courts, and of organized police force were established. In economic organization also the conquerors, by establishing roads and communication, safeguarding safety, and policing the whole empire, stimulate commerce and the interchange of goods, the need of which is brought about by the divergence in the productive abilities of the two groups.

Religious and scientific ideas are exchanged and cross-fertilize each other.

We must emphasize that when war functions creatively, the centralized political organization resumes once more its positive role as protector of the people. It is in the measure that national or tribal unity, which is established by conquest, can show a higher cultural development and political, legal and administrative efficiency that conquest becomes of real evolutionary importance. In the general appraisal of the cultural effects of war, that is, its function in the widest connotation of this word, we can say that a war which in its results produces through conquest, federation, or amalgamation a wider cultural framework may play a constructive part in human evolution. In its results, therefore, it can create a wider scope for collective and individual freedom within the new culture or the new commonwealth through this abrogation of freedom.

The creative period of political conquest and cultural cross-fertilization belongs to the early stages of human development. As we have seen, war in the full cultural sense of this term has been absent from the longest and most important stage of human evolution: the ages during which humanity gradually had to emerge from its animal state, develop the beginnings of civilization, establish the principles of law and order, and discover the earliest arts and crafts. This stage probably covers some nine tenths of human evolution in time reckoning, and 99 per cent of the great and real inventions, creations, and principles. It is well to remember that the rapid vertiginous progress of today is a progress in which we are immensely aided by all the past achievements. The early efforts of mankind were unaided, heroic, and truly creative. These achievements were not done sword in hand, they were not done through the use or abuse of armed force. They were done under conditions of peace and of peaceful co-operation.

The dawn of written history falls into the evolutionary stage of constructive conquest. No wonder the historians, who were not able to look at humanity beyond the written records, developed theories of primitive aggressiveness, and a complete warlike beginning of all things in civilization. Even one of the early Greek philosophers believed that "war is the father of all things." In the light of modern science of evolution, this is a completely false and exploded mythology.

Looking at the history of human development, we see that the establishment of larger cultural entities is also a danger point in history. The wider such a unit, the more dangerous it becomes with regard to other large units in the use of force for aggression. With the formation of the earliest military tribe-state, there are co-existent two factors of oppression; one, the use of violence and destruction in warfare between the two hostile tribes; the other, as a by-product of war, in the exploitation by the victors of the vanquished. Let us analyze these two elements *sub specie libertatis.* We have defined freedom as an attribute of co-operative activity. People who undertake an activity by agreement and on free choice of purpose, who control their own actions according to the rules of the game, and who share the profits of an enterprise, are free. War between two enemies by means of armed force, fighting or a combat are also forms of co-operative enterprise. Yet enemy use of violence in human behavior changes fundamentally the nature of the co-operation. The arbitrament of force, the use of coercion as an argument, creates a situation in which one side must lose so that the other gains, whereas in every constructive action all free participants gain. The use of force even in its most elementary forms as between two playmates, between the stronger and the weaker, in any transaction between the robber and the robbed or between the tyrant and his subject, means inevitably the gain of one at the expense of the other. In lieu of a carefully planned enterprise, of an adequate organization and implementation of concerted activities, of reward for productive behavior, we have here a phenomenon in which one individual or one group bears the whole brunt of work and then is deprived of it in one act of coercion.

When this procedure is implemented, where it is institutionalized into warfare, it creates the form of "co-operative transactions" in which victory gives all the gains and defeat means a total loss. The price of defeat may consist in losing one's life or one's freedom, or in becoming conquered as a whole community. It is however hardly necessary to point out that the freedom to be eaten, to be decapitated and have one's head pickled or one's scalp taken, is not one which we would register as an enjoyment of the results of an enterprise.

Thus the sociologist who looks at war as a type of transaction between two parties has to register that it implies always that abrogation of freedom to the vanquished which results from a completely non-distributive character of the reward.

On the debit side of conquest is the heavy price paid in terms of human misery, individual destruction and degradation, and the temporary dislocation of normal activities. We see the exaction by the conquerors of loot and tribute from the vanquished, and their reduction to a state of slavery. On the side of the victors also, conquest brings about conscription, expenditure and military discipline. Thus both in preparedness, that is, the political organization for war, and in the process of acute political action which takes place in wars of conquest, the problem of freedom enters a new phase.

War is functionally constructive only when in the long run

both sides are compensated by an integral gain, and when violence is the only means to break down barriers so that the cultural processes can develop. Nowadays no violence is needed for the breaking down of barriers and the development of the cultural process. The disastrous nature of modern war is due to the fact that its positive function can now be achieved by means of peaceful discussion and negotiation at the council table; while its destructiveness has increased to an extent which is incompatible with the maintenance and continuance of civilization.

Before analyzing more fully the abrogations of freedom resulting from conquest, we must draw attention to the fact that there is one type of war which can never lead either to the formation of greater political units, still less to the cross-fertilization of cultures. This is civil war. Civil war occurs within the same culture and within an already established political unit. It is a war in which the human substance of a culture is being wiped out by attrition. Such a fratricidal war is always an unmitigated calamity, since by destroying the common patrimony of both parties, it cannot add to the interest of either. It attacks indeed that organic unity of interests which makes cultural and political integration of value to a group.

At present, an international war, like World Wars I and II, is a civil war of mankind divided against itself. Modern technical developments, and the international systems of communication, economics and trade, have made the whole world one. War nowadays cannot be isolated. As yet however no criminal law exists which can effectively be applied to nations at war; and there is no organization which could enforce such law. The only hope for the future is that after this war is over, the peoples of the world will agree to become one in the political sense, even as they are now one in many of their cultural interdependencies.

6

War and Slavery as Main Denials
of Freedom

THE political principle in the sense of military force exists in
the whole domain of cultural history, and as we know, the results
of the use of political force can either be constructive or can
bring about disaster. War has two aspects, that of waste and that
of creativeness. Thus there are two types of war: the war of cross-
fertilization, and the war of extinction which is without any
creative or constructive after effects. All civil wars are wars of
extinction, for which the only remedy is their prevention forever,
by means of a federation of states. The main positive function
of war is its unifying cross-fertilizing effects through the creation
of larger sized units which thus have a greater scope for development through bringing different cultural units into closer relationship.

With genuine war, that is, the international use of arbitrament
by force, we enter on a new stage in human evolution, a stage in
which both state and nation assume new roles. Here we can for
the first time register aggressive nationalism or imperialism.
Here also we meet the phenomenon of conquest in its full historical and cultural sense. Conquest in this form is the submission
by military victory of one culture to another and the incorpora-

tion of its territory, its population, and its economic resources and other forms of national wealth into a new political system. Conquest, the integral control of one culture over another by means of force, gives the victors many advantages, including those of loot, slavery and increase in political power.

Victory once gained, the side which has won the argument by force obtains the reward of more power. This, as we know, can be used for mere destruction; or for the culinary use of the vanquished or for their transformation into trophies. The permanent use of a vanquished people by the victors results in a fundamental abrogation of freedom to the vanquished, and transforms them either into slaves or into a subject class, or into a lower caste. In all such conditions they become dependent on the will of their victors. They become means to the end of those who can impose their will as they like. Indeed, we find in human evolution and history an infinite variety of forms under which slavery, political oppression, tyranny, methods of spiritual inquisition and serfdom obtain.* All these forms have the one principle in common, which denies freedom and human rights to the oppressed caste or class. The human being turned into a slave has no share in the initiative of action, nor yet any claims to its results. He is only allowed, and indeed constrained, to carry out that part of a free man's activity which is really burdensome and which no free human being undertakes without purpose, motive, or drive: the exercise of muscle, the expenditure of energy, the effort and strain of manual and nervous work.

This doctrine has to be accepted in a slave-ridden community by masters and slaves alike. Its acceptance by the masters is

---

* For fuller information consult H. Nieboer's *Slavery As an Industrial System*, The Hague, 1910. The problem of earliest stratification of human societies is well discussed in G. Landtmann's *The Origins of the Inequality of the Social Classes*, London, 1938. An interesting chapter on slavery will be found in E. Westermarck's *The Origin and Development of Moral Ideas*, London and New York, 1906-08.

easier to understand, although it carries also its own dangers. They have only to recognize their intrinsic superiority and the right to wield law and morals in a discriminative manner. They may claim that certain human rights are inalienable. In practice they have to alienate these inalienable rights from others. To the slaves a doctrine that he has no right to act as he chooses is not so agreeable or acceptable. It implies also, however, that he has no right to think or to feel. Thoughts and feelings, as we know, are worthless unless they can be translated into action. The slave can only pray for favors from his master, or else if he acts against his master's will he becomes a criminal.

In actual history and evolution the lot of slaves was hardly ever quite as harsh and degraded as the legal charter of slavery declares. Self-interest tempered even cruel masters. Many, indeed most of them, were not naturally cruel, and humane and benevolent treatment made the conditions of slaves far from intolerable. Domestic slavery as practiced by some primitive peoples is indeed at times hardly different from domestic service, and often even akin to a relation as between the rich and poor relative in our community, when the rich person does not avoid the poor one. All this explains the endurance of the institution. It does not explain away or attenuate the principle as a norm of human conduct.

The legal principle, indeed, becomes the more stringent and inhuman, the higher the culture in which we find slavery, the less personal the relations between master and slave, and the greater the number of slaves. As an industrial regime in our modern Christian civilization slavery was at its worst from every point of view, not excluding the ethical. Were it now reintroduced by the totalitarians on a world-wide scale it would be a denial of human rights to humanity on an unprecedented scale.

It would degrade the slave portion of humanity and it would destroy the last vestiges of human decency in the master folk.

Have we any intellectual justification to substantiate our ethical reaction to the principle of slavery? In our analysis we have found that man as an animal, and indeed every living organism, is determined in his behavior by his biological needs. He carries out the instrumental activities which his species has developed through the adaptation to the environment, to satisfy the basic needs of his organism. The animal is free, when, within the environment to which it is adapted, it can both pursue its instrumental activities and reach its organic satisfactions with an unimpaired bodily outfit and without any trammels extraneous to its natural adaptive environment. This is freedom in the animal sense and it is closely related to the survival of the species. Man continues this tradition of freedom. He satisfies his needs, basic and derived, within the artificial environment of culture. The essence of this satisfaction consists, as we know, in freedom and here the essence of freedom is that all determinants of a behavior should come primarily from the organism itself and result in the organism's own benefit. The charter of both war and slavery contradicts this central organic determinism of man. War is the direct denial of the freedom of survival since its essence is killing. Slavery is the denial of all biological freedom except in the self-interest, not of the organism, but of its master. The slave also is deprived of all those satisfactions which culture guarantees to man as the price paid for the trammels which it imposes. The slave does not enjoy the protection of the law. His economic behavior is not determined by profits and advantages. He cannot mate according to his own choice. He remains outside the law of parentage and of kinship. Even his conscience is not his own.

Such a doctrine is not and cannot be accepted by the slave

class. Only in so far as it is completely transformed in practice, as has been the case in many of the more primitive forms of this institution, does it become bearable.

Returning now to the principle of slavery as the typical abrogation of freedom and underlying all forms of its denial, let us compare the charter of this institution with other charters of human co-operation. In our definition of freedom we have analyzed the essential constituents of human action into purpose, performance, and reward. Freedom consists, as we know, in the full access by all members of an institution to the sharing in purpose, to the control of action and to the benefits of the rewards. Slavery consists in the substitution of force for organic drive or free chosen motive. The slave participates only in the middle phase of our chain. He has to work, to toil, and accept the control of his work under the lash of the overseer. The work which he does he has not chosen, nor yet accepted of his own volition. He is compelled to work by fear of punishment or by compulsion. The punishment may not be immediate and actual, nor yet do we always need to imagine a slave working under a raised whip. The slave may play his part obediently, to all appearances willingly and with full submission if he has been drilled into the acceptance of his condition.

This introduces the question of indoctrination for slavery; the question of how whole classes of people are made to accept the status of becoming means to an end. One point, however, must be made directly. Acceptance of slavery and continuance in this status are no proof that human beings readily submit to it. The acceptance usually means that the actual conditions of existence had been administered not with a full stringency of the legal principle, but largely meliorated by the human nature of the master. The institution becomes worse in the measure in which it is numerically stronger, industrially significant, and organized into large enterprises. The modern slavery which ended less than a century ago by its abolition in the United States was probably the most oppressive that ever so far existed.

In all rigid forms of slavery we find that large groups of human beings are submitted to conditions of life where no individual interest or initiative, creativeness or constructiveness can be developed. Their standard of life depends on the calculations of an industrial enterprise. Free people contribute their sweat, their tears, and their blood when the end is cherished and the purpose chosen. The slave has to work as hard as he is bidden for reasons which are not his own, and for ends in which he will never partake.

The fact that slavery has existed for ages, that it has been accepted by many religions, even the highest, and had the support of moralists and philosophers, is a significant problem in any evolutionary treatment of culture. It is a parallel to such problems as that of war, prostitution, and at lower levels cannibalism, infanticide, customary sexual perversions and excesses, and headhunting. The anthropologist does not approach such questions from the point of view of moral zeal. As regards war we have already offered an explanation. War is always a catastrophe, since its essence is killing and destruction. Insofar as it is an instrument for the breaking down of cultural barriers and the cross-fertilization of human achievements, it has fulfilled in its time a positive function. We could show the same about prostitution, infanticide, or cannibalism. War nowadays has become disastrous because its positive function has been taken up by other agencies, and its destructiveness has increased to a degree incompatible with the continuance of civilization. Slavery is an institution which is based on the principle of the fundamental denial of freedom and of human rights to the slave class. It had also its contributions to make towards human progress. Under conditions where large numbers of human beings were necessary for the performance of engineering tasks on a great scale, slave labor was an asset. The coercion of force can be the most effective short-cut in certain human activities.

What is the price which every human system has to pay in cultural values for the institution of slavery? When this principle is rigidly enforced, it relegates the slave to a class which remains outside the human group which carries and exercises its culture. The slave class is by law deprived of all rights and privileges of organized life. It therefore becomes also devoid of all cultural interests, of all sense of value and identification with the group. Slavery introduces an antagonistic and disloyal element into the group. It is an element where protests and rebellion have to be suppressed by strong supervision and a constant exercise of coercion. Vigilance is not only the price of freedom, it is also the price of slavery. And vigilance means the development of an organized class of overseers, police and coercive agents which become an additional burden on a community.

In cultures which were relatively safe because of their small size, and in cultures which were as powerful as those of the Roman Empire or the monarchies of the Ancient Orient, slavery was not a great disruptive danger. Yet we can find throughout the development of history that the slave class always produced the traitors, the rebels, the elements of disruption and disunion in any community under conditions of strain and stress. We can say, therefore, that the principle of slavery implies potential dangers to the cohesion of a group to the degree to which this principle is fully enforced. Only when slavery ceases to be slavery and becomes a form of division of labor under a charter which may be legally discriminative but is not enforced, does it lose some of its integral dangers.

We have still to deal with an apparent inconsistency in our

argument. It was demonstrated that freedom is an essential factor in the cultural process. Here on the other hand we are showing that slavery also contributes at certain levels of development, and under certain conditions of culture, towards human efficiency and progress. The contradiction is similar to the one which we find in discussing war as a type of human activity which in its time has contributed towards the advancement of humanity. It would be hardly necessary to prove that abstention from killing one's neighbors is essential to the process of culture. A simple reflection shows that killing one's neighbors in small primitive groups—and doing that as a legal, culturally implemented form of behavior—would have led to an early extermination of the whole of humanity. Hence war occurs only at fairly late stages of human development, and it occurs only as a sporadic, rare, and numerically insignificant affair. The principle of *bellum omnium contra omnes* used to describe the primitive state of mankind is nonsense. At higher levels, however, serious wars occur occasionally. They levy a heavy toll in human lives, in substance, and in moral values. In conquest, however, they subserve an important function; that of forming larger human groups politically united and culturally cross-fertilized. This constructive period of war occurred at a relatively early stage of human history. The really important point to be remembered in such an argument is that in the phase of its cultural flourishing and relative beneficence, war is not total. It is not a pursuit which leads to the abrogation of all other activities. It is an occasional affair. And it is destructive in its principle of mass murder but not in its consequences which play themselves out under conditions of peace.

The same refers to slavery. Under primitive conditions it does not exist. It has no economic basis at a time when a pair of hands can produce only as much and no more than one mouth consumes.

It comes into being when the cumulative results of labor can be stored, or integrated into large works of construction. Under such conditions the slaves never constitute the sum total of any group. Perhaps the most positive function of slavery was the creation of a leisure group. The aimless, unwilling, and unpurposeful labor of some gave others more scope for the development of culture. However amoral this may sound, it is a fair description of facts. Thus returning to our concept of freedom and to its sociological referent we can solve the contradiction easily. The answer to it is that freedom is as necessary in a slave-ridden community for the exercise of its culture as it is in a group of free men. But in a slave-ridden tribe or nation, culture is carried on, transmitted, and maintained exclusively by the master class. Slavery, indeed, gives them more freedom for this pursuit; and unless and until slavery becomes a large scale industrial system, it does not even levy the toll in terms of organized coercion and the debasement of certain values which is its inevitable by-product.

This argument implies that a substantial majority within such a nation or institution must remain masters, for the master class have not only to maintain and develop the culture, but they have also to maintain slavery, which is always a job demanding vigilance, organization and effort. Beside this they must supply the military backbone of the community strong enough to fight foreign aggression, as well as the inner disruption made possible by slave rebellion.

We have not yet discussed the influence of slavery upon the master class. The system means for the master class a complete denial of the fundamental principles of human dignity to their slaves. This denial has to be accepted, enjoyed, used, and fostered by the masters. Concepts of human freedom, of equality, and of brotherhood may be the cherished principles when applied between master and master. They become false, immoral, and pernicious as between master and slave. The combination of such Christian principles as the "universal brotherhood of man" with the institution of slavery must have always put considerable strain on the general moral outlook in a civilized community. How to combine the inalienable rights of man with the chronic, palpable, and thorough-going alienation of these rights, must have created a mental conflict in any thinking and sensitive man. Undoubtedly, part of the conflict was solved by making the exercise of master's prerogative as humane as possible. A complete segregation as between masters and slaves; a universe of humanistic discourse in which two humanities had to be assumed, was another moral and intellectual anodyne. The study of Christian and rationalist apologetics for slavery which flourished in the time of its abolition is fascinating and profitable reading, which brings us nearer to the understanding of why some of our contemporaries sympathize with Hitlerism while calling themselves good democrats. A good summary will be found in Westermarck's chapter on the subject, already quoted.

That slavery became incompatible with the level of civilization reached by this country in the middle of the last century has been proved by history. The fact is that the institution was undergoing a profound change and, had the Civil War not interfered, the South would have abolished it, probably in a manner more profitable to the slaves than that of the Civil War. While it lasted, slavery implied a moral isolationism, the segregation of two sets of principles of justice, decency, and humanity which today, like most isolationisms, would be impossible to a thinking man.

And yet we are faced today with the stark reality that if the totalitarians win, we shall be submitted to a system of abrogation of freedom and the fundamental rights of man far worse than any slavery of the past. It is always difficult to argue the obvious, and even more so to preach what might appear to be a moral commonplace. It seems enough to state that the Nazis want to enslave the world, to produce the necessary reactions of horror in the minds of many a good democrat. Unfortunately, not all people fully realize that we are faced with real facts and not with metaphors, and some people still suffer from that moral isolationism which allowed civilized people and good Christians to make peace with slavery, even as some would like to do business with Hitler now, or till recently. Appeasement is not quite dead yet, and just because it is almost completely silenced and leads an underground existence, it is still sufficiently dangerous to be treated as a menace.

7

Totalitarianism, the Enemy of Freedom and Culture

ANOTHER and new phase in the evolution of collective violence is marked by the appearance of total war. Totalitarianism can be defined as the supreme mobilization of national resources for war efficiency. It revives revolution as the means of change, and war as the only instrument of international policy, in face of the fact that the common interests of a nation rule out war. The avowed ends of totalitarianism are world domination, and the imposition of National Socialism on humanity as a whole. This is not a temporary condition, for the purposes and during the time of preparedness and war, but a complete reconstruction of humanity and civilization. It is the extreme example of aggressive nationalism or imperialism bent on conquest. To live, totalitarianism has to create crises where these do not exist.

In a dictatorship, there is a systematic establishment of the principle of violence. The anthropologist diagnoses totalitarianism as the exaltation of human omnipotence, aiming at the achievement of power and wealth; promising dazzling success and the satisfaction of national pride at the expense of others. Totalitarianism consists in the substitution of organized brute force for all other sources of cultural inspiration; and in the placing of one institution, the state, above all others, at the expense of their very existence. It has constructed an apparatus of force and constraint which is essential both to the internal workings and to the external success of totalitarianism. In Nazi Germany, this supremely effective machinery of force is combined with a doctrine of the crudest mysticism. By means of force, trickery and indoctrination, the bodies, souls and pockets of all within the nation are reached, and the manpower, wealth and spirit are mobilized.

The ethics which pervade the teaching and the line of action of Nazism are the glorification of force at the expense of justice; the exaltation of war as against peace; the gospel of preparedness for destruction as against negotiation at the council table. The Nazi faith is a pragmatic doctrine of spiritual and physical aggression, a dogma of arrogance and superiority. It produces a recrystallization of society on one principle, and towards one end, that of war. The very fact that this doctrine has delivered the goods in terms of real achievement—that is, conquest; the violation of human rights within the nation and in the conquered countries; and the destruction of free independent communities— makes it a menace to the whole of civilization. It has brought death and destruction to millions; but still worse than this, it has brought about a disastrous decay of all human values and the disorganization of legitimate human strivings and efforts.

The essential difference between any previous military system and the present-day total militarization of Germany is that at present our technical means both allow and demand that such a transformation must be integral, for modern war is inevitably total, world-wide and culturally all-embracing. Total war requires a complete mobilization, spiritual and economic as well as political, of the national resources, so as to produce the necessary striking power. The achievement of Nazi Germany lies in this extreme concentration of purpose, individual and social, on one end, that of world conquest. The totalitarian doctrine lives on promises which cannot be fulfilled, for no nation, however powerful, can dominate the whole world; it is stultifying, for it has destroyed the independence of judgment on which German culture throve for centuries.

Totalitarianism therefore affects not merely the constitution of the State and its political machinery. It is a phenomenon which embraces a revolution in the whole economic life of the nation, in its educational systems, in the manner of administering law, and in the methods by which artistic, scientific and religious activities are molded. Totalitarianism is thus primarily a cultural revolution. It is intimately associated with the integral subordination of all cultural activities for the emergency of war, revolution or counter-revolution. As a system it is essentially destructive, because its doctrines and its promises are at variance with the empirical truths of science, with the ethics of traditional religion, and with the very texture of modern social organization. It is the most fundamental revolution which has ever occurred in human development. Totalitarianism thus is an evil which carries the seeds of its own destruction and has destroyed the world's peace. But it has forged two formidable weapons. It has achieved through the illegitimate but effective means of force and indoctrination a social unity and a spiritual discipline which make the organized German state, backed by its machinery of force and destruction, a grim foe to face. We must not forget however that this machinery has not been produced by National Socialism, but by men, institutions and factories which had been built up by Pre-Nazi Germany. The condition of Germany which led to the victory of National Socialism at home must not be forgotten. Towards this condition the organized democratic commonwealths have substantially contributed.

The pervading use of the combination of force and indoctrination within the German nation enters into all aspects of life—the home, the school, the law court and church. Under totalitarian rule, the state takes over control of all relevant faiths, of science, education, and the dictates of justice. Thus it abolishes the effective and creative autonomy of church, school, research, religious organizations, free courts and free discussion. It abolishes the independence of the family, municipality, and free association. Totalitarianism, indeed, is an attempt, not merely at the control, but largely at the annihilation of the other institutions and the replacement of all of them by dictated state control. Through this system the normal, traditional, peaceful way of life of the nation is destroyed, and finally, the nation itself. Extreme aggressive nationalism is thus Enemy Number 1 of nationhood; for the nation, as a democratic cultural unit, is composed of individuals dedicated to their way of life.

Pre-Nazi Germany was proud of its *Kultur* and justly proud of it. The centuries-old German civilization has a wide range of achievement in art and in craftsmanship, in music and in science, in poetry and in philosophy. Germany has been for ages renowned for its industry, its love of knowledge and its appreciation of spiritual culture. Apart from national talent, this was largely due to the great differentiation of the country, regional and religious, historical and racial. In spite of the puerile pretenses of its modern, politically inspired pseudo-anthropology, the German nation consists of assimilated Slavs and Scandinavians; it is a mixture of the Dinaric, Alpine and Mediterannean stocks. It was the diversity of innate racial qualities and the value of interbreeding which has contributed to the productive greatness of Germany, even as it made the melting pot of the United States culturally creative. And let us not forget the part of the Jews in German history. Musicians like Mendelssohn, Mahler and

Schönberg, not to speak of the innumerable conductors, performers and patrons; men of science like Hertz, Kirchhoff, Ehrlich and Einstein; thinkers like Marx and poets like Heine cannot be forgotten or ruled out without stultifying and impoverishing the cultural patrimony of the German nation. In solid fact, the Jews are part and parcel of German cultural history in all the best that it has given the world.

The highly differentiated and culturally creative social background has been destroyed by the Hitler oath, by the steam-roller of Gleichschaltung which results in the extinction of all effective regionalism, by the verbal spellbinding of Nazi magic preached at the end of a machine gun, and by the constant vigilance of the Gestapo. There is only one gospel, one limited set of ideas, and one aim which is taught in the elementary schools and workshops, in labor camps and universities, in factories and in barracks. In modern Germany, we can always discern behind the fusillade of bombastic words the clatter of machine guns. The binding of the spirit runs parallel to the bruising of the flesh. Totalitarianism, in fact, has changed a community of creative individuals into a human machine preparing for economic autarchy, military effectiveness and the gospel of dominance, hatred and destruction. Totalitarianism thus destroys the substance of its own culture and transforms the nation into a blind instrument of power, a gigantic human factory of force.

This transformation, however, was not carried out by propaganda and education alone, by unaided preaching and indoctrination. Side by side with the perversions of truth, the twisting of ethics and the organization of free human beings into mechanized groups, we have a pervading, insidious and powerful system of police, with ruthless and brutal sanctions of violence. Propaganda is one of the most powerful weapons of the totalitarian state, which creates the mental attitude of complete submission to the leaders.

The essence of Nazi propaganda lies in the fact that it is carried out at the point of the bayonet on communities who have machine guns trained at their backs and a pervading system of espionage as the atmosphere in which they think, feel, and move.

Now in Nazi Germany political power is replacing domestic discipline, and in replacing it, obviously destroys it. Training is no more in the hands of the autonomous institutions but is centrally controlled in the school and university and in the workshop. It is also determined politically. Thus in all institutions, technical and financial, in places of learning and places of worship, the career of an individual and his advancement is determined by political adherence to the hierarchy. With such a system, the development of first-rate workmen, technicians, overseers, and even first-rate university professors becomes impossible, because this system is based on violence and constraint. Trust in others and loyalty to them cannot exist except among those agents who are loyal because they are dependent upon the party, and their self-interest lies in its continuance. Hence both in Italy and Germany we find this absolute replacing of the differential influence of parent and institution and of individual initiative, by the power of the party and adherence to it. In most totalitarian regimes the submission to the iron discipline of the party and loyalty to the leader are the only qualifications for a place in the hierarchy. Thus influence lies in the hands of people who are sufficiently unscrupulous as to place their own interest above all other considerations.

Can we build a civilization in the long run on this, on a system composed of individuals who by definition have lost the power of criticism and the power of initiative? Can we have a sound social texture when there is only one loyalty, a loyalty which is inspired by force and cannot have been inspired by love? Even assuming that all Germans are sufficiently stupid, sufficiently inhuman to have developed a passionate attachment to Hitler, it is obviously impossible that this could replace the loyalty between parent and child, the love between husband and wife, and the solidarity of people and friends who work together because they are engaged in a common occupation or constructive task. The Nazi mechanization of humanity is not due to any moral deficiencies in their victims, but to the requirements of a system, where violence and violence alone, politically organized, has to supplant all the diverse qualities of men and women.

This is not a new phenomenon in human evolution. Systems similar to totalitarianism have occurred frequently in the past. The psychology and civilization of the predatory bands of Cossacks and Tartars which for centuries lived on the southeastern border of Poland and invaded it, were very similar to the Nazi doctrine, psychology and ethics. Such groups have developed the megalomaniac attitude of dictators. The more fully we study the elements of the Nazi German culture the more clearly we see that it is determined from the outset by most efficient preparedness and the use of force, and by a doctrine and philosophy embodying these principles. The end in view is the greatness of the people, the greatness of its one leader, and the fact that all good Germans must live for the enhancement of Germany.

Let us then indulge in a Nazi daydream, taking our cue from the famous song "Today Germany belongs to us; tomorrow we will be the masters of the world". We need only to remember the charter of the Nazis' "moral" doctrine and of their religion. The divinity of Adolf Hitler is unquestionable. This is not a metaphorical statement. Apart from the fact that he has been compared in words, printed, written and spoken, to Jesus Christ, and at times even made to supersede the Jewish Jehovah, Hitler, the misbegotten mediocrity of Upper Austria, is treated functionally and pragmatically as God. People pray to him; people greet in his name as they did in the name of God. He is the ultimate fountainhead of all German truth; his icons are carried in processions, and actual forms of ritual, indeed sacraments, are carried out in his name. From this position of vantage, he has revealed to mankind—and this consists of the German people alone—that there is only one race which is fully human and one nation which is destined to be the master of the world. Within this master race of supermen there exists still an upper class of supermasters, that is, members of the party, who again are topped by the leader.

The ethics of this religion are simple, but have become ominous for the world and history. The duty of the masterclass was for a time to transform an industrious, independent, and civilized people into a total war machine. The second chapter of Nazi ethics was to carry out what they had prepared for. This we are witnessing now in World War II. This is a crusade; the world's legitimate masters are fighting the rest of humanity to impose on them the new revealed religion. As the by-product of this and as the realization of one of its main dogmas, humanity has to become the slaves of the Germans.

It was necessary to draw the outline of the Nazi daydream primarily to show that what we are now fighting for is nothing short of the survival of culture and humanity. Any of our slogans which appear somewhat ambitious are really understatements as regards the evils which the democracies now are opposing by force of arms. This nightmare which we have carelessly allowed to creep upon us is now so near that only a supreme effort can prevent it. The danger of another such disaster must at all costs be prevented.

The principles upon which the Nazis have transformed Poland, Czechoslovakia, Yugoslavia, Greece and other parts of conquered

Europe into actual slave communities are neither temporary nor metaphorical. The German nation, partly through the cunning trickery of the Nazis, partly through brutal coercion, partly willingly, partly through indoctrination of the young, have accepted their historic mission of masterhood. They have paid and are paying for it an enormous price, for they themselves have been transformed into real slaves of the Nazi king. They are waiting now to be reimbursed. Those of us even who refuse to admit that a whole nation can in a space of some six or seven years be completely corrupted from top to bottom, have to recognize that sufficient willing and effective tools—human tools—have been found and produced in Germany to carry out, not only the fighting, but much more significant, the brutal, inhuman, unyielding task of oppressing the subject nations. Those of us who have lived in Germany and have seen the working of the Nazi regime as it was applied to the Jews and dissenters, know that nothing comparable to it has ever been produced by men turned into machines and machines used by inhuman men.

Let us try to imagine the world under the rule of the Nazis. There are those who suggest that in the long run such a system would undergo a gradual progressive change and work itself out into a regime, different perhaps, but comparable to a modern democracy. This was the argument of the "wave of the future" apologists and other Nazi sympathizers, and this argument still lingers in the minds of many. Had the Nazis not added the claim that "tomorrow we will be masters of the world", not only in their song, but in their practice, this might have been a correct argument. Nazism, however, from the very beginning and in its very foundations, was a regime made to turn Germany into an assemblage of inhuman machines, or better, of interchangeable parts of a military machine. This machine has now been turned loose to subjugate large portions of the world, or indeed the whole of it. A regime which lives by force within its own nation has to cultivate force and to prepare the nation for international conflict. And international conflict must bring the reward of conquest, or else it will lead to internal mutiny.

Now, contemporary conquest is either completely meaningless, or it means the transformation of conquered peoples into slaves. It is meaningless if we really form a united Europe based on principles of equality and collaboration. Such a result could have been obtained by Hitler or any one else in power, through a wholehearted backing of the League of Nations. Having exacted from his own people an unprecedented toll in wealth, blood and sacrifice, having indoctrinated his slaves with the belief that they are a master race and master nation, the Nazi leader has to offer them a big price, far bigger than even a leading place in the united commonwealth of free nations. Freedom, moreover, is a word and a practice incompatible with the inner structure of Nazism. Were it given to others, it would be a constant disruptive and demoralizing influence to the regime.

The application of our concepts gained from anthropological analysis to the present world situation allows us to clarify the real and fundamental distinction between totalitarianism and democracy. Totalitarianism means slavery of most human beings and mastery by one nation, or, more exactly, by a small group within this nation. Unlike all previous forms of bondage, Hitler's New Order attacks the spirit and the flesh in every aspect of human activity. The mechanical perfection of our modern means of control—and this control refers not only to the human body and to human wealth, but pervades also the human spirit—on a nation-wide and world-wide scale, threatens culture in its very foundations. World-wide slavery is not a type of organization compatible with the adequate mobilization of originality, initiative, talent, and loyalty. The slave caste under this modern pervasive type of control must naturally atrophy. The master class transformed into an enormous world-wide secret police would become even less fitted to supply mankind with leaders of originality, talent, and inspiration, leaders who would lead in virtue of their intrinsic ability. It is here submitted that such a system would destroy what remains of our civilization, both in the slave nations and even in the master-folk itself. This is the most vital argument, the supreme value which makes the New Charter of world-slavery under Nazi German rule as futile and destructive, as it is abhorrent to us personally.

This modern slavery cannot be justified either morally or functionally. It is not the oppression of a group, however large, for the benefit of the whole culture. It is really the gradual but inevitable destruction of the whole for the benefit of a small component part, constituted not by any intrinsic superiority but by the accident of party membership.

Thus, if Germany wins, the constitution of the future world would be based on the denial of freedom to the slave nations. This would also mean inevitably the permanent transformation of Germany into a community which has to develop an internal constitution on a new charter of militant world police. This is the reason why the present rigid hierarchy, determined not by talent, competence, or skill, but by adherence to the party system, would have to be maintained. It would have to be developed into an even more ruthless and brutal instrument of oppression. The abuses of the Gestapo in Germany and within all the Concentration Camps and Brown Houses, combined with espionage, torture, and fraud, were tempered and limited by the fact that persecution was applied to fellow members of the master nation. When applied to slaves, it will be infinitely more degrading to tyrants and victims alike, and since the job of playing Gestapo will be world wide, the whole German nation would have to be transformed into a nursery of supremely degraded police agents.

The new German system would mean a slavery numerically so strong that it could never be really quelled. Let us remember that the nations which Germany wants to enslave are sufficiently strong, numerous and developed to continue their culture, their education and their public opinion, and to fight even as now the Poles, the Norwegians, the Czechs, the Hollanders, the Yugoslavs, the Greeks, and even some of the French are fighting. The German nation would have to continue the battle against its slaves. The picture is so fantastic that it baffles our imaginations, but if Hitler wins this will be the reality, even as all the unthinkable horrors of this war are a reality. Hitler however will not win.

To press our main point once more: the main danger to freedom today comes from international anarchy, in which the danger of international slavery has been bred, and is now upon us as the greatest threat humanity ever had to face. The creation of a superstate is indispensable. The totalitarian solution, in which force is substituted for inspiration, initiative, loyalty, and devotion to ideals, is not a way out of our difficulties. We do not like it. We cannot approve of it morally. Scientifically we have come to see that it is an impasse leading straight to a precipice.

Democracy is freedom in action and freedom is the guarantee of spiritual, social and technical creativeness and advance. Freedom and democracy are essential because they are indispensable to all aspects of culture with one exception; efficiency in war. The final value judgment rests with the private taste of each individual. If he values more highly the short-run privilege of violence, of mastery of the moment, and of victory in war, then let him join the Nazis. Even this we hope does not guarantee that the moment will last. If the individual values more highly the full range of culture—family life, praying to whatever God he chooses, science, art, and the ability to pursue happiness and to live among happy people—then let him fight the Nazis on every front he can for ultimate victory in the war of nerves, blood, steel and fire.

The fundamental difference between democracy and totalitarianism is that democracy supplies us with all the means to deal with any serious threat to freedom. Totalitarianism denies freedom and substitutes force as the only effective inspiration in human conduct. If totalitarianism, in its twofold dimension of military force and the doctrine of brutality, is allowed to continue, the end of civilization is inevitable. Only a world-wide organization for order and for peace can save us, and the strong and live belief in our ideals of democracy, in the equality of every individual nation and race, and in the conviction that man is on this world to produce and create, and not to destroy and kill. This faith must play the same part in our system as the crude mysticism of magic plays in that of the totalitarian states. If this belief is dead, then all is over with the world which we loved and valued, in which we are able to live and work for the advancement of civilization. But indeed, I am deeply convinced that our belief, pervaded by science and religion, by the ethics of free citizenship and the independence of moral and intellectual judgment, is still alive. The scientific indication of freedom attempted in this analysis vindicates all our personal preferences, the dictates of our common sense, and of our moral sense also, since it shows in cold dispassionate analysis that our democratic regime is a sound mechanism of progress, while totalitarianism must inevitably kill not only freedom, but also the gift which it has given humanity, that is, culture.

Epilogue: The Foundations of Democracy and Freedom to Come

W E HAVE rambled across the world and ranged over centuries, ages and eons in our search for freedom. We were able to establish certain principles, not perhaps startling or original, but badly in need of being reaffirmed. Indeed, we were deliberately interested in finding the foundations of the Old Order, in discussing values and truths which, being basic, cannot be new. Starting from the actual problems of today, we found that a clear understanding of what freedom means is necessary for a fighting democracy. Freedom is our main ideal, our watchword, and the source of such inspiration as must lead men into battle if they are to believe that they are fighting for positive values rather than defending an outworn system.

In our anthropological outline of what freedom means in evolutionary perspective, we were able to see that culture—the complex instrumentality of social organization, mechanical invention and spiritual values—is the real context in which human freedom is born and by which it is specifically limited. Culture gives freedom to man in that it allows him to control his destinies. Man frames his purposes in terms of cultural instrumentalities. In this he not only has to be taught tradition, he not only receives the values of his tribe or nation; he also works these out, works them over, and in each generation he has to reaffirm, renew and revitalize his cultural heritage. From the very beginnings of civilization, freedom has been the prerequisite of all constructive work in the maintenance and development of culture. It can also, therefore, be stated that culture is the gift of freedom at the beginnings of humanity and throughout its development.

We have seen that the basic freedom of survival is the indispensable condition of all other freedoms; human beings must first and foremost be able to survive, to go on living, to reproduce and then, and then only, to have a leeway for other enjoyments. Through culture, the species gains its freedom to overcome environmental trammels. Man becomes more mobile, able to change environment, to penetrate regions for which he is not anatomically or physiologically directly equipped. His behavior from the specific, one-dimensional adaptation becomes many dimensional. He enlarges his freedom to survive, to adapt, to move. He learns to fly, navigate oceans, penetrate deserts and arctic ice fields. Thus the freedom of culture is the initial and integral installment of control given to primitive humanity over and above animal freedom.

This freedom is bought at the price of submission to a new type of norms and rules—those resulting from cultural determinism. Technique, knowledge, law, custom, ethics and ritual all dictate constraints on behavior in the interests of cultural adjustment, co-operation, and submission to the laws of the universe. Man has to organize and equip for all enterprise, which means submission to additional laws and restraints. Organization also implies a material or mechanical outfit, and rules for using it and dividing the contributions to the work, as well as distributing the results of the concerted action.

Our analysis of instrumental and implemented action has

led us to the recognition that human beings always organize for a purpose. The specific way in which this mobilization of human energies and resources on cultural lines occurs is through institutions. The individual achieves his career, his maintenance, his emotional fulfillment and his ambition by participating in several institutions, and he enjoys his personal freedom insofar as the institution gives it to him.

In this context we have seen that authority is indispensable in any form of organization; there must always be someone who takes the initiative, who gives orders, who resolves conflicts and acts as moderator in opposing claims. Such authority exists in every one of the component institutions within a community, where it becomes the distribution of power through initiative, control of the material and mechanical outfit, and control of responsibility and loyalties. No individual, as against any other individual or all others, is ever free from trammels, restraints and temporarily unlimited submissions.

In the narrowest sense, freedom is generated in the partial or total submission of individuals or groups to authority. In every instance we have found that freedom consists in a set of opportunities in which individuals and groups can mature their purposes, enact them successfully, and enjoy the fruits of their labors. Freedom, therefore, is an attribute of action. At the same time, we have seen that all action is a temporary surrender of freedom.

Perhaps the most important distinction in the problem of freedom and bondage is between those intrinsic constraints which cannot ever be eliminated from purposeful human action, and those arbitrary constraints, on the other hand, which are imposed on human beings, groups and communities by the abuse of power, whether this be economic, legal or political. We have found that the essential distinction between the rules of freedom and rules of servitude hinges around the use of brute force in human affairs. When personal authority and its coercive application is imposed by cultural determinism in a process where participation occurs in choice, in control of the means, and in sharing of the rewards, we have a constraint necessary for the freedom of order and successful activities. When force is substituted for initiative and inspiration; when it is used to control work and to spur people on to effort against their wishes or interests; when it enters in the more or less masked form of robbery to deprive people of what they have earned, we have the incidence of slavery or servitude as a principle. The measure of freedom depends, therefore, on the degree of one-sided and excessive concentration of authority within an institution; the freedom of a community depends both on personal authority and on the politically wielded co-ordination of specific institutions. We see, therefore, that freedom can also be denied by culture. Whenever we find institutions in which there is embodied a principle of discrimination as well as compulsory membership, we face abrogations of freedom culturally established. Freedom dies when human nature is denied to man. Thus the problem of freedom is synonymous in its cultural, that is, historical and sociological sense, with the problems of authority and violence in human organization.

There occur both institutions and types of personal or individual status in which freedom is completely denied. In all societies we find restriction of freedom to members who, by their conduct, have proved their inability to co-operate or to live together with others; in primitive groups this occurs through ostracism, expulsion or direct execution, and in higher civilizations by the various sanctions of criminal law. At one extreme of the political scale, we have in human development certain negations of freedom like slavery, the caste system and serfdom.

In our analysis of anthropological facts, we were able to observe certain general trends of evolution. The earliest cultures live in what we term protodemocracy, which we found to be associated with the tribal organization on the cultural, that is, the national principle. A tribe-nation is the widest group exercising a common culture, and united by the same language, customs, tradition, law, and economic techniques. A nation is intrinsically a peaceful and constructive unit organized on the basis of a common culture; it is a type of integrated community where freedom flourishes. Equally important is the recognition that the coercion of force does not occur in primitive communities on any large scale, and that freedom as the full access to the benefits of culture obtains fully, since it is necessary for the maintenance of culture.

As soon as the political principle, that is, the legalized use of force, enters, a new entity, the tribe-state comes into being. Political organization implies a central authority and a military force which sanctions the decisions of the authority. In its beginnings and throughout its development, the state acts as a general arbiter and moderator between its component institutions and individuals. It also assumes control of the military power and carries on internal policing, as well as defense and aggression.

A comparison and even a certain equation has been made between the conditions which must have obtained in primitive humanity and those which determine the processes of our modern cultures. There is one principle which they have in common. The earliest groups of mankind had their integral unity imposed on them by the simplicity of their culture and by the imperative of total participation. This, as we have seen, was indispensable to the maintenance of simple cultures by small groups. Today we have the total participation of mankind, of each nation, and each group, imposed by the high development of our technical means, of intellectual communication, transport, and interdependence. Universal education, which is not an act of good-will from those above to those below, is fundamentally necessary to our industrially determined culture. With this, however, is brought about the participation of the masses in present-day concerns, political, economic, and cultural. Culture today has to be accessible and wielded by every member of a nation.

In our evolutionary survey we also found the two-phase principle of human organization. In times of peace, human beings are integrated on the cultural principle; they form national groups engaged in the constructive and creative tasks of the exercise and development of culture. Such conditions are controlled by the principle that freedom is indispensable for the maintenance of tradition, for the mobilization of talent, and thus for the advancement of culture. In times of war, human beings are integrated on the political principle, that is, the legalized use of violence. The political state is intimately associated with war, and the use of violence as the main argument and drive to action is essential to war. Before violence can become effective as a political principle, it must first be used within institutions. War again, in the military preparedness which it implies, in its main activity of fighting, and in its aftermath of victory and subjugation, is the permanent source of all the curtailments of freedom.

The element of force, as we have seen, exists in all types of human organization. Force is vested at the beginning in each differential institution and in its development it becomes vested in the local group, the regional unit, the tribe-state and tribe-nation, and finally in the large federation it increases and becomes gradually liable to abuse as the mechanical instruments of violence increase in perfection. With the development of mechanical means of constraint, with the accumulation of wealth, and with the extension of means of communication, there comes into being the defensive and aggressive crystallization of military power. The relation between man and machine at the point where a monopoly of control can be established is probably the essential problem of freedom in human evolution.

The main thesis of this analysis hinges on the concept of violence as the greatest enemy of freedom. All freedoms are dependent on the elimination of collective violence. We see that most of the restrictions, diminutions and abrogations of freedom are specifically related to those temporary, man-made crises in evolution and in history which are connected with war; and that all major crises are the danger foci of freedom and democracy. With the appearance of war and military organization, which incidentally started very late in the course of evolution, there occurs for the first time in history the full denial of freedom through the substitution of force for the other means of persuasion and initiative. War creates slavery, the need of military discipline, the caste system, serfdom, and bondage; and it is fed in turn by the advantages which individuals and restricted groups of people in the positions of power can derive from the unrestricted use of armed violence. The worst abuse of power occurs when a culture is transformed into an apparatus of destruction. In our present world, this is the real problem which we have to consider: now that humanity is in many respects one large interdependent community, must we still insist that war is the only means of establishing justice and equality between nations, or can we dream and think of some political and legal substitute for war?

In order to answer this question, let us consider culture as a whole and direct our focus on modern civilizations and modern conditions. A culture in its normal working conditions implies certain uniformities of action, a degree of predictability, conventionality, and standardization in human beings, and democratic, universal education. The development of common mythologies, traditions, ideals, and sentiments is indispensable for the unity of a nation even under normal conditions, for these provide the body of traditional lore and traditional values. Here, as we have seen, the greater the uniformity, the more we increase practical efficiency and national cohesion. Human beings become interchangeable parts of an enormous machine which runs best to the tune of the abrogation of personality. At the same time we have here obviously an important corrective. There are limits to the "one mold", "one pattern" principle. Culture advances by inventions. Culture lives by individuals and by institutions. Society as a whole delegates its powers to differential institutions. More correctly and concretely, society is the co-ordinated system of interdependent institutions, composed of the individuals within an institution with their loyalty, dependability, ethical character, and specific differential ideals. Any system of education which suppresses criticism, personal initiative, independence in views or outlook kills inspiration, originality, and inventiveness. A type of social organization which attempts to foster and bring out loyalties, solidarity and comradeship by dictated sentiment to be felt under coercion creates an *esprit de corps* which will not endure under any considerable strain. Any system of indoctrination in human values, ideals, and morals which leaves no room for the small still voices of conscience, which suppresses enthusiasms and coerces joy, happiness and self-realization, will not implant values and ideals in the mind of the individual strongly or permanently.

We can formulate this in concrete terms of our previous analysis of protodemocracy. A sound culture must live, that is, develop, change, readjust. This implies the existence of an independent spirit, of a critical intelligence, and an emotional life which has a wide scope in choice and in range, that is, a wide scope of freedom. This is only achieved in human societies by a diversity in spiritual influence, in technical training, and in social organization. Thus, we postulate a cultural constitution of society based on a large measure of independence granted to all the institutions, traditional or new; the privilege of organizing into institutions, under charters chosen by the members, though sanctioned by a co-ordinating central authority. Criminal, pornographic, and vice-seeking institutions must be excluded since every society must think first of its existence, the bodily health of its members, and their spiritual sanity. But apart from these limiting factors, full scope must be left to the diversity of institutional organizations and to the autonomy of each institution. The multiplicity in diversified by-laws, that is, rules prevalent in a given institution; the diversity in multiple and autonomous systems of training and inventing; the diversity and independence of legal institutions, economic enterprise, and the educational system—all these are attributes of modern democracy but are rejected by totalitarianism. The freedom of conscience has to be implemented or translated into the freedom of organization for the exercise of any religious, metaphysical, or political creed.

State control is necessary; but state control in democracy is invariably carried out through the division of powers, by legal institutions which are independent of direct central regulation. The armed organs of the state are also subject to law and can be arraigned before courts of law. The modern democratic state delegates not merely a great many of its powers to special administrative departments which are not subject to party politics or centralized policies; it also allows independent organizations for the carrying out of education, of religion, of economic enterprise, of professional training and control, and of the exercise of many satisfactions, interests, and recreations artistic or intellectual, as well as providing control to ensure that these are not criminal or subversive. Institutions for the defense of civic liberty, of minority rights, or of anti-scientific, anti-religious, anti-political views are fully tolerated; they ought to be.

In all this we find that the essence of democratic freedom is the scope given to people in the control of their own lives, and lies for the individual in the immense range of choices which are before him as regards every phase of his existence, every decision which he can make in matters of career, of creed, of love or hate, of competition or possible associations, in the choice of a mate, and the choice of an ideal.

Thus it seems clearly indicated by all the facts and arguments that we must establish the maximum autonomy for all purposes, all organized activities. A fair latitude should be given to the working out of conflicts by freely accepted compromise through agreement. So long as the central authority acts partly as advisor, partly as co-ordinator and moderator, it can exercise its harmonizing role without impinging on the creative activities of the institutions, through which culture is exercised in the last instance. The most direct way to the achievement of democratic methods therefore is the guarantee given by a central administration for the fullest institutional autonomy. The state under a democratic system must follow always the principle of indirect rule, that is, advise and restrain too far growing developments in economic power.

Above all, however, we must lay down the principle that we cannot have any well-ordered democratic state if there is no security in the world at large.

Throughout this argument we have linked up the present conflict of democracy and totalitarianism as two opposite principles which have existed through the development of the human species. The application of our conceptual outfit to the present world situation helps us in clarifying the real and vital issue between totalitarianism and democracy. Modern democracy, as we have seen, is the heir of the oldest, most fundamental, and essentially most constructive principle of constitution in human societies. In certain very basic ways we, in our democratic commonwealths, live under the same essential charter of existence under which earliest humanity established culture, maintained it, and gradually developed it. The same charter of peaceful, constructive collaboration, in which rules, customs, and laws functioned under the sanction of effective activity, has always been in vigor under conditions of constructive peace. The peaceful and constructive organization on the basis of common culture we have labelled as the principle of nationhood.

Totalitarianism denies all these principles; the main indictment which can be made against it by the student of culture is that it induces a centralized control referring to all phases of human existence, and eliminates all the other institutions through this monopoly of control backed by violence, to the exclusion of initiative, criticism, differences of opinion, deliberation and debate. In its chronic preparedness for war in the interests of war, totalitarianism means the complete enslavement of a nation and all its members.

Against this complete transformation of a whole population of a community into willing and perhaps enthusiastic slaves of the doctrine of violence and war we rebel not merely with our moral sensibility, but as sober and non-partisan students of human behavior, of society, and of culture. Our common sense as well as our conscience suggest that this is the greatest betrayal of everything that civilization and progress have given to humanity within the last centuries. The complete standardization of human beings engenders a process of psychological and social corruption which is incompatible with the exercise, still more with the advancement, of culture. Again, when the ultimate values of such indoctrination must lead to hatred, to racial contempt, to national inflation of vanity, pride and aggression, and finally to war on a world scale, the destructiveness of such a regime assumes a magnitude baffling to our imaginations. Unfortunately, those of us who foresaw this danger and warned of it, find that the concrete results of the catastrophe supply a shattering text for our imaginations.*

The chronic, critical condition of a group engaged in war or threatened by war, or on a footing of hostility with its neighbors, fosters unquestioning and unreasoning obedience to any command by a leader and a military hierarchy within the community, as well as the imposition of force upon its enemies. The modern totalitarian state is the heir of this system of life. It proclaims war once again as the main aim of nations and individuals. It does it at a moment in human history, indeed at the stage of evolution, where the only creative function of war—the forming of larger cultural units—is no longer necessary.

Humanity has now become one and united through means and mechanisms which have nothing to do with conquest. Conquest also nowadays ceases to be feasible, since even a primitive tribe in Africa, Asia, or the Pacific must be educated if it is to be useful to its conquerors. Universal education and the spread of news and ideas has now imbued the whole world with the legitimate claims of national, that is, cultural independence, voiced by each group.

The great democracies have learned the lesson. In the British Empire there has been dominant, since the beginning of the century, the trend of devolution and decentralization in political, financial, and doctrinal control. The British Empire is now a combination of self-governing dominions, of mandates, and of crown

* Compare the present writer's "The Deadly Issue" in the *Atlantic Monthly*, December, 1936.

colonies where the principle of indirect rule, that is, regional independence under supervisory control, is being progressively instituted. The United States has discarded the policies of the big stick, of dollar diplomacy, and of manifest destiny, and has adopted the system of good neighbor relations. Here also we find that under pressure of conditions combined with democratic wisdom, the conquests of the Spanish War have been partially subject to devolution. The Republic of Cuba and the Philippines were granted independence or are on the way to it; while in the internal policy of this country we find, not ideal conditions of freedom, of course, but a definite and systematic progress towards it, even as regards the Negro minority.

The Germans have with a single-mindedness, clarity, and brutality, associated with Prussian history since Frederick the Great, reversed all the principles of wisdom, experience, and humane ethics which have been put into practice by the English, the Americans, and the French. It is a policy repulsive to our ethical sense. This is a value judgment; but it is maintained, however, that this value judgment is in complete accordance with the conclusions of the scientific analysis of facts. War at present is unnecessary. It is not compatible with all the inherent trends of our culture, and it is so destructive to our present world-wide Great Society, that is, humanity at large, that unless we abolish it we have to plan for another large-scale immersion into a new era of Dark Ages.

War can be abolished and must be abolished. Assuming that the United Nations win in unity, will this unity remain for the formation and continuance of peace? The fundamental points for the assurance of peace is the employment of force as a protective element, and its control when force becomes an aggressive factor. Total war has become the civil war of mankind divided against itself. The concept of nationality has allowed us to establish the distinction between civil wars and national wars. Civil war insofar as it disrupts and decimates the carriers of the same culture is on the historical black list, and is anti-functional. Only insofar as civil war leads to union or to federation and thus establishes a wider protective group for collaborative work, can it be functionally accounted for.

Thus, in the analysis of the character and function of war, we have always to make reference to the cultural unity or cultural differences between warring groups. Here we find another vindication of our indictment against total war. War nowadays is total on two lines. It is total insofar as it mobilizes all the resources of the nation, human, material and spiritual; and insofar as it mobilizes humanity as a whole. Humanity as a whole is now in many aspects one enormous interrelated system of interests. It is united by the need of economic exchange, of a common share in raw materials and in markets, of a stable currency and some protection from violent crises and "economic cycles". Unemployment, slave labor and large economic disruptions in one part of the world spread like an infection to all others. Most of these are caused by the striving for autarchy, political sovereignty, and cut-throat, state-engineered competition, which produces chaos, anarchy, and disintegration, with terrible counter-revolutionary reactions like Hitlerism, Fascism, and the rule of Pétain in France. These are dangerous not only to the country itself, but to the whole world. World-wide planning, therefore, is indispensable.

The main obstacle to this is the state and its sovereignty, for the nation as such would benefit by planning. There is no doubt that the state, with its present monopoly of power, is the main seat of potential dangers as well as the main guarantor of freedom. Deprive this authority of the manifold guarantees which we label as democracy, which work more or less efficiently, and are capable of indefinite improvement, and the state becomes an obvious and patent danger to the outside world, as well as to its own members.

The state today has to abrogate some of its sovereignty, rather than increase the use of mechanized power for enslavement within or without. There is no psychological, social or cultural basis for totalitarianism, unless we assume that collective violence on a world-wide scale is the only argument, the inevitable argument, and the permanent argument. We must abolish war once and for ever. We must reconsider the structure of humanity from the standpoint of nationhood. The power of the state has become extended too far, and must be limited by world control and by the effective and sanctioned outlawry of war. There is nothing Utopian in this proposal, provided the states are ready to pay the price; the strongest states must surrender most but will gain accordingly.

The Good Neighbor policy, which consists partly in a definite guarantee of non-aggression but also of the give and take of a mutual exchange of duties, obligations, services and concessions, is a step in the all around abrogation of state sovereignty on this continent. The best neighbor never gives without asking to get. The one appeal which must be made to the citizens of the United States of America is to abolish in their minds the imaginary Maginot line which runs in unrealistic fashion down the Atlantic and somewhere in the Pacific. It has been abolished through this war, by this war and for this war. It cannot be reproduced in peace.

The prevention and outlawry of war is the concern of all humanity. This cannot be achieved without the formation of some central institution; for as we know, no achievement can ever be realized without being embodied in a full-fledged, well-implemented, purposive institution. Hence the need for a federation of mankind, a superstate, League of Nations, or commonwealth of peoples.

We here put forward some concrete suggestions as to a federation of nations in which a cultural regeneration could be combined with the abrogation of state sovereignty on the following points:

1. The complete disarmament of everyone except for internal police and militia.
2. The establishment of an international world police force, in which even the smallest unit would have to be international. The most effective branch of the international police force would be its air force. There must be several centers of command with special arrangements for curbing any attempt at misuse.
3. The principle of the division of powers.
4. The establishment of an international court.
5. International executive offices, such as existed in Geneva.
6. There would be an unquestionable and absolute right of secession of one national group from another, within the Federation. A larger confederation composed of small cultural groups or nations would benefit for many reasons, though every small group would lose in influence within the Federation.*

A federation of nations on this basis would produce an enormous quantity and quality of new liberties for each institution, each cultural group, each region, and the whole of humanity. As regards the so-called preliterate peoples, these would have to be given a minimum tutelage, on the basis of what is called by

* The following further idea on World Federation was among Prof. Malinowski's notes and is therefore included here.

"The principle of priority in inverse ratio to the aggregate population, wealth, production, and vested interests of each country. This plan of anti-populational representation, giving the weakest nation as much or more control than the strongest, seems to me to be the soundest guarantee for future peace. This would not only give more influence to small states but also might induce and justify a projected dismemberment of Germany. It would balance and obviate the problem of rivalries between British and American imperialism. It would make Russia or China less dangerous as potential reservoirs for totalitarian mobilization."

the British "indirect rule" or "independent rule"; an exception would have to be made regarding certain restricted areas where raw materials exist which are necessary for mankind as a whole. The preliterate peoples would enjoy an even greater amount of autonomy, tribal or national, than they now have, for they would be allowed to federate and combine, to fuse or to separate. A special colonial committee composed primarily of anthropologists might be set up for the purpose of advising and assisting such groups. The treatment of colored labor would have to change fundamentally, since one of the requirements of this plan is equality as well as freedom in the future of living.

* * * * * * * * *

Freedom is an indispensable ingredient of civilization. It guarantees the flowering of those spiritual qualities of man, primitive and civilized, which give birth to inspiration, to creative ideas, to the criticism of the old so that new knowledge, new art, and a finer moral quality may emerge. It is essential to the formation of social loyalties and group solidarity, through spontaneous choice and not by coercion. Freedom cannot be really established unless there is a premium on intellectual originality as well as on integrity, and on devotion to ideals.

To substitute the principle of mechanical force for that of the human spirit spells the death of civilization. The use of force as political control is indispensable. It must, however, be limited to the legitimate balancing and moderating functions which it had from the very beginnings of culture and which are necessary wherever conflict occurs or a crisis arises. Political force, the force of a state, must always follow established laws and freely accepted agreements. The proper function of force is negative.

When a complete or total tyranny and suppression of freedom is planned for the future, we see that it would spell the gradual extinction of culture. We need not consider this eventuality, however. The democracies will win the war. No appeasement is possible, no temporizing and no compromise. Yet, as we have constantly seen, victory is not enough. It has to be translated into a regime fundamentally opposed to totalitarianism on every point and on every principle. Instead of the doctrine of a master race and master nation, we postulate complete independence to be given to all races or nations and all cultural minorities. A culturally united, integrated group is not and cannot ever be a menace to any of its neighbors, provided that it is deprived of military force.

The absence of political freedom destroys all other liberties. The greatest task of contemporary science and statesmanship is the use of force for the control of the abuse of violence, in such a way that it can only be used in the backing of administrative authority, and not for the subjection of whole nations to their governments. The world must choose between a state of international anarchy or of international law. Since law cannot exist without sanctions, and sanctions must be embodied in a political organization, we need a Superstate, a World Federation, or a Commonwealth of Nations in order to have freedom anywhere and everywhere.

Bibliography

Annals, American Academy of Political and Social Science. Vols. 179-180; 1935. Vols. 199-200; 1938. Philadelphia.

Freedom in the Modern World, edited by Horace M. Kallen, New York, 1928.

Freedom, Its Meaning, planned and edited by Ruth Nanda Anshen, New York, 1940.

Forever Freedom, Josiah C. Wedgwood and Allan Nevins, New York, 1940.

Fountainheads of Freedom, Irwin Edman with the collaboration of Herbert W. Schneider, New York, 1941.

Principles of Social Reconstruction, Bertrand Russell, London, 1917.

Liberty in the Modern State, Harold J. Laski, New York, 1930.

The Method of Freedom, Walter Lippmann, New York, 1934.

What Is Freedom?, Dorothy Fosdick, New York, 1939.

Liberty, Its Use and Abuse, Ignatius Cox, 2 vols., New York, 1936, 1937.

The American Leviathan, Charles A. Beard and William Beard, New York, 1937.

A Grammar of Politics, Harold J. Laski, London, 1925.

The Conditions of Enduring Prosperity, James T. Shotwell, The Carnegie Endowment for Enduring Peace, No. 267, Worcester, Mass., 1931.

Freedom, Its History and Meaning, James T. Shotwell, The Carnegie Endowment for Enduring Peace, No. 350, New York, 1939.

The Heritage of Freedom; The United States and Canada in the Community of Nations, James T. Shotwell, New York, 1934.

Slavery As An Industrial System, H. Nieboer, The Hague, 1910.

The Origin of the Inequality of the Social Classes, Gunnar Landtmann, London, 1938.

The Origin and Development of the Moral Ideas, Edvard Westermarck, London, New York, 1906-1908.

War As A Social Institution, Thomas Childs Cochran (co-editor), New York, 1941.

Les Rites des Passages, A. V. Gennep, Paris, 1909.

Stammeslehren der Dschagga, Bruno Gutmann, München, 1932-1938.

Das Recht der Dschagga, Bruno Gutmann, in *Arbeiten Zur Entwicklungspsychologie*, Vol. 7.

Primitive Society, Robert H. Lowie, New York, 1920.

The Origin of the State, Robert H. Lowie, New York, 1927.

Chaga Childhood, Otto F. Raum, London and New York, 1940.

Hunger and Work in a Savage Tribe, A. I. Richards, London, 1932.

Altersklassen und Männerbünde, H. Schurtz, Berlin, 1902.

Primitive Secret Societies, Hutton Webster, New York, 1908.